**DK**

# The Only Guides You'll Ever Need!

THIS SERIES IS YOUR TRUSTED GUIDE through all of life's stages and situations. Want to learn how to surf the Internet or care for your new dog? Or maybe you'd like to become a wine connoisseur or an expert gardener? The solution is simple: Just pick up a K.I.S.S. Guide and turn to the first page.

Expert authors will walk you through the subject from start to finish, using simple blocks of knowledge to build your skills one step at a time. Build upon these learning blocks and by the end of the book, you'll be an expert yourself! Or, if you are familiar with the topic but want to learn more, it's easy to dive in and pick up where you left off.

The K.I.S.S. Guides deliver what they promise: simple access to all the information you'll need on one subject. Other titles you might want to check out include: Playing Golf, Wine, Playing Guitar, Yoga, the Internet, Photography, and many more.

## GUIDE TO

# Fishing

## ROBERT ROTH

Foreword by **Scott Bowen**
Associate Editor, *Outdoor Life*

A Dorling Kindersley Book

LONDON, NEW YORK,
MUNICH, MELBOURNE, DELHI

**DK Publishing, Inc.**
**Senior Editor** Jennifer Williams
**Copyeditor** Susan Aufheimer
**Editorial Director** Chuck Wills

**Dorling Kindersley Limited**
**Senior Editor** Caroline Hunt
**Managing Editor** Maxine Lewis
**Managing Art Editor** Heather M^CCarry
**Production** Heather Hughes
**Category Publisher** Mary Thompson

---

Produced for Dorling Kindersley by **Sands Publishing Solutions LLP**
4 Jenner Way, Eccles, Aylesford, Kent ME20 7SQ, United Kingdom

**Project Editors** David & Sylvia Tombesi-Walton
**Project Art Editor** Simon Murrell

**Picture Research** ilumi

---

2  4  6  8  10  9  7  5  3  1

Published in the United States by
DK Publishing, Inc.
375 Hudson Street
New York, New York 10014

**Library of Congress Cataloging-in-Publication Data**

Roth, Robert, 1945 Oct. 9-
    KISS guide to fishing/ author, Robert Roth.-- 1st American ed.
    p. cm.-- (Keep it simple series)
    ISBN 0-7894-8421-8 (alk.paper)
    1. Fishing.  I. Title: Guide to fishing. II. Title. III. Series

SH441 .R8 2002
799.1--dc21

Color reproduction by ColourScan, Singapore
Printed and bound by MOHN media and Mohndruck GmbH, Germany

See our complete product line at
# www.dk.com

# Contents at a Glance

## PART ONE

### All You Need to Start Fishing

## PART TWO

### Basic Tricks of the Trade

## PART THREE

### Between Reel and Bait

## PART FOUR

### Baits

# Contents

## PART THREE   Between Reel and Bait

## PART FOUR   Baits

## APPENDICES

# Foreword

WHEN I FIRST STARTED FISHING, *my father bought me one of those little Golden Press books at a garage sale. It was called A Guide to Fresh and Salt-Water Fishing, published sometime in the 1960s. I still have it in a drawer of my desk, and there is still a thing or two it tells me whenever I flip through it.*

*Robert Roth's K.I.S.S. Guide to Fishing is that kind of book – one you'll keep nearby, and one that will show you something new every time you open it. It is a real trove of information, but it is written and organized carefully for the person it wants to reach: the novice angler. It's also the kind of book novice adult anglers can read with their novice child anglers (who always stand a good chance of outfishing mom and dad).*

*Fishing was once an act of survival. But sometime during its evolution, the notion of sport was introduced; a roughly equal emphasis was put on the methods of pursuit as was put on the results. A technical craft arose to produce the gear with which a person pursued fish. Eventually the would-be angler faced terms such as "snap swivel," "monofilament," and "crankbait." Beyond the vocabulary are basic issues of hardware: rods, reels, hooks, and lines. Can't we just fish?*

*Yes, of course we can, and that is what Mr. Roth's book will get you to do. After working through the basics (and obtaining a valid license), you can make your fishing as easy or sophisticated as you wish, based upon what you learn from this book. You may have seen bass- or walleye-fishing tournaments on television, but fishing is not naturally competitive the way tennis or baseball is.*

You will sometimes compete with yourself or the elements, but a day on the water without catching a fish is not necessarily a bad day, whereas a day without touchdowns is a bad day for a football team. Some days you may catch just one fish, and it will be one very good fish that makes the day perfect. And sometimes you will be bringing them into the net like you just can't miss. That's the day you won't get home until late.

Fishing is a great global pursuit, undertaken by millions of people in thousands of places. When you start casting and catching fish, you will have joined that world. It's a fun place. You'll probably meet new people. You'll realize you have responsibilities to the environment that you never considered before. Fishing is a lifelong sport, and also a learning process. Five, ten or twenty years from now, what you learn from this book will still be with you but you will have built upon it a hundredfold. The more you learn and the more you fish, the more you'll enjoy it.

*Scott Bowen*

SCOTT BOWEN
ASSOCIATE EDITOR, *OUTDOOR LIFE*,
AND AUTHOR OF *THE MIDNIGHT FISH*

# Introduction

THE PURPOSE of the K.I.S.S. Guide to Fishing is to turn the novice angler into a successful fisherman. It attempts to provide all the essential fishing information and instruction that a book can supply while still keeping it simple. Admittedly, some currently available books have already done this job, and done it well. Unfortunately, these very informative, honest efforts look like fishing-equipment catalogs and read like fishing encyclopedias.

The quality that makes the K.I.S.S. Guide to Fishing unique is that, not only are first things covered first, only the necessary things are covered first. It's not a book that must be read in its entirety before you wet your fishing line. Part One contains everything you need to know about fishing to get started. After reading it, you not only can but should start fishing.

The remaining three parts of this book are more conventional. They will deepen and widen the knowledge you gained from Part One, covering all the different methods and tricks without turning novice anglers into catatonic basket cases.

This book is no wishy-washy preview of all the fishing possibilities before you. Do you really want to start out by reading a chapter on the history, idiosyncrasies, and proper use of ice-fishing equipment? Do you really think the first fishing reel you should get your hands on is an unlimited-class trolling reel the size and weight of a bowling ball? If so, then what you have in your hands right now is the wrong book. Save yourself some time and money by putting it back on the shelf.

The first thing a novice fisherman should learn is how to catch fish. Afterward, he or she can learn the advantages of specialized gear and how to use it. Too many would-be fishermen get this order reversed. They end up walking away from the sport with some barely used fishing equipment and no fish.

*Believe me, I can receive no greater compliment than to hear that you are only halfway through the K.I.S.S. Guide to Fishing yet already using Chapter 1 to wrap fish. And if your fishing skills overtake your reading skills – necessitating your fish wrapping be done with unread pages – the more power to you!*

*One thing I hope you will learn in the end, you can't learn from this book: The people we go with are at least as important as the fish we go after. That's why this book is dedicated to seven real fishermen: Murry and Charlie Davis, Vernon and David Leer, Morris Cappel, Alex Targonsky, and Jerold Roth.*

*Good friends mean good fishing.*

ROBERT ROTH

---

### A NOTE ON THE UNITS OF MEASUREMENT USED IN THIS BOOK

Throughout this book, you will notice that I have consistently used the imperial system of weights and measures, talking about weights of fish in pounds and lengths of line in feet and inches. I understand that some readers may be unfamiliar with these units and use the metric system instead. So here is some information to help you convert from my measurement units to yours.

1 ounce is 28.35 grams
1 pound is 0.454 kilograms
1 inch is 2.54 centimeters
1 foot is 30.48 centimeters
1 yard is about 8.5 cm less than 1 meter

1 mile is 1.609 kilometers (5 miles=8 km)
Lastly, 1 US pint is just over 47 centiliters, whereas 1 UK pint is almost 57 centiliters. I will use US liquid measurements.

# What's Inside?

*THE INFORMATION in the* K.I.S.S. Guide to Fishing *is arranged from the simple to the more advanced, making it most effective if you start from the beginning and slowly work your way to the more involved chapters.*

## PART ONE

Part One starts out by telling you exactly how to start out – what type of fishing reel to buy, how to get a good one, how to set it up, how to use it. Equally important, it will tell you how to find that very first place to fish, and what to do when you get there. It will take you through becoming a successful fisherman step by step. Even if you have already passed these stages, read the chapters anyway. I have a feeling you'll pick up a new trick or two. By the time you finish Part One, you'll be ready to start fishing.

## PART TWO

The greatest advantage *most* fishermen have over fish is superior intelligence. Yet every fisherman has days when this advantage does not seem to work. That's the time to ask yourself if you're taking full advantage of this edge, if you're using your intelligence to apply the tricks of the trade. Part Two will teach you many of these tricks – when to go fishing, where to present your bait, how to attract the fish to it, and how to take your bait to the fish.

## PART THREE

One way to look at all the components of your fishing tackle between reel and bait is as links in a chain. Of course, a chain is only as strong as its weakest link, but strength is not our primary consideration in Part Three. Compatibility is – link to link and chain to purpose. When choosing your line, hook, sinker, bobber, swivel, and leader, one poor choice can cost you a fish or any chance at a fish. The chapters in Part Three will explain how to make the right choices.

## PART FOUR

The next time you catch yourself thinking, "They just ain't bitin'," ask yourself, "How do I know?" If you're sure there are fish, are you presenting your bait where they are? Are you using the right bait? Have you tried all the logical, available baits? Are you presenting that bait as it should, and all the ways it could, be presented? The more carefully you rig and present your baits, the more likely they will catch fish, and, more important, the more likely you'll remember exactly how you did it so you can do it again.

# The Extras

THROUGHOUT THE BOOK *you will notice a number of boxes and symbols. They are there to emphasize certain points I want you to pay special attention to, because they are important to your understanding and improvement. You'll find:*

### Very Important Point

This symbol points out a topic I believe deserves careful attention. You really need to know this information before continuing.

### Complete No-No

This is a warning, something I want to advise you not to do or to be aware of.

### Getting Technical

When the information is about to get a bit technical, I'll let you know so that you can read carefully.

### Inside Scoop

These are special suggestions that come from my own personal experience. I want to share them with you because they helped me when I was learning to fish.

You'll also find some little boxes that include information I think is important, useful, or just plain fun.

### Trivia...

*These are simply fun facts that will give you an extra appreciation for the uniqueness of the sport of fishing.*

### DEFINITION

*Here I'll **define** words and terms for you in an easy-to-understand style. You'll also find a glossary at the back of the book with all the angling lingo.*

### INTERNET

**www.dk.com**

*I think the Internet is a great resource for fishermen, so I've scouted out some web sites that will add to your enjoyment and understanding of the sport.*

# PART ONE

GOOD FRIENDS MEAN GOOD FISHING

# Chapter 1

# Your First Rod and Reel

THE CHOICE OF A FIRST ROD AND REEL is in some ways similar to the choice of a first lover. Either choice can have permanent consequences, and permanent consequences are often unfortunate ones. Furthermore, poor first choices, in love or fishing tackle, may lead to second and final choices of abstinence. For this reason, I'll lead you slowly, carefully, and logically to a choice of fishing tackle I have, with much thought and effort, already made for you. For your first rod and reel, you have five types of tackle from which to choose. To keep it simple, we'll ditch four of them as quickly as possible.

In this chapter...
- ✓ Ice-fishing tackle
- ✓ Conventional tackle
- ✓ Spincasting tackle
- ✓ Fly-fishing tackle

# Ice-fishing tackle

WHEN LOOKING *for your first rod and reel, we can quickly reject ice-fishing gear for the simple reason that so few of you reading this live within the climates, or within dogsledding distance of the climates, that make ice fishing possible. Even if you're so fortunate, you may still lack the stomach necessary to hold down the 90-proof spirits that make this type of fishing bearable. Though the latter has never been a problem of mine, I unfortunately lack another necessary attribute – a frost-proof posterior. My tropical variety turns blue when I even think about ice fishing, which is reason enough to quickly move on.*

*Alcohol and serious fishing never mix, especially when the alcohol is inside the person fishing. I know of no instance when alcohol ever contributed to the success of a day's fishing, and many instances when it worked to its detriment, sometimes disastrously.*

■ **It's gonna be real cold** *out there on the ice! If you can easily get to a suitable location for ice fishing, make sure you have the appropriate clothing.*

## Trivia...
*The origin of the still-common term "fishing tackle" is another still-common term, "block and tackle." The latter refers to the pulleys, ropes, and cargo hooks used to lift heavy, often unwieldy loads. Today, we continue to lift fish in nets with block and tackle. We also "lift" them by means of other tackle – rods and reels. These days, fishing tackle refers to just about any type of fishing equipment.*

# Conventional tackle

FOR THE NEWCOMER, *a far better choice than ice-fishing gear would be* **conventional tackle**. *However, it wouldn't be good enough. For certain specific purposes, such as bass fishing and* **trolling**, *conventional reels are the reels of choice, and rightly so. The reasons for this, interestingly enough, are the very same ones that will force you to look elsewhere for your first rod and reel.*

Conventional equipment comes in many different varieties, and baitcasting and trolling are just two of these. Put simply, if the gear in question is not fly-fishing, spinning, spincasting, ice fishing, or a plain old fishing pole, it's highly likely to be conventional tackle.

CONVENTIONAL REEL

*The fact that conventional reels sit above the rod, as opposed to spinning and fly-fishing reels, which hang below, enables the fisherman to place his or her thumb directly on the reel's spool. Doing so gives the fisherman both an extraordinary feel for and control over what occurs. This feature is a main reason certain models of conventional reels are the most sensitive reels available.*

CONVENTIONAL REEL
POSITION

SPINNING REEL
POSITION

FLY-FISHING REEL
POSITION

## Specialized level-wind reels

There are different level-wind reels for saltwater, freshwater, beaches, piers, bottom fishing, trolling, and *jigging*. Over the years, these types have been perfected in their specializations to a point where they hardly overlap. No trolling reel would do for bass fishing – unless you were actually trolling for bass, of course. For sure, no bass reel would be of use if you were trolling for marlin.

**DEFINITION**

*The term **jigging** means to work a lure with sharp jerks of the rod.*

*Any conventional reel severely limits the types of fishing you can do with it. And this is not even the most important reason for looking elsewhere.*

**DEFINITION**

*Even the most perfect cast is worthless if it ends in a **bird nest**. Similar in appearance to actual bird nests, these objects are often found sitting atop conventional reels. They are constructed by anglers from fishing line, usually at the end of a cast or an attempted cast. These tangled masses, though constructed in an instant, can take enormous amounts of time, and sometimes a knife, to deconstruct. Both the bird nest and its method of construction are commonly referred to as **backlashes**.*

A single reason stands far above all others for not choosing a level-wind reel for your first – the difficulty in learning how to **cast** one. Be assured, we're talking about the very models specifically engineered for casting. Admittedly, this engineering has taken some extraordinary leaps, such as the inclusion of magnets to help prevent that number-one casting problem – the *bird nest*.

**DEFINITION**

*To **cast** is to send your bait, with the help of your fishing rod, through the air to the place you want it to enter the water.*

At the end of a cast, when your bait has hopefully hit its target, the spool of a conventional level-wind reel keeps revolving. Since your bait is no longer pulling line out through the line guides, you must stop the spool with your thumb at exactly the right moment. Learning when to do so takes time and practice. Much of this time is wasted untangling bird nests, and would be better spent catching fish. Until you learn the latter, there are easier ways to go than conventional. Needless to say, I favor the easiest way, and I hope to drag you along with me.

*Despite the drawbacks of conventional level-wind reels, if you start doing any specialized type of fishing, your first choice for a second rod and reel is likely to be conventional.*

■ **When casting** *a conventional reel, you must know exactly when to stop the revolving spool with your thumb.*

# Spincasting tackle

MANY PEOPLE CLAIM *that* **spincasting** *tackle is the easiest way to go. I'm not one of them. My own very first tackle, acquired when I was a kid, was spincasting. I hadn't used my shiny new close-faced reel for more than 2 minutes before a tangle caused me to remove the very cover that qualified it as close-faced. A second later, this cover disappeared forever in some very dark water beneath a bridge. My first fishing reel was no longer close-faced. Neither was my second.*

Like the conventional reel, the close-faced spincasting reel sits atop the rod. This enables the fisherman to release line simply by pressing a button. Line comes off the end of a fixed, nonrevolving spool, as with the spinning reel, facilitating easier casting with less danger of tangles.

## It's easy, but . . .

The spincasting reel is the easiest of all reels to cast, but not by much when compared to the spinning reel, which we will discuss in Chapter 2. Plus, spincasting gear is more prone to tangles, especially after line is reeled in under tension. These tangles occur beneath the face cover, which then has to be removed to get at them.

■ **Spincasting tackle** *may be the easiest to cast, but that doesn't necessarily mean that you should choose it for your first rod and reel.*

*Although spincasting gear is fine for some types of freshwater fishing, it's practically useless for trolling or anything more than the lightest saltwater fishing. Spincasting tackle offers no advantage great enough to compensate for the limits it places on your fishing possibilities.*

# Fly-fishing tackle

*WELL, WE'VE FINALLY REACHED that type of fishing equipment for which many of you, including those unavoidable few snobs and literati, have been waiting. Admittedly, if any type of fishing approaches an art form, it's fly-fishing.*

In certain situations, fly-fishing gear makes any other equipment appear clumsy and primitive. Practically every accomplished fisherman eventually tries fly-fishing. The large majority comes to respect and enjoy it, and a significant number comes to prefer fly-fishing to any other method. There are reasons for this. Only in a small minority of cases are these reasons the desire to pose rod in hand, pipe in mouth, contemplative expression on face.

Mastering fly-fishing is more difficult than mastering any other type of fishing. That said, the task is surprisingly easier than it appears. Any halfway coordinated person with a minimum amount of perseverance can learn how to fly-fish in no more than a handful of sessions. Expert instruction can help. In some cases, it proves indispensable.

## Casting the line

The fly fisherman is unique in that he or she actually casts the line itself. The fly on the end of it, an almost weightless bait, merely comes along for the ride. This differentiates fly-fishing from all other methods, where either the weight of the bait or added weights enable the cast.

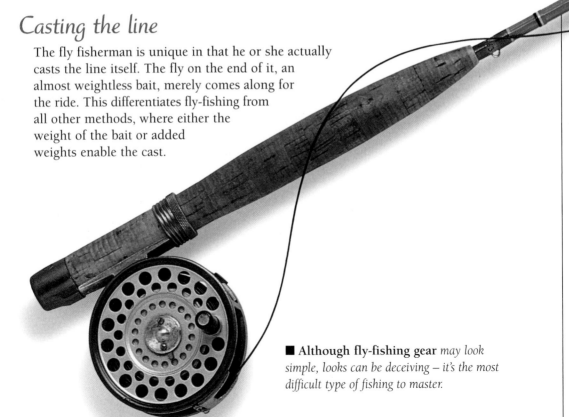

■ **Although fly-fishing gear** *may look simple, looks can be deceiving – it's the most difficult type of fishing to master.*

With one inferior, almost inconsequential exception we will take up later, fly-fishing is the only viable method to cast a weightless bait. Unfortunately, it's no way to cast a weighted bait.

Fly-fishing is, far and away, the method of choice for streams and shallow water. However, the aspects of fly-fishing that prove advantageous in these environments often turn into handicaps in other situations.

**INTERNET**

### www.orvis.com

*This fishing equipment manufacturer's site should prove extremely interesting to prospective fly fishermen. It even has an interactive fly-casting lesson.*

*Fly-fishing in environments harsher than idyllic mountain streams can add to the challenge and excitement of such fishing, even in situations where it would seem impossible to add any more excitement, such as the pursuit of tarpon.*

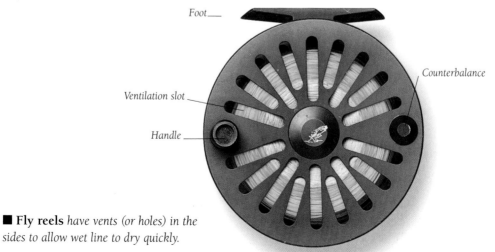

Foot___

Counterbalance

*Ventilation slot*___

*Handle*___

■ **Fly reels** *have vents (or holes) in the sides to allow wet line to dry quickly.*

■ **There's no way you can fully appreciate** *the serenity of fly-fishing in an idyllic mountain stream until you've first spent an entire day on a noisy sportfishing boat.*

These days, tackle and methods have even been perfected to enable fly fishermen to successfully challenge larger quarry such as sailfish. However, when you do find sailfish, you may also find a wind stiff enough to make fishing impossible without some very intrusive boat handling.

## Give it a go

I hope someday you'll try fly-fishing. It wouldn't bother me a bit if you never went back to any other method. Fly-fishing may give you a peace of mind and sense of fulfillment that no other type of fishing can. However, now is not the time.

*I feel very strongly that you should not start your fishing experience by trying to master the intricacies of fly-fishing. Concentrate first on learning how to catch fish, doing so with the most easy-to-use, versatile equipment available.*

## A simple summary

✓ Ice-fishing tackle is suited for that and only that.

✓ Conventional tackle, as a whole, is the most versatile of the five main types of fishing equipment. However, conventional gear has become so specialized that any particular rod and reel is ill-suited for much more than its intended specialty.

✓ Spincasting tackle is extremely limiting. The advantages it offers the fisherman do not in any way compensate for its inherent disadvantages.

✓ Fly-fishing tackle holds an honored yet limited place. Wherever that place is, however, it is not in the hands of the novice fisherman.

✓ The first thing to learn is how to catch fish, doing so with the most versatile, easy-to-use equipment available.

# Chapter 2

# Your First Rod and Reel, for Real

CONGRATULATIONS! By the process of elimination you've chosen spinning tackle for your first rod and reel. I agree with your choice wholeheartedly. Still, there's little that can be done with a spinning outfit that can't be done at least slightly better with more specialized gear. I hope that someday you'll have the resources, opportunity, and competence to experience various types of fishing with the style of rod and reel best suited to each, but spinning tackle is the most versatile all-purpose gear you can own. It's the least troublesome and the easiest to master. You chose well.

*In this chapter...*
- ✓ *Casting ability*
- ✓ *Versatility*
- ✓ *Balance*
- ✓ *Range of baits*

# Casting ability

ONLY SPINCASTING TACKLE *casts more easily than spinning tackle. However, the difference is slight, almost inconsequential, and it comes at a substantial cost. That cost includes, among other things, a shorter casting range and a greater tendency for tangles.*

*The foremost advantage of spinning gear is the ease with which you can learn to cast.*

The main reason for spinning tackle's ease of casting and infrequency of tangles is its fixed spool. When you cast a conventional level-wind reel, the weight of your **terminal tackle** sets the revolving spool in motion by pulling line from your reel. During a cast, the spool of the spinning reel remains stationary as line uncoils off its end. If any excess line does come off the spool, it's not nearly enough to result in a bird nest.

Foot

Handle

Bail

Spool

Spool skirt

Drag knob

SPINNING REEL

*One of the unique features of a spinning rod is the larger line guides. They decrease in size from the very large one closest to the reel to the small, normal-sized tip guide. These guides are necessary because the line comes off the spool in a corkscrew pattern. Larger line guides lessen friction, which increases casting distance.*

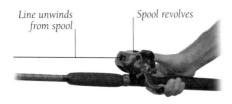

Line unwinds from spool

Spool revolves

CASTING WITH
CONVENTIONAL TACKLE

Line uncoils from spool

CASTING WITH
SPINNING TACKLE

SPINNING
ROD

# Versatility

*WITH THE PUSH OF A BUTTON or the twist of a knob, you can switch spools on a spinning reel in seconds. This places a variety of line strengths at your fingertips, and a wide spectrum of fish within the range of those line strengths. A medium- to heavy-size spinning outfit can be taken to the lake to catch bass or to the coast to catch shark. And, if you can get offshore, combining it with some nifty boat handling can catch you a sailfish.*

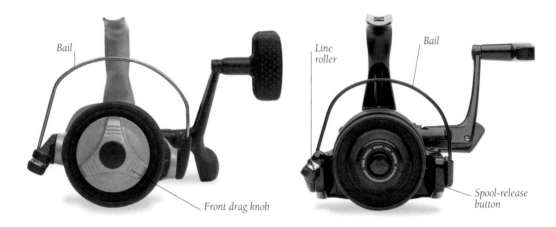

Bail

Line roller

Bail

Front drag knob

Spool-release button

■ **Changing spools** *with a spool-release button only takes a second. Doing so by unscrewing a front drag knob only takes a few seconds more.*

## Quick retrieval

The versatility of spinning tackle encompasses not only the size of the fish you can catch, but also the ways in which you can catch them. Spinning reels enable you to retrieve your baits faster than other reels do. This added speed is sometimes essential in enticing a fish to strike (attack) your bait. For long-distance surf casting, spinning gear works great. It works well for trolling, too. With spinning tackle, you can fish the surface, the bottom, or cover the whole water column in between.

*The faster retrieval rates of spinning reels are due to their higher gear ratios. These come at the cost of some power to reel in the fish. However, the lost power is of no use if you can't retrieve your bait fast enough to induce a strike in the first place.*

27

# Balance

*A MATCHED SPINNING ROD AND REEL are a pleasure to use. The reel hangs below the rod, exactly where gravity wants it. This makes both casting and rod handling easier – an advantage of spinning gear impossible to fully appreciate until you've spent a long day fishing with a heavy conventional outfit, struggling to keep the reel balanced atop the rod.*

*Never use your spinning outfit holding the reel above the rod shaft instead of hanging naturally below.*

Despite the seemingly obvious advantage of balance, eventually you will come across some novice, wrong hand working the handle, fighting to keep an upside-down spinning reel sticking awkwardly above its rod. This is a habit that should be broken as soon as possible, if not sooner. Aside from looking ridiculous, it is a less effective method of fishing. In addition, a spinning rod is designed to bend with its line guides on the inside of the curve. The reason for such awkward misuse of spinning tackle is usually that the novice is left-handed. Well, this reason is not good enough – not when a perfect solution to the problem exists. We'll get to it shortly.

■ **Combine a view** *such as this with the comfortable balance of a spinning outfit, and you'll be able to cast all day without getting tired.*

# Range of baits

*THE EASE WITH WHICH line leaves a fixed spool enables the spin fisherman to outcast the fly fisherman by a wide distance. It also gives him or her a far greater choice of what to cast.*

At one extreme, the fly fisherman is limited to almost weightless flies. At the other extreme, the conventional-reel fisherman needs heavier terminal tackle to cast at all. The spin fisherman can cast smaller baits and lighter models of the same size lures (artificial baits). Less weight creates less disturbance upon hitting the water, thus decreasing the chance of spooking the fish. The spin fisherman's possible choices of terminal tackle cover the spectrum from flies on up.

*The spin fisherman can sometimes outfish the fly fisherman in the latter's own backyard — the trout stream. When the current is strong and the water dirty, the fly fisherman still has to stick with flies, while the spin fisherman can cast the more suitable spinners and spoons (see Chapter 23). These lures get down faster, with more flash.*

## A simple summary

✓ The only tackle that casts more easily than spinning tackle is spincasting tackle, but, when compared to spinning gear, the difference is inconsequential.

✓ Spincasting tackle's drawbacks compared to spinning include, among other things, a shorter casting range and a greater tendency for tangles.

✓ Spinning tackle is the most versatile gear available.

✓ The position of the reel, hanging below the rod, lends spinning tackle a comfortable, balanced feel that adds to its ease of use.

✓ Spinning, above all other tackle, affords you the effective use of the widest range of baits.

# Chapter 3

# Finding a Good Fishing Spot

I'M ASSUMING you have no fishing mentors willing to share their fishing spots. If I'm wrong, no matter. The advice in these next few pages, though no more than common sense, is uncommonly put into practice. Read and apply it: you'll be rewarded. Finding your own fishing spots requires experience. For now, try instead to find someone willing to share his or her favorite spots. This person must either be generous, stupid, or have an ulterior motive. Of these three types, the easiest to find is the one with the ulterior motive. In fact, this dude is already looking for *you*. I'll save both of you some trouble by telling you exactly where you can find this guy first – at your local tackle store.

## In this chapter...

✓ First stop, the tackle shop

✓ On the way to the fishing spot

✓ Full stop at the fishing spot

✓ Plan B

A QUIET FISHING SPOT MAY NOT BE A GOOD FISHING SPOT, BUT AT LEAST IT'S QUIET

# First stop, the tackle shop

*THE TERM "LOCAL TACKLE STORE" does not refer to your average 1-mile-square Universemart Mega/Super Discount Store. Sure, you can save some bucks there, the lighting will be better, and it will certainly smell nicer than any real bait-and-tackle store. Just don't expect to find a clerk who can give you worthwhile fishing advice. In fact, don't expect to find a clerk.*

The guy who wants you to be a successful, satisfied fisherman, the guy who personally needs your steady business, is the guy in the small tackle shop. It's in this guy's interest to sell you bait and lures that work, and to send you to good places to use them.

## Finding the right tackle store

Entering a new type of store – a type into which you've never set foot before – can be pretty daunting. It needn't be. That's why I've put together these step-by-step instructions. Following these points will help make your first trip to the tackle store a more pleasurable experience.

 Get out your Yellow Pages, and make a list of your local tackle stores, nearest ones first.

■ **The tackle-shop owner** *will want you to feel comfortable enough to keep coming back time and again. And you may meet neighbors there that you wouldn't meet anywhere else.*

**2** Enter the first store and glance around as if you're familiar with what you see. Don't walk right up to the clerk or owner. That would be a sure tip-off that you're going to ask some dumb questions.

**3** You want to get the guy's attention and whet his appetite with the impression that you're about to make a nice purchase, so head for the spinning gear.

**4** Pick up a rod-and-reel combo and give it a slow, knowing once-over. Hold the rod upright and give it a quick wrist shake or two to examine its action (flexibility). After no more than a few shakes, the salesman or owner will be standing next to you, trying to keep from salivating all over his shirt front. His opening remark will be something such as, "Nice outfit you picked out." This will be true no matter what rod and reel you "picked out" (which is sales-speak for, "already decided to buy"). Don't hold this cliché against him. He is just being polite and trying to make a halfway-honest buck.

*When examining a fishing rod, do not stick the rod tip between the blades of that ever-present ceiling fan. If it isn't hanging directly above the rod rack, this fan is sure to be within a fishing rod's distance of it. Determining damages is never the best way to start a friendly conversation.*

**5** There is no need for you to lie or play games. Just tell the owner or salesman straight, "I'm going to need a good outfit, and all the extras that go with it. The problem is, I don't have a boat. So first I want to be sure there are some places around here to use it." You can bet that he or she will assure you there are plenty. That's when you get serious and say, "Tell me where they are. I'll check them out right now. If you've treated me right, you'll have yourself a steady customer." If the owner bites, make sure you get the exact locations. Before checking them out, try a few more tackle shops. Put all the locations on a map.

*If a tackle store's staff can't give you worthwhile advice on where to fish, there's no reason to believe their advice on what tackle to buy would be any more worthwhile.*

It should be much easier to find a helpful tackle store owner than to find a good fishing spot by yourself, especially if you're new to fishing. Just make sure you reward the tackle shop that proves most helpful.

# On the way to the fishing spot

*THE FIRST TRIP to a potential fishing spot is a reconnaissance patrol, not an attempt to fill your freezer with fish. I would advise against bringing along any distractions such as fishing tackle.*

## Safety first

Your first consideration when examining fishing spots should be your safety. Your car's safety should also be a consideration. Don't drive down a road unless you're sure you'll be able to drive back out. If you're not sure, do your exploring on foot. And make certain you leave your car in a spot that's as dry at high tide as it is at low. No matter how good the fishing, a bridge where a careless step backward can land you in a traffic lane is never worth the risk, most especially if children are with you. Even if you're confident you won't make a possibly fatal mistake, can you be equally confident about all the passing drivers? Do you care to bet your life that not one of them has had a drink too many?

Another place to avoid is one that can be reached only by hopping from boulder to boulder. It's just a matter of time until you or a friend end up between two of those boulders. If the space between them is covered by water, you'd better be damn sure that high tide won't leave you stranded, or that a change in wind speed or direction won't leave you drenched by breakers and hopping back over some now wet and slippery rocks.

■ **An idyllic** *fishing spot can also be a dangerous fishing spot. Be aware.*

# Full stop at the fishing spot

THE FIRST THING YOU WANT TO SEE *at a prospective fishing spot is a few people. You don't want to see a crowd, unless a lot of them are catching fish. What you do upon arrival depends on what you want. If what you want is to get thrown into the water, go right up to a fisherman and start telling him or her better ways to catch fish. If, instead, you prefer a mere cold shoulder, grill the fishermen with all the questions you can think up, as fast as you can think them up.*

However, if you really want to know if you've found a good spot and, equally important, how to fish it, then try this: Just stand around watching for a while. Let the fishermen get used to you. Notice who is catching the most fish, and figure out how they're doing it.

Do more than watch – study. What kind of rod and reel is he or she using? If it isn't spinning tackle, keep an eye on the most successful spin fisherman too. Try to

■ **This must be a good sign:** *If there are this many fishermen present, they are there for a reason . . . and the reason is fish.*

decide if choice of rod and reel is the difference. What kind of bait seems to be working best? How are the fishermen presenting and using this bait? Is it down to differences in technique? Figure out as much as you can and reserve your questions for the rest.

*When approaching fishermen for information, never do anything that would give the impression that you're a psychopath or, worse yet, out to steal their bait.*

I guarantee, if you sidle on up to someone catching fish with a fishing rod in your hands, a thought similar to this will come to his or her mind: "Here comes a jerk that thinks I got all the fish in the world lined up here in front of me. Bet he tries to set up right between my legs." However, if you instead walk up with a cold drink in your hand, he just may think, "Maybe he's got a cooler with another one of those."

*Don't go back to the tackle store until you've covered every spot on your list. Only then will you know how helpful the people there have been. You'll also have a far better idea of the equipment you need to buy.*

# Plan B

**IF ALL THE TACKLE SHOPS FAIL YOU,** *take consolation in the fact that you can now save some money on your fishing gear, then move on quickly to Plan B.*

## Ask around

Try to get some information about good fishing spots from your relatives, friends, and neighbors. Keep an eye on the newspaper for any mention of fishing hot spots. Pictures of people holding fish are often captioned with the location. You can even telephone your local paper about a story, or for information in general. Nothing they can say to you will draw blood. Find out if there are any fishing organizations or clubs in your area. Chances are they're not very exclusive. Be alert for the arrival in town of any fishing clinics. Read fishing magazine articles about your area or areas like it. If a fishing tournament is held nearby, hang around and see what you can learn. Better yet, volunteer to help the organizers.

## Find fishermen in action

A good way to find fishing spots is to look for fishermen. If you see any along a road, stop to check how they're doing. If you can't stop right then, make a note to come back. Go a little out of your way to recheck interesting locations. Finding fishermen who have found fish is usually easier than finding fish yourself. And when it's easier to find fish, you have no need to find other fishermen!

**INTERNET**

**www.sosin.com**

*Mark Sosin's outstanding web site lists fishing guides, fishing tips, fishing articles, and much more. Check it out.*

# Charter a fishing boat

In theory, and only in theory, when you charter a boat it is at your disposal. Actually, the captain may, with emphasis on the may, give you a choice of a few types of fishing. If a choice is what you want, you must state so clearly when first making arrangements. Charter boats usually take out from one to eight fishermen. They can get you a lot of excitement and some very nice fish. Expensive as these charters are, you may still find the experience well worth the cost. Keep in mind that it's very difficult to book the best charter captains for the best seasons. Those dates are reserved by, and sometimes for, their steady clientele.

If you are a complete novice, I do not recommend charter boats as a learning experience – not unless you own a boat on which to apply the lessons you learn. All charter captains and fishing guides say they like teaching beginners, and I am sure most of them do, in theory. However, that theory rarely holds true for more than the first few hours of the charter (unless you're an attractive member of the opposite sex). Good captains judge themselves by their success in teaching you, which comes down to the fish you catch.

### Trivia...

*Tipping after a fishing charter, in appreciation of effort and results, is customary all over the world. Even if the captain declines acceptance, he will almost always direct you toward his crew.*

■ **Charter boats** *can provide the fisherman unequaled excitement. However, they are usually not the best learning experience for the complete novice.*

If the fish aren't biting, the charter's atmosphere can take a dive. Still, don't judge the captains too harshly. No one does fishing charters to get rich or because they're lazy. Once you get some practice fishing, it would be a pity if you didn't take a few charters for the uniqueness of that experience, its inherent excitement, and as a learning tool.

## Party on

**Party boats** are usually much larger than fishing charter boats, and far better suited to beginners. You don't charter them. You buy a place at the rail, alongside the other fishermen. Party boat trips are rarely expensive, and, if the crew does its job, usually a bargain. You can gauge the crews by showing up at the dock when the boats come in. Fishermen usually bring their catch home, so you can see what they caught and the looks on their faces. Don't be embarrassed to ask questions. The novice on a party boat can learn a lot from just watching the other fishermen and listening to the crew.

> **DEFINITION**
>
> **Party boats** *take out large parties, anywhere from two dozen fishermen on up. They anchor or drift, with the fishermen lining the rail. These boats usually supply everything needed, including bait and instructions.*

■ **Party boats** *are probably the best offshore experience for the novice. They supply equipment and instruction at an affordable price.*

*Whenever you're at a marina, check out the fish-cleaning tables. You'll see what's being caught, and you may find out how and where. Also, there may be some nice fish swimming around behind the tables, where they are so used to living easy off discarded scraps that they've stopped bothering to check for hooks.*

## And finally . . .

Last but not least, check with your local fish and game department. People there know where the fish are being caught. More important, they're usually courteous enough to tell you. Sometimes they can even supply you with maps.

*No matter where you are, you'd be foolish not to take advantage of what you can learn from others. Have patience. Watch, study, and copy as much as you can before you get creative.*

Without a doubt, a good fisherman must learn how to innovate. However, most innovation fails. Still, learning what not to do is almost as important as learning what to do. In any case, the easiest method of becoming an accomplished fisherman starts with instruction and imitation.

If none of the above advice helps you locate someone else's fishing spot, don't worry. In Chapter 11, I'll explain how to find your own spots.

## A simple summary

✔ The best place to get fishing information about your area is your local tackle shop.

✔ Be safety-conscious when you are choosing a fishing spot. Remember, a trophy fish is not worth injury or worse.

✔ At a prospective fishing spot, make sure you observe all you can – only ask other fishermen questions that you can't answer yourself.

✔ Keep your eyes on the media for any information about fishing organizations, clinics, or tournaments in your area.

✔ Keep an eye out for fishing fishermen. Wherever they are, they aren't there to get away from fish.

✔ Charter boats and party boats can both be exciting. However, as a learning experience, party boats are superior.

# Chapter 4

# Buying the Right Reel

YOU NOW HAVE a general idea about the equipment you will need. Head for the Mega-Super Discount Store, and you may save 10 or even 20 percent. You can also get the wrong tackle, worthless tackle, or tackle you don't need. On the other hand, at your local bait-and-tackle store you may pay a little more, but good advice can save you time and money in the long run. Go first to the dealer who let you in on the best fishing spots. Look for a reel in the mid-price range. You don't yet know enough to get the most out of an expensive one, but you don't want one so cheap that you'll completely abandon it when you do gain experience.

## In this chapter...

✓ The right size reel

✓ Testing the drag

✓ Are parts easily available?

✓ Extra spools

✓ Reel options

AN ELONGATED SPOOL MEANS LONGER CASTS

# The right size reel

THE FIRST THING TO CONSIDER *when choosing a spinning reel is size. By size, I'm referring to line* **test** *rating, not physical size, though they are, of course, related. Some of the large saltwater spinning reels have the muscle to handle 30-pound test line. On the other extreme, some of the very smallest, ultralight spinners are smooth and precise enough to use 2-pound test. In case you didn't know, you are not interested in either of these extremes.*

Remember, the two main reasons you chose spinning tackle were its ease of use and its versatility. At the extremes in size, you lose both of these advantages. Catching trophy fish on 2-pound test is neither easy nor likely, unless you're an expert. Thirty-pound test spinning tackle also restricts versatility. Stronger gear means heavier gear. A rod and reel beefy enough for 30-pound test line are not built for a long day of casting. The term "ease of use" won't come to mind when your arm feels ready to fall off. Also, casting distance decreases as line test increases, unless you also increase the weight of your terminal tackle. Heavier terminal tackle restricts the types of fish you can target and can make it harder to attract, fight, and ultimately catch them.

<u>The First Golden Rule of Fishing</u>: *"Less is better, if it can get the job done." The lighter your line and the terminal tackle attached to it, the more fish you will fool.*

## Choosing a reel by doing the math

Your first reel is going to be your only reel for a while. Different target fish often mean different line strengths. No reel comes close to covering the spectrum from 2-pound test to 30-pound test. You'll have to give up some options at one or both extremes. Now, if you intend to do a lot of freshwater bass fishing, you want to be able to get down to at least 8-pound test. If you plan on spending a lot of time chasing sailfish in a maneuverable boat, you can do quite well with 20-pound test. Right there you've already narrowed your original 28-pound range (30 pounds minus 2 pounds) by almost 60 percent, to a range of 12 pounds (20 pounds minus 8 pounds). By splitting the difference, we arrive at an optimum line test rating of around 14 pounds.

# What's right for you?

However, before rushing out to buy a reel with a line-strength range centered near 14 pounds, let's make sure that this is the optimum range for you. If you're going to spend most of your time chasing sailfish, 40-pound salmon, or 30-pound catfish, you may want to go up a few pounds to a reel with a range centered at 15- or 16-pound line strength. If you're going to spend most of your time catching 2- and 3-pound bass, you definitely want to go down a few pounds in line test, to a reel with a range centered at 12-pound test or less.

Understand that neither 12- nor 16-pound test is necessarily ideal for any of the species just mentioned. Still, a quality reel rated for 12-pound test should be okay for 10-pound and, quite possibly, 8-pound test. A quality reel rated for 16-pound test should be okay for 20-pound test. Your choice, if made correctly, will give you the best all-around reel for the types of fishing available to you.

Most reels are more or less rated by their manufacturers; this rating can sometimes be found on the reel itself. However, what you have in such cases is not strictly a rating – it's a range of capacities for different line tests. It's fairly safe to assume that the optimum line for the reel shown below is 12 pounds. It's not quite as safe to assume that the reel will work well at the extremes of the listed range. To further confuse matters, a quality reel may work acceptably slightly beyond the listed range. If the range of acceptable tests is not printed on the reel itself, it may be found in its manual or the manufacturer's catalog. If not, then you may have to depend upon the judgment of the tackle-store owner. In any case, no matter what the manufacturer or store owner says, you'll have to make the final and definitive test of your reel's range yourself, through use . . . a lot of it.

■ **Many reels** *have a range of line-strength capacities printed right on the spool skirt. These reels are likely to work best at the middle of the listed ranges.*

**INTERNET**

### www.asafishing.org

*The American Sportfishing Association is, among other things, a conservation organization. Amazingly, it loans fishing equipment to novices in the same manner as libraries loan books. Log on to find out if there's a branch in your area.*

# Testing the drag

**YOU WANT TO TEST** *a reel's* **drag**, *if possible, before you buy it. If this proves impossible, you still want to test it before a fish does.*

## What a drag?

Before we discuss the drag, it would help to see its components, and at the same time get a glance of all the parts that make up a typical spinning reel. The exploded view below is merely for reference. Don't try to memorize the parts. You'll learn the ones you need to know soon enough, through use and despite yourself. Do refer to this illustration if a part unfamiliar to you is mentioned in subsequent chapters.

*Never oil your drag washers. If it's necessary to remove rust from the metal washers in between them, remove all excess rust inhibitor before replacing these metal washers.*

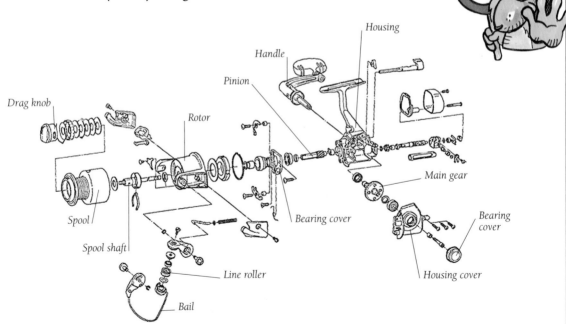

■ **There are so many parts** *to a spinning reel that it really isn't worth trying to learn them all. Also, it's not a good idea to start taking your reel apart to see how it works. Your reel will consist, more or less, of what you see in this diagram.*

---

> **DEFINITION**
>
> *A spinning reel's* **drag** *is a set of washers and a spring, plus a knob to adjust the pressure on them. How it is set determines the force a fish needs to apply in order to take out line.*

# Why a drag?

You'll never know how good your reel's drag is until you hook a fish with the speed, strength, and determination to test it. However, a simple test done inside the tackle store may be enough to expose a poor-quality drag. Before we get to that test, it's appropriate to first explain the function of a drag and why you need a good one.

Let's assume you have an 11-pound fish on a 10-pound test line. Now, an 11-pound fish weighs much less than 10 pounds when in the water. Just take my word for it, for a few more chapters anyway. So if this fish were not in the mood to fight, you would have no trouble bringing it to the water's surface. However, if you lift it out of the water into the air, your fishing line could easily snap. Still, keep in mind that even though this fish does not weigh 10 pounds in the water, if it wants to fight it can still break your line. By using the power in its tail to swim away fast and forcefully, by leaping out of the water and away from you, or merely by shaking its head, this fish could put more than 10 pounds of pressure on the line, thus breaking it. In order to prevent a fish from doing just that, the drag was invented.

*The purpose of the drag is not only to prevent a fish from breaking your line, but also, at the same time, to wear down this fish until it loses the strength to do so.*

For example, say you're using 10-pound test and you set your drag at 5 pounds. A fish can't run away until it increases the pressure it puts on the line to over 5 pounds. The drag then allows line to escape as opposed to letting the fish increase the pressure on the line to over 5 pounds. This means a fish is not allowed to place enough pressure on the line to break it.

At the same time, every inch of line it pulls from the reel costs the fish energy. Eventually, it will tire and become so weak that not only will it lack the strength to apply the 10 pounds of pressure needed to break the line, it will even lack enough strength to apply the 5 pounds of pressure needed to pull more line from the spool. Then you can reel it in.

Today's drags, through advanced technology and engineering, make it possible for fishermen to catch a fish many times heavier than their line's test strength. In fact, the *IGFA* has a 5 to 1 Club, 10 to 1 Club, 15 to 1 Club, and 20 to 1 Club for fishermen skillful enough to have caught a game fish weighing five to 20 times the test strength of the line they used to catch it. These are elite circles that many accomplished fishermen strive to join. Don't be in too much of a hurry to try out.

> **DEFINITION**
>
> *The International Game Fish Association, or **IGFA**, is the arbiter and keeper of all international fishing records. Among other things, it works to protect the oceans and the fish in them. A year's membership costs less than a cheap rod and reel. Every sportfisherman should join.*

# Testing for smoothness

There are three very important qualities of a drag that we can test – smoothness, sensitivity, and range. Smoothness in a drag means that, once set, the amount of force needed to pull line from the reel remains constant (over short distances, but we'll get to that later). The more sensitive a drag, the more precisely drag tension can be adjusted. The larger a drag's range, the larger the range of line strengths that can be used effectively on that reel.

The best way to test a reel's drag is with the reel filled with line and attached to a rod. Sometimes you will find such a combo ready for sale in a tackle store. Sometimes a store will have the same rod and reel you're interested in purchasing set up and available for rental. In either of these two cases, consider yourself lucky. If the sales clerk starts raving about a drag, you can agree to buy the reel if he or she allows you to test the drag first. The clerk just may fill the spool and attach it to a rod. If not, don't hold this against him.

*Pull on line to test drag*

If you are lucky enough to get the chance, here's how to test a drag:

1. Thread the line through the line guides, and place the rod and reel in the rod rack so your hands are free.

2. Tie the end of the line around a pen or pencil. (This will prevent you from cutting your hands.)

3. Adjust the drag by turning the drag knob, which is either at the top of the spool or the rear of the reel. Set the tightness so that the line comes off with little effort, but the rod tip bends a least a foot from the vertical.

4. Pull on the line. You must do this at the most uniform speed and pressure you can manage.

If your pull is even, then the bend in the rod tip should remain uniform. In other words, it should not bend and straighten, bend and straighten. An unstable rod tip indicates that the reel is giving up line in irregular spurts, and therefore the drag lacks smoothness.

*Rod held firmly*

### An alternative test

If you are not able to test a drag with the reel attached to a rod, don't let that stop you. There's another way.

**1** Cut a length of monofilament 6 inches shorter than yourself.

**2** Tighten up the drag.

**3** Reel the line onto the spool.

**4** Hold the end of the line over your head with the reel dangling in front of your face.

**5** Slowly, in very small increments, loosen the drag until the reel falls.

If the drag works smoothly, the reel falls smoothly. If the reel stops and starts, find one that doesn't.

*During a drag test, never lower your hand holding the line below eye level. You cut this line 6 inches shorter than yourself to keep the reel from hitting the floor. This is a drag test, not a bounce test.*

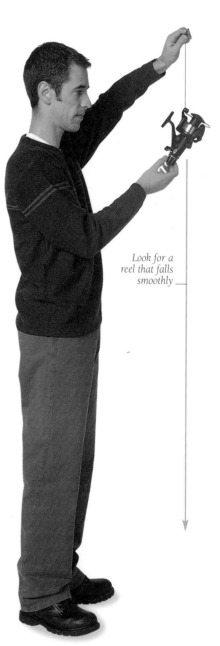

*Look for a reel that falls smoothly*

If the drag can't pass the smoothness test, then it will not put even pressure on a fish. This means the fish has a better chance of throwing (getting off) the hook or breaking the line. When the rod bend suddenly increases more than it should, we describe the drag as "sticking." This places the line in danger of snapping, because the drag refuses to let out line while the fish is applying more than the set pressure.

When the rod straightens more than it should, we say that the drag is "slipping." The fish can then run away without fighting the drag. If it takes out all the line, the drag is then useless and a fish can snap the line. In any case, the more line the fish can strip from the reel, the better its chances of getting away.

## Testing for sensitivity

The more sensitive a drag, the more accurately and easily it can be set. You must make numerous drag adjustments during a day's fishing, and if you fish long enough, one of these days you will have the displeasure of trying to adjust a worn-out or worthless drag. Most likely this will happen when you're fighting a trophy fish. The drag will be too tight. To keep the fish from breaking your line, you turn the knob a touch counterclockwise to lessen the tension. Suddenly all drag resistance is gone. The fish explodes forward. If it remains hooked, it takes a mile of line with it.

The opposite scenario occurs when the fish is already stripping your reel of line. To slow the fish and make it work harder, you turn the drag knob just a touch clockwise to increase drag pressure. Before you can take your hand off the knob, your fishing rod bends double and your line snaps. The reason you now lack a fish on your line is the unfortunate fact that your drag lacked sensitivity. Instead of possessing a wide range of settings, it was pretty much an on/off switch – either giving out line under the slightest pressure or not giving it out at all.

*Drags washers are most often made of leather, fiber, or Teflon, with metal spacers in between. Each type has its disadvantage. Leather heats up quickly, fiber is unreliable under light pressure, and Teflon loses reliability under heavy pressure.*

### Drags wear out

If your first fishing reel does not have a sensitive drag out of the box in the tackle store, it never will have. Drags eventually wear out and need to be replaced. By "wear out," we usually mean lose sensitivity.

*The greater the sensitivity of your brand-new reel, the more likely it contains a quality, long-lasting drag.*

You check drag sensitivity by gently tightening the drag until you have real difficulty pulling line from the spool. Slowly, in increments, loosen the drag by turning the knob slightly counterclockwise. Keep rough track of the amount you are turning the drag knob. Is the drag becoming lighter (looser) in small, uniformly progressive increments? Keep opening (loosening) the drag until it gives no tension at all. Try again, this time retightening the drag.

Adjust the drag to what you think (guess) would be the right setting for the line test now on the reel. Pull enough line off to get a real feel for this setting. Give the drag knob a good turn in either direction. Now see if you can find your preferred setting again. If you can, easily, you have yourself a reel with a sensitive drag.

*Fiber drag washers wear out when their surfaces harden and get slick. You can then get a little more use out of them by rubbing their surfaces gently on medium sandpaper.*

## Testing for range

The fact that the line capacities for 8-, 12-, and 16-pound test are printed on a reel's spool housing or in its manual is no guarantee that that reel performs acceptably using this range of line strengths. The name of a quality manufacturer on the reel, or the assurances of a knowledgeable, reputable dealer might appear to lend credence to this claim. Still, there is no harm in checking out the reel for yourself. The ideal way to do so would be to fill your spool with both the lightest and heaviest test strengths listed, then check the drag for sensitivity at the necessary settings. In other words, see if the drag offers, for each test strength, a wide range of settings between the one that will release line with almost no tension and the setting that will break the line before releasing it. Of course, you can't very well set up shop in a tackle store. However, once the reel is yours, you should definitely check the drag's range before you let a fish do it for you.

# Are parts easily available?

*A REEL CAN LAST FOREVER, but eventually you will need to replace some of the parts. When deciding upon a reel, knowing that parts and service are available locally is a big plus. When they are available at your neighborhood tackle store, that's a bigger plus.*

*Never buy a reel unless parts and service will be easily available.*

You can order parts by mail for most reels on the market. To do so, you need two things – a diagram showing all the reel's parts and an address to send your order. These can be found in the reel's manual or possibly on the Internet. Never buy a reel if the manual is missing and unavailable. Aside from a parts list, you may also need some maintenance instructions, especially reassembly after a cleaning. There is nothing superior to a parts diagram for identifying leftover parts. Believe me, no parts inside a reel are spare parts. Each one has a purpose, and it's a good idea to figure out that purpose without the help of a fish on the other end of your line.

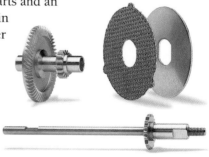

REEL PARTS

# Extra spools

*THE FIRST SPARE PART you should buy is an extra spool. As I said before, a prime feature of spinning tackle is its versatility. Having a couple of spare spools makes it even more versatile. For reasons I will cover later, you should always start your day fishing with the lightest line you can get away with. If you lose a fish and want to change to heavier line, no problem. With spinning tackle, all you do is snap or screw on a spool filled with higher test.*

You may want two extra spools – three choices of line strength or two choices and a spare of your favorite. Don't buy the extra spools right away. Just fill your reel with the line test you think suitable for the fishing you intend to do. After a few days of fishing, you'll know whether your spare spool should be filled with heavier or lighter line, or if you need one spool of each.

EXTRA SPOOLS CAN BE A GREAT BENEFIT

# Reel options

*DISCUSSING THE ESSENTIAL QUALITIES you need in your first reel, I got a little more involved than I would have liked. Now, when discussing options, I'm going back to keeping it simple. Many options now available will soon disappear from the face of the earth. Deservedly so. Of the numerous worthwhile options, I'll limit myself to the examination of only three.*

## Corrosion resistance

Many spinning reels qualify as saltwater-proof. However, if there is a completely corrosion-proof spinning reel, I have yet to come across it. Still, there are numerous spinning reels made with enough care and quality materials to far outlast the fishermen who own them, which, it should be noted, will not do these fishermen much good. Of course, even these reels necessitate some reasonable care and maintenance.

If your first reel is strictly for freshwater use, it does not have to be saltwater-proof. However, try using a freshwater reel in saltwater, and you're going to end up with a corroded mess with no moving parts. Rust, oxidation, and pitting invisible to the naked eye can cost you fish. When it occurs on a part such as the bail or spool lip, the added friction will weaken and wear out your line. If you have to prevent corrosion through the heavy use of protective lubricants, you'll end up lubricating line, lures, bait, and other terminal tackle.

■ **If you're planning to use** *your reel for saltwater fishing, it's important that you buy one that is saltwater-proof. If it isn't, no rust inhibitor can help it.*

*The Second Golden Rule of Fishing:* "Never contaminate your line or terminal tackle with lubricants, insect repellent, sunblock, suntan lotion, or any other substance that will repel fish." These substances are known, for a fact, to take away a fish's appetite.

Save yourself some fish and maintenance. Buy the most corrosion-proof reel you can afford, and rinse it thoroughly after each use, especially after any contact with saltwater.

*Never wet your drag washers when rinsing off your equipment. Prevent this by first completely tightening down your drag. When you're done rinsing, back off your drag completely, so as not to weaken its spring or flatten the softer drag washers.*

### Trivia...

*There exist fishermen so determined not to contaminate their terminal tackle that they don rubber gloves before touching it. Your author is not one of them. This is one of the few things he won't do in order to catch a fish. Resigned to the fact that the need for lubricants, insect repellent, and sunblock will sometimes result in contamination, he strives to keep this to a minimum, and sleeps well despite it.*

## Skirts are in

Another desirable option is a skirted spool. You can see the difference between this and a regular spool by comparing the pictures on this page. One of the reasons you chose spinning tackle over the other types of equipment was its trouble-free operation.

REGULAR SPOOL

SKIRTED SPOOL

*A skirted spool makes a spinning reel even more trouble-free. It does so by preventing your line from finding its way beneath the spool.*

The remedy for this mess involves removing the spool, untangling the line, removing any damaged sections or junking it entirely, and putting your reel back together again, all the while dropping a minimum of parts into the water.

I realize that to the uninitiated, getting line underneath the spool seems impossible. Believe me, it isn't. I guarantee that you won't have to use a standard-spool spinning reel very long before *Faure's Law* applies itself.

Don't let me give you the wrong impression. Millions of fishermen have used the standard spool and survived. Many of them have even thrived. So let's assume you've narrowed your choice down to two reels, one skirted and one unskirted, and cost is a major factor in your decision. The skirted is almost sure to cost more, as will its extra spool. If the reel with the unskirted spool is clearly a better buy, go with it. You'll do fine. I have faith in you.

**INTERNET**

home.icdc.com/
~vernonsk/

*Maybe it's premature since we're talking about buying your first reel, but this is a quirky little site about collecting antique reels!*

## Convertibility

There is one option that is unimportant to the majority of fishermen, yet extremely important to a minority of them. Most styles of fishing reels are either right-handed or left-handed, and the left-handed ones are hard to come by, except by special order. This often means at a premium, and never means at a discount. However, many, if not the majority of, spinning reels can be converted from left- to right-handed merely by unscrewing the handle from one side and screwing it in to the other. If you're left-handed, make sure you get a convertible model.

## Optional options

There are numerous other options I could discuss, but there's no real need to do so yet. An elongated spool will give you slightly longer casts, but unless you find it on a reel you otherwise prefer, forget it. Worry about the quality of the drag, not its location or mechanics. A special release lever for live bait is nice, but you can survive without one on your first spinning reel.

*Remember, all you need is a reasonably priced reel that is sturdy, operates smoothly, and possesses a quality drag. The next thing is to get out of the tackle shop and over to the fishing spot.*

# A simple summary

✓ The First Golden Rule of Fishing: "Less is better, if it can get the job done." The lighter your line and the terminal tackle attached to it, the more fish you will fool.

✓ The Second Golden Rule of Fishing: "Never contaminate your line or terminal tackle with lubricants, insect repellent, sunblock, suntan lotion, or any other substance that will repel fish." These substances are known, for a fact, to take away a fish's appetite.

✓ The "right" reel is sturdy and can handle the range of line tests necessary for the fishing you intend to do.

✓ Don't buy a reel unless you're sure parts and service are available.

✓ Keep your drag washers dry and free of lubricants.

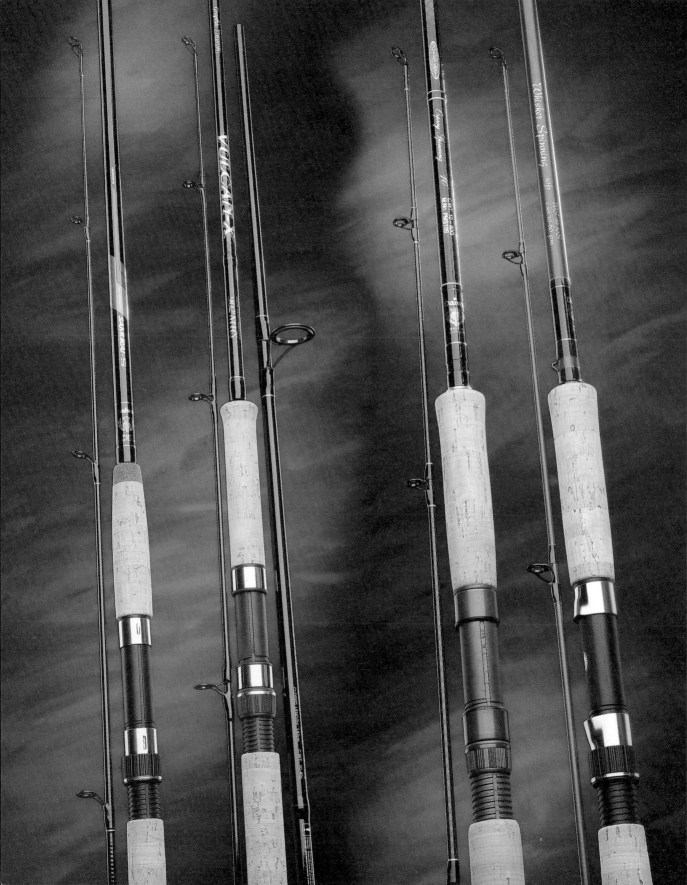

# Chapter 5

# Buying the Right Rod

THE MAIN QUALITY you look for in your first fishing rod is the same one you were looking for in a spinning reel – versatility. Stay away from specialized models such as the long, surfcasting rods. Find an all-around rod to match your reel. The first and foremost aspect to match is line-strength rating. Doing so is important because of the functions the rod serves – as a shock absorber that protects the line, as a spring that tires the fish, and as a lever that draws the fish closer to you. To serve these functions, your rod must not be either too stiff or too limber for the test (strength) of the line being used.

## In this chapter...

✓ The rod as a shock absorber

✓ The rod as a spring

✓ The rod as a lever

✓ Rod options

# The rod as a shock absorber

*SAY YOU'RE USING 15-pound test line and have hooked a 30-pound fish. Now, if your drag is set to 5 or 10 pounds, you shouldn't have to worry about the fish snapping the line. You shouldn't have to, but you should worry anyway. The line could be damaged. More to the point, the drag could stick, especially at that very first instant it's supposed to give line. Also, it could slip, letting the fish take out way too much line. You may have no choice but to tighten the drag, perhaps even beyond the line's breaking strength. All will not necessarily be lost – and, by "all," I mean your 30-pound trophy fish.*

## The right rod for the job

The pictures on these pages show the same person, the same reel, the same 15-pound test line, and the same stubborn fish on the other end. The only difference in the drawings is that the rod on the left is rated for 4- to 8-pound test, the middle one for 10- to 20-pound test, and the rod on the right for 25- to 35-pound test.

*Rod is bent to its maximum*

These illustrations catch a moment during the fight when the fish is applying close to 15 pounds of force on 15-pound test line. This means the drags are set way too heavy for some reason (likely for purposes of explanation). In less than a second, the fish will give a short but ferocious shake of its head that will add another 3 or 4 pounds of force to the line, enough to surpass its breaking strength. Something has to give.

The 4- to 8-pound rod is already bent as far as it will go. There is no way it can give any more.

*When the fish increases the force over the line's breaking strength, the line will snap. This is not good. I repeat, not good.*

4- TO 8-POUND
ROD

Let's skip to the 25- to 35-pound rod. It's hardly bent at all. The slight increase in force that the fish is about to apply won't increase that bend in the fish's direction much. Again something's got to give, and it will be the line – SNAP!

Now let's look at the 10- to 20-pound rod, a perfect match for the 15-pound test line. Notice the nice bend in the rod tip. That bend can get a lot bigger before the line reaches its breaking strength. If the fish increases the force it's exerting over the fishing line's strength with a sudden jerk of the head or a jump, there's a good chance that the rod will act as a shock absorber. It will bend just enough to dampen this sudden pressure and prevent it from breaking the line. If the fish goes on a long, sustained run, there is less of a chance the rod can help, but a significant chance all the same. And this is why the rod's function as a shock absorber is important.

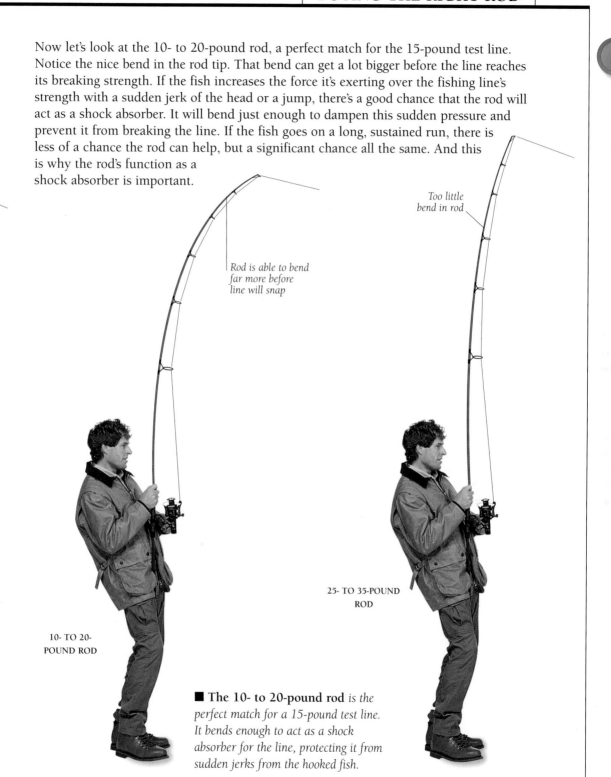

*Too little bend in rod*

*Rod is able to bend far more before line will snap*

25- TO 35-POUND ROD

10- TO 20- POUND ROD

■ **The 10- to 20-pound rod** *is the perfect match for a 15-pound test line. It bends enough to act as a shock absorber for the line, protecting it from sudden jerks from the hooked fish.*

# The rod as a spring

**THE SAME QUALITIES** *that make a fishing rod a good shock absorber also make it a good spring. The phenomenon I'm describing is the ability of a fishing rod to store and release energy.*

*In order for your rod to act as a shock absorber or a spring, you must hold it in a position that allows the fish to bend it. Pointing it directly at the fish is not the way to go.*

Think of the spring in the fishing rod as attached externally and secured at a point directly opposite the fish. When the fish exerts no force, the rod remains straight and the spring remains contracted. When the fish exerts enough force to bend the rod, it also expands the spring, which now wants to contract, pulling the fish back toward it. So, just to stay put, the fish has to work against the force it stored in the spring. If it tires for even an instant, it's pulled closer and the fisherman can reel in some line.

The energy expended by the fish to fight the spring tires it in the same way as drag pressure tires it. Interestingly, the rod working as a spring gives you an advantage that the drag does not. When the fish loses strength, the rod straightens (the spring contracts), pulling it back toward you. A drag does not do this. It tires the fish, but at the cost of giving out line. You don't get the line back automatically, as when the rod straightens. You have to reel it in, with a heavy fish on the other end.

Look back at the pictures on the previous two pages. Too limber a rod, such as the 4- to 8-pound one, can't help you fight the fish. Its spring effect is too weak. You would merely give the fish an enjoyable workout, sculpting its physique. Too stiff a rod, like the 25- to 35-pounder, does not help because the fish is too small to really bend it.

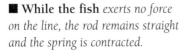

■ **While the fish** *exerts no force on the line, the rod remains straight and the spring is contracted.*

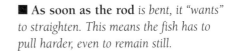

■ **As soon as the rod** *is bent, it "wants" to straighten. This means the fish has to pull harder, even to remain still.*

# The rod as a lever

THE APPROPRIATE FISHING ROD *will also act as a lever, helping you draw a fish toward you and retrieve line. You don't need this advantage when fighting a small fish, a tired fish, a lazy fish, a suicidal fish, or a fish anxious to meet you. However, some day you'll have the good fortune to hook a big, strong, stubborn fish with none of the previous accommodating traits.*

There will arrive a crucial point in the battle, usually with the spool almost empty, when that fish can no longer pull line from the reel but you can't regain any line either. Whenever you turn the reel handle, the drag slips and the fish doesn't come an inch closer. This is when you have no choice but to use the rod as a lever. You must pump and reel.

## The pump

You start by pulling back the rod until it is about 10 degrees from the vertical. This step is referred to as pumping the fish up or toward you. It must be accomplished smoothly and steadily. Otherwise you can yank the hook out of the fish's mouth, or slingshot the fish forward, thus giving it enough slack to throw the hook.

Jerking the rod can also place enough sudden pressure on the line to break it. Notice how the rod is bent, often referred to as loaded (with energy or force).

## The reel

The next step in the pump and reel is, not surprisingly, the reel. You're going to lower your rod until, as illustrated, it's about 80 degrees from the vertical. Notice I didn't say lower the rod smoothly and steadily. This is a much quicker move than the pump, and for good reason.

THE PUMP AND REEL

_The Third Golden Rule of Fishing_: "Keep your line tight." Give a fish slack and you give it a chance to throw the hook. Also, in order to tire a fish as quickly as possible, it's important that you always maintain maximum pressure.

When you lower the rod, the bend in it almost disappears. This illustrates the fact that the rod is not maintaining the same amount of pressure on the fish as during the pump. You must compensate for this loss by applying pressure with the reel to gain line. The reel phase must be completed quickly, while keeping the line tight. You do so by starting to reel an instant before you lower the rod, and by reeling like crazy until an instant after you start the pump.

## The reason why

The purpose of the pump is to draw the fish closer. By lowering the rod and reeling, you gain back line. Then you start all over again, using the rod as a lever to draw the fish closer. If you can't see why this is more effective than keeping the rod stationary and merely cranking the reel handle, then keep cranking the handle until you meet a fish tough enough to enlighten you. When that handle-cranking wrist of yours feels pulverized, and you see your drag slip a half turn for every $\frac{1}{8}$ inch of line you gain, you'll start pumping and reeling despite your suspicions.

## Match the rod to the reel

Afterward, as you sit trying to regain your strength, think about what happened. Those little gears in your spinning reel gave you an advantage when collecting line. Still, this advantage was small compared to that offered by a lever the length of your fishing rod. In addition, when reeling you used mainly your hands. Pumping, your arms did the work. Which is stronger?

Returning for the last time to the pictures on pages 56–57, it should be apparent that the undersized 4- to 8-pound rod wouldn't be of much use as a lever, not with a fish on strong enough to bend it into a pretzel. As a lever, the stiff, oversized 25- to 35-pound rod would be tops, if you don't mind snapping your line in the process.

The importance of matching your reel with an appropriate rod is indisputable. A good one will usually have its line-test range printed right on its shaft. This range should approximate that of the reel. If it does, your first fishing rod will bend and act like a shock absorber to protect the line, a spring to work in concert with your drag to wear down the fish, and a lever to draw the fish closer. Don't misunderstand me – you won't want to pump and reel every fish. Unless there is a need to, it is often a safer and more pleasant experience to take your time. There is no need to fight every bass the same way you fight a marlin.

# Rod options

**WHEN IT COMES TO FISHING ROD COMPONENTS,** *the variety of styles and materials on the market is enough to make even a professional rod builder dizzy. Don't waste your time trying to become an expert. Just find a fishing rod or two that work for you. Depend on one fact – a cheap rod will have cheap guides. Another thing you can depend on, but with less certainty, is that a top-of-the-line rod by a quality manufacturer will have excellent guides. For your first fishing rod, try to find one in the mid-price range.*

## Comparing the parts

First, take a look at the most expensive spinning rod in the store. Examine the guides, the reel seat, the butt, and the grip. These are what you want. Examine these same features on the cheapest rod in the store. These are what you don't want. Now check out the mid-price, medium-***action*** rods. A valuable clue to their quality is how their components compare to those on the most expensive rods. Keep it simple by concentrating on the more important and telling components – the guides and the reel seat. You can use the butt and the grip for tiebreakers if necessary.

> **DEFINITION**
>
> *A fishing rod's **action** refers to its flexibility. This depends upon the blank, which is the unadorned shaft of fiberglass, graphite, and so on. You are looking for a flexible tip with some backbone (stiffness) beneath it. Only experience, and a lot of it, will teach you how to judge a rod's action.*

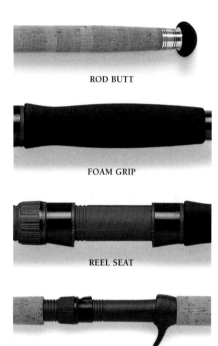

ROD BUTT

FOAM GRIP

REEL SEAT

TRIGGER GRIP

COMPLETE BROKEN-DOWN ROD

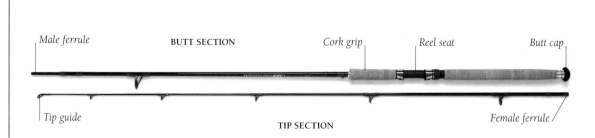

*Male ferrule*     **BUTT SECTION**     *Cork grip*     *Reel seat*     *Butt cap*

*Tip guide*     **TIP SECTION**     *Female ferrule*

## The right guides

Spinning rod guides are most often made out of hardened metals or hardened ceramics. If you can gauge the quality of fishing rod guides merely by looking at them, then you should be writing this chapter, not reading it. When you find a mid-price rod with the same guides as (not knock-offs of) a top-quality rod, you've found a very persuasive buying point. Check out any written material that comes with the rod, especially those cardboard tags hanging from a line guide. The better the guides, the more likely that the manufacturer will make some claims about them.

Butt guide

Intermediate guide

Tip guide

**SPINNING ROD GUIDES**

No rod guides are perfect. Metal guides that don't rust may oxidize or pit. Ceramic guides can chip and crack. To the amateur fisherman, wear is only a problem with the cheapest guides. You wear out a quality guide, chances are you've lived a long life, getting your money's worth out of more than just your rod guides.

*To check a guide for defects or damage that can, in turn, damage your line, run a piece of nylon stocking through them. If there's a problem, the nylon will catch it, literally. A fourth of a stocking will do fine. A pair of panty hose is overkill. It will get stuck in the smaller line guides and may raise some eyebrows to boot.*

Pay special attention to the care with which the rod guides are attached to the rod. A rod manufacturer that skimps on epoxy almost certainly skimps elsewhere. Still, where glue is concerned, quantity is no assurance of quality either. If it is too thick, the glue is more likely to crack. An extra **wrap** underneath the glue is worth more than an extra gob on top. Look for neat, clean work.

> **DEFINITION**
>
> A **wrap** is a layer of thread attaching the feet of a line guide to the rod shaft. The use of tape in place of thread is a sure sign of poor quality.

*While intricate rod wraps are a sign of extra care on the part of the rod builder, watch out for two reasons. First, you may be paying extra for a nonessential. And second, too decorative a job on lighter, faster rods can actually dampen their action.*

If you're the type of person who will religiously rinse and apply corrosion inhibitors to metal guides, and who will also take great care not to chip or crack ceramic ones, then either hardened metal or ceramic is fine for you. If you're going to do a lot of saltwater fishing, ceramic guides have the edge. Just be careful how you carry them around – in the car and in your hand. Also, when reeling in your line, try not to hit your ceramic tip guide with metal swivels (see Chapter 6). You can chip it or knock it right out of its setting. Check your rod guides often for defects that can damage your line.

*Until you get used to a ceramic rod tip, keep a soft bead on your line just above the swivel. It will come between it and your rod tip. If you see you don't need the bead, get rid of it and anything else on your line that you don't need.*

## It's called a ferrule

"**Ferrule** or no ferrule?" that is the question. More precisely, the question is whether the added safety and convenience of a two-piece fishing rod is worth the disadvantages. The answer is yes. Car doors zero in on rod tips the way tornadoes find trailer parks, and with similar results. A rod that can be broken down to half its size is easier to safely transport and store.

> ### DEFINITION
>
> A fishing rod **ferrule** is a male–female connection that allows the rod to be broken down into two or more pieces. It can be two pieces of metal glued onto the two halves of a rod shaft, or it can be a connection molded into the rod shaft itself.

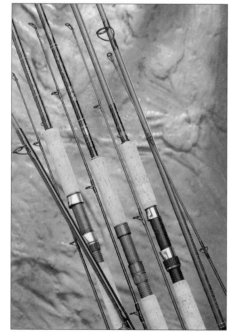

FERRULE

■ **A ferrule is worth the extra cost:** *It will make travel easier for you and safer for your rod.*

One drawback to ferrules is that they dampen and distort the action of the rod blank. However, the effect is small, except on lighter rods. It takes an accomplished fisherman to notice the difference. I hope some day you will be so accomplished. Another drawback is that two-piece rods yearn to be one inseparable piece. Store your rod in two pieces. Every time you put it back together, first lubricate the male half of the ferrule with a few soft strokes of candle wax or a touch of WD-40. Otherwise, you'll end up with none of the advantages of a ferrule and all the disadvantages, slight as they are.

*Never lubricate a ferrule with grease or oil. Grit will stick to it, causing almost as much trouble as corrosion.*

■ **Be sure to** *lubricate your ferrule every time you put your rod together. Just put a couple of drops of WD-40 onto the male part.*

The real reason I recommend a ferrule is the same reason I steered you away from fly-fishing gear: I don't want you to get discouraged enough to quit fishing. Rare is the fisherman who has not busted off a rod tip at exactly the wrong time. Usually there's enough rod left to stick on a replacement tip. Still, the crunching sound is sickening, repairs are a hassle, and the rod is never the same. When we were kids, we used to work our way down fishing rods as if they were sticks of beef jerky. If, after a discouraging day of fishing, or perhaps a few in a row, your subconscious decides to top things off by turning your one-piece rod into a two-piece after all, you just may get discouraged enough to quit fishing before you master it. Prevent this. Get your two-piece rod ready-made.

## Choosing your seat

In our discussion of reel seats, I'll keep it simple. Your basic choice is between metal or one of the miracle composites. In the mid-price range, you should be safe with either. A top-of-the-line metal reel seat gives you more strength, but a quality composite is stronger than many metal reel seats. It should be plenty strong enough for anything you can land on spinning tackle. With a metal reel seat, double locking rings are a nice plus. You don't have to tighten them down as hard, and they're more likely to stay tightened.

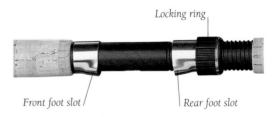

*Locking ring*

*Front foot slot*

*Rear foot slot*

**REEL SEAT**

**INTERNET**

**www.fishingworks.com**

*Claiming to "help fishermen navigate the Web," this site contains information on pretty much every aspect of the sport, including buying fishing rods.*

■ **You have your rod and reel,** *and it won't be long till you're out fishing with it!*

## A simple summary

✔ The Third Golden Rule of Fishing: "Keep your line tight." Give a fish slack, and you give it a chance to throw the hook. Also, in order to tire a fish as quickly as possible, it's important that you always maintain maximum pressure.

✔ The "right" spinning rod for you will be one that matches your spinning reel.

✔ Your rod can and should be used as a shock absorber, a spring, and a lever.

✔ Your first rod should have a medium action and decent line guides.

✔ If you can't gain line by reeling, then pump and reel.

✔ Two-piece rods are the way to go.

# Chapter 6

# Tackle-Box Essentials

WE'RE GOING TO START at the end of your fishing line and work our way down to the hook. Keep in mind the First Golden Rule of Fishing: "Less is better, if it can get the job done." You want as little as possible between you and the fish. If you don't need something, get rid of it. If you do need it, use the smallest size that will do the job.

## In this chapter...

✓ Snap swivels

✓ Leaders

✓ Hooks

✓ Baits

✓ Sinkers

✓ Bobbers

✓ The bare essentials

# Chapter 7

# Rigging Your Gear

IN THIS CHAPTER, I'll cover all preparation necessary, from the moment you get home with your new equipment, until the moment you walk out the door to go fishing. The staff at your tackle shop should have helped you do much of this preparation. This was one of the reasons you paid a little more than you would have at the Super-Duper-Mile-Square Discount Mart – not for having the tackle shop do the work, but for the opportunity to learn how to do it by watching them. The time and care they took after the sale should influence any decision about giving them your business in the future. After reading this chapter, you should be able to do it all yourself and do it right.

In this chapter...
- ✓ Assembling the rod and reel
- ✓ Filling the spool
- ✓ The most essential knots
- ✓ The most essential leaders

READY TO RIG

# Assembling the rod and reel

*THERE ARE MANY STYLES of reel seats found on spinning rods, and the seat of the reel is also the seat of a few of the fisherman's most annoying problems. If the reel seat is metal, the reel's foot is invariably made of a different metal, and at the place where they meet, they usually also meet up with corrosion.*

Corrosion can cause the locking ring to freeze. This will leave you with a very aggravating, time-consuming job. To prevent this problem, you must rinse and apply a rust inhibitor to your reel seat both before and after exposing it to the elements, especially when those elements include saltwater. Now is the time to start. Spray any metal components with WD-40 or a similar solution. Pay special attention to the threaded parts and the reel foot slots.

## SECURING THE REEL TO THE ROD

To secure the reel to the rod, follow these few simple steps:

1. Slide the front foot of the reel into the front reel foot slot.

2. Holding the reel in place, slide the rear reel foot slot forward until it holds the reel in place.

STEP 1

3. Screw the locking ring up against the back of this sliding reel slot, but don't tighten it yet.

4. Jiggle the reel, at the same time centering and pushing it gently forward as far as possible.

STEP 4

5. Hand-tighten the locking ring as tight as you can.

*Never use any type of wrench on reel-seat locking rings.*

STEP 5

# I'm warning you . . .

Now I've given you the procedure for securing a reel seat, here are the scare tactics to make sure you follow it. If the reel foot isn't centered, when you tighten the locking ring enough to hold the reel steady, you just may tighten it enough to distort the reel foot slot. Once the foot slot is distorted, the reel will never stay steady for long. Then every time you retighten the reel seat, you further distort it. This process continues until you end up with the choice of holding the reel in place with stainless steel hose clamps or throwing away the rod. Either way, you have proved *Finagle's Law.*

> **DEFINITION**
>
> **Finagle's Law:** *Once a job is fouled up, anything done to improve it just fouls it up worse.*

*Keep your reel seat lubricated and in working order. Check it for tightness before and during each day's fishing.*

## Missing screws

No matter how carefully and well-tightened a reel seat, it may somehow loosen by itself. Boat vibrations are notorious for perpetrating such mischief. Once, on my way to do some trolling, I was surprised to notice that a few of my reel's screws were a thread or two away from falling out. Upon closer inspection, I was more surprised to notice that another half dozen had already left the scene of this impending disaster. If I hadn't been able to salvage a few screws out of the bilge, a day's fishing might have been ruined.

*Supposedly, screws get unscrewed when the pitch of an engine matches the pitch of a screw. This is the reason many of the old-time boat skippers jiggle their throttles every so often. They prefer a boat load of loose screws to a few missing ones.*

## Damaged seats

Getting back to reel seats, there's another common way they get damaged. Large fish have an uncanny knack for finding the rod with the loosest real seat, even if that reel seat is hardly loose at all. During the ensuing battle, the reel will loosen further, enough to fall off if something isn't done first. The fish by itself can usually manage more than enough damage, even before the angler joins in on the demolition job by trying to tighten down the reel. Pressure from the fish will keep the reel improperly seated. If the fisherman succeeds in tightening the reel, there's a good chance he or she will also succeed in ruining the reel seat for good.

*If you're not a stickler for looks, and insist on added insurance that your reel will not work loose, take a few turns over the locking screw with duct tape.*

# Filling the spool

*IT MAY HAVE IRRITATED YOU that the previous topic, "Assembling the rod and reel," took about five times longer to read than to accomplish. No fear. Filling the spool will take five time longer to accomplish. However, don't assume you'll find it any less irritating. In the tradition of keeping it simple, I'll lay down the law and say that there's only one type of line you want to use on a spinning reel – monofilament. We'll delve deeper into this subject in Chapter 15. All we need to consider now is that monofilament, often referred to as "mono," has* **memory.**

> **DEFINITION**
>
> *Monofilament fishing line, when unwound from a spool and allowed to hang without tension or weight, retains the* **memory** *of the spool by hanging in a corkscrew pattern. A long, hard fight from a big, strong fish can straighten out mono and give it amnesia. However, winding it back onto the spool again will cure the line's amnesia and return its corkscrew memory.*

## Giving your line amnesia

If we wind the mono onto the spinning reel's spool with its memory of the manufacturer's spool it came on even somewhat intact, then this line may not want to stay on the reel's spool. Every time we open the bail to cast, the line may spring off and cause a mess. For this reason, we first eliminate as much of the line's memory as possible. We do so by soaking the mono in hot water, then winding it tautly and neatly onto our spinning reel.

Soak the line for about 10 minutes in very hot, but not scalding, water. Brace or have someone hold the manufacturer's spool sideways, so the line comes off the end of it. This line should uncoil in the direction it will be coiled onto the reel's spool. If you find this hard to understand, just remember that if the helper is holding the manufacturer's spool in his left hand and the line coming off it in his right, then the line should be coming off the top of the spool, not the bottom. If this is not the case, he has merely to turn the spool 180 degrees so the other end is facing the rod and reel.

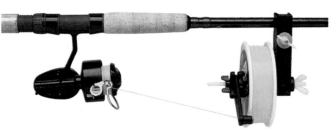

■ **When you fill your reel's spool,** *you don't need a willing helper or a brace to hold the manufacturer's spool. However, if you don't have either one, you'll soon wish you did.*

# Reel preparation

Turn the reel handle to see if it moves in both directions. If it does, you just had a 50-percent chance of winding on the line backward. This is certainly an experience your ego can do without. To avoid it, flick on your reel's anti-reverse lever or switch. If it's not located on your reel in the same place as in the picture (*right*), there's a good chance your reel's instructions provide some clues as to its whereabouts. After you're sure the reel handle now turns in only one direction, thread the line through the rod guides, or at least use the bottom guide. Now flip open the bail. Tie the mono on the spool using the arbor knot, which we will be coming to shortly.

ANTI-REVERSE SWITCH

*Sometimes the bail won't lock open. The rotor may have stopped on the one spot that prevents this. Turn the reel handle a touch and try again. If the bail still won't lock, clean the bail spring with a shot of a rust inhibitor such as WD-40, then apply a few drops of oil.*

Close the bail by turning the reel handle. If the handle will not turn, do not try to force it. The rotor may be resting right up against the bail-release trigger. Give the handle a quick jerk backward, then immediately forward. It will hardly move back at all, but even a little play may supply enough momentum to trigger the bail release. If not, click off the anti-reverse lever and turn the handle in reverse about ¼ of a revolution to back the rotor off the bail trigger. Then slam the handle forward. As soon as the bail snaps closed, flick the anti-reverse lever back on and start filling the spool.

*Never, never try to close the bail by hand. If you succeed, you have probably also succeeded in breaking your reel, or at least bending the bail out of shape.*

■ **Opening the bail** *allows line to leave the spool.*

If you ever forget to first flip open the bail before tying the line to the spool (which you will, more than once, I guarantee it), when you turn the reel handle the bail will still revolve nicely around the spool as it should. However, it will not be winding any line onto it. The novice usually solves this problem by cutting the line off the spool, opening the bail, and retying it. You won't. Instead, you'll unsnap the spool, open the bail, replace the spool, and start winding.

## Filling the spool

You must wind on the line tightly. If you don't have a device to supply the necessary tension, your thumb and first finger will do fine. However, to avoid third-degree burns, work slowly and move the line around between your fingers. Better yet, wear a glove, preferably leather. Whatever you do, make sure to hold the line away from the rod shaft.

*Never let running mono rub against a rod. And don't even think about supplying winding tension by pressing line against the rod shaft instead of between your fingers. Running line can create enough heat against the rod shaft to ruin both line and rod.*

## How full is full?

This question has been plaguing fishermen since way back to the days when they first found themselves with too much time on their hands. Overfill a spool and the excess line will jump off at an inappropriate moment and possibly cause a tangle. Underfill a spool and you'll pay in casting distance (thoroughly discussed in Chapter 8). The great fishing authorities all agree that, when full, the line should lay level on the spool – no bulge in the middle or anywhere else. However, they can't agree whether it should lay level $1/8$ or $1/16$ of an inch (or however many millimeters) below the spool lip.

Your humble author will offer his own take on this controversy, admittedly influenced by the fact that he could not distinguish $1/8$ of an inch from $1/16$ even with a ruler. He aims for maximum casting distance and blithely fills his spools right up to the lip. If, during some practice casts, his line jumps off his spool, he jettisons the part that does until it doesn't. Until it doesn't, he stays away from the more time-consuming knots.

**INTERNET**

www.kenschultz.com/ articles.asp?article=41

*This article, "How to Spool Line," is found at KenSchultz.com, "the angling authority™." It covers spinning gear, as well as spincasting, baitcasting, and fly casting, and should be worth a look.*

# The most essential knots

*THIS BOOK DOESN'T AWARD merit badges for knowing all the different fishing knots. It will never even test your competence. All testing will be done by fish, usually at the most critical times. There's not a fisherman alive who hasn't failed at least a few of these tests. You will too. Your drag will be perfectly set, or perhaps even too loose. You are even thinking of tightening it when . . . SNAP! There goes your line, your fish, your trophy, and, more important, your supper. To add recrimination to injury, there's a suspicious little curlicue on the end of your line. Consider this a failing mark on your last knot.*

The weakest point on an undamaged line is the knot. Any time you tie a simple overhand knot in a fishing line, you weaken it by 50 percent. So, if you're using 10-pound test and you tie an overhand knot in it, you'll then be using the equivalent of 5-pound test, with none of the advantages of that lighter line. You doubt me? Take 3 feet of mono, 20-pound test or less, and tie an overhand knot in the middle.

■ **The overhand knot** *has proved invaluable to fishermen. Master it.*

## Tying an overhand knot

Take the **tag end** underneath the **standing line** to form a loop. Pass the tag end through the loop from above. Pull the tag end and the standing line in opposite directions to tighten the knot.

## Test the line strength

Wind each end a few times around a foot or so of broomstick. Hold the two broomsticks so the line has some slack in it, then yank your hands apart in a quick, sudden jerk. If you are by yourself, the line will snap exactly at the knot 100 out of 100 times. If you are demonstrating this fact for someone else, your success rate will be only slightly lower, except on the first try or two.

*Some knots are much stronger when the pressure is applied slowly. Other knots are better able to absorb sudden jerks. When using knots susceptible to sudden pressure, a sensitive rod tip acting as a shock absorber proves a valuable asset.*

> **DEFINITION**
>
> *The* **tag end** *of the line is the end that you are using to tie the knot. The* **standing line** *is the bit that remains still.*

> *Trivia...*
>
> *Once you've halved the strength of your line by tying an overhand knot in it, additional overhand knots will not cost you any more line strength. Hence, all additional knots are free.*

## Only learn what you'll use

There is no point in wasting time learning more knots than you need. You'll quickly forget how to tie the ones you don't use. The following few knots are easy to learn and will allow you to attach line to spool, line to leader, and line and leader to hook. These knots will be sufficient to get you started fishing.

### Every monofilament knot must be moistened before being tightened.

Start each knot by measuring off the length of line with which you will be working. Run this line quickly through your mouth to moisten it. If you find the idea of this distasteful (pun most definitely intended), let me warn you that a moment later, when the knot is drawn fairly tight and ready to be tightened down completely, you must pop it into your mouth, activate your saliva glands, and slosh it around with your tongue before spitting it out. Then, and only then, do you pull it completely tight. The lubricating and cooling effect of the moisture both protects the line and helps you get a tighter knot. If a knot is not tight, it is more likely to fail when a big, strong fish volunteers to tighten it for you.

You may now be thinking, "I'll get my knots plenty tight without slobbering all over them." Well, I'm not going to argue. However, I assure you that there will come a day when you lose a beautiful fish and see from the pretty curlicue on the end of your line that your knot has failed. You won't waste a lot of time reflecting on this failure. Instead, you'll waste your time rerigging your outfit while everyone else around you is hauling in beautiful fish. And when you have your nice, new knot pulled almost tight by your filthy, stinking-of-fish, black-fingernailed hands, you will then pop that knot into your mouth as quick as a peanut. Many years later, you will think back upon that moment and say to yourself, "Yes, that was the day I became a fisherman."

## The arbor knot

You'll use the arbor knot to tie your fishing line to your reel spool. Remember, before you start, take the tag end of the line and run the last foot of it through your mouth to wet it.

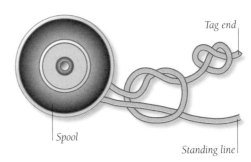

*Tag end*

*Spool*

*Standing line*

**STEP 3**

1. Tie a tight overhand knot close to the tag end.

2. Wrap the tag end around the spool to meet the standing line.

3. Tie another simple overhand knot, this time circling the standing line.

4. Wet the knot and pull fairly tight.

**5** Pull on the standing line until it's tight around the spool.

**6** Keep pulling until the two overhand knots are up against each other.

**7** Keep on pulling until either the first overhand knot prevents the second from sliding or the arbor knot comes undone.

## The improved clinch knot

You can use the improved clinch knot to tie your line to your hook, your leader to your hook, and your line or leader to a swivel. Remember, if you want your *barrel wraps* uniform and even, before you pull this knot tight you'd better slobber profusely all over it. This is the last time I'll remind you to wet the line, but do so for every mono knot every time. If your knot doesn't turn out as neat and pretty as the one shown here, clip it off and start again.

**1** Pass the tag end through the eye of the hook or swivel.

**2** Take the tag end under the standing line and then back over it to form a complete turn.

**3** Repeat step 2 until you have made four to six turns around the standing line.

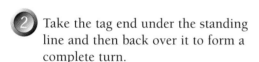

**4** Pass the tag end through the loop nearest to the eye.

**5** Pass the tag end through the large loop made in the previous step, and pull on the standing line slowly and steadily. If necessary, at the same time, pull gently on the tag end to remove any slack.

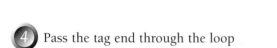

**6** Trim the tag end to ⅛ of an inch.

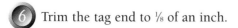

# The blood knot

You use the blood knot to connect two lines of equal or very nearly equal diameter. To be more specific, you use it when half your line is in the water, and a mangled section of it is in your hands. You will then cut out the mess and rejoin the two now distinct parts of your line, hoping that some fish with impeccable timing doesn't choose that moment to dine.

**1** Overlap the two tag ends.

**2** Wrap the tag end of one line around the other standing line about six times.

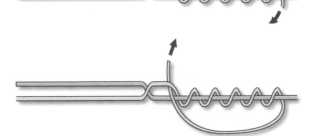

**3** Loop the same tag end back, passing it between the lines on the other side of their crossing point.

**4** Hold the tag end and the crossing point between two fingers and repeat the previous step with the other tag end. Note that this tag end must go through the same loop as the other, but in the opposite direction.

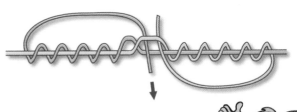

**5** Gently pull on both standing lines until you have two neat, tight, and adjacent barrel wraps. Trim the tag ends to ⅛ of an inch.

**INTERNET**

**www.fishingcairns.com**

*This interesting Australian web site offers instruction on the tying of numerous knots – some I've covered, some not. It also offers much information about fishing in Australia.*

# The surgeon's knot

The surgeon's knot is used to connect lines of dissimilar diameters. You'll use it to connect your leader to your line in situations where you don't care to use a swivel. One such situation occurs when you want to use a long leader, say 15 feet, but you don't want to end up with your swivel trying unsuccessfully to squeeze its way through your rod tip guide while 15 long feet of leader lie between you and your fish. A surgeon's knot will slide right through your line guides, allowing you to reel in the entire leader.

**1** Take the two lines by their tag ends and overlap them by about 6 inches.

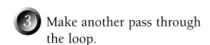

**2** Tie an overhand knot in the overlap, but don't pull the loop closed.

**3** Make another pass through the loop.

**4** Close the loop by pulling on the overlapped lines.

**5** Pull on the standing lines until the knot is tight, and trim the tag ends to ⅛ of an inch.

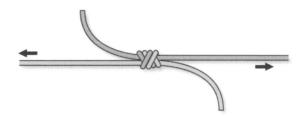

## The surgeon's loop

You tie the surgeon's loop on that end of a leader that will be attached to your fishing line, the opposite end from the hook.

**1** Double the tag end of the line.

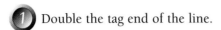

**2** Tie an overhand knot in the doubled-up line, but don't pull it closed.

**3** Pass the end loop through the overhand loop again.

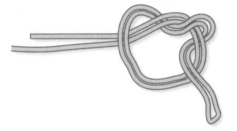

**4** Slide the knot up or back to set the size of the loop.

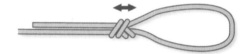

**5** With one hand, pull on the loop; with the other, pull on the standing line and tag end. Trim the tag end to ⅛ of an inch.

*Use a nail clipper to trim your knots. Don't get an expensive one you have to keep sprayed. Rust inhibitor will stink up your line and terminal tackle. Get two cheap ones. Keep one tied to your belt or in your pocket or both. Rinse it off with plain water when necessary. Keep the spare clipper dry and protected in your tackle box. You'll need it sooner than later.*

# The uni-knot loop

The improved clinch knot or any tight knot can restrict the action of some lures. It's preferable to attach them with a loop such as the uni-knot loop. A large fish will often close this uni-knot loop. No matter, the loop has already done its job by allowing the lure to function properly and attract that large fish. It should not bother you at all to merely clip off the old knot and tie a new one.

**1** Lay the tag end parallel to the standing line for an inch or two.

**2** Form a loop extending back to the eye.

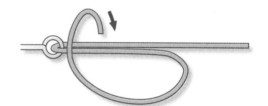

**3** Starting at the eye, take five turns around both parallel lines and between them and the loop.

**4** Gently pull the tag end until the barrel wraps are uniform and snug, but not tight.

**5** Hold the barrel wraps between two fingers of one hand. With your other hand, gently pull on the standing line until the loop is the size you desire.

**6** Lock the loop by pulling hard on the tag end with pliers. Trim the tag end to ⅛ of an inch.

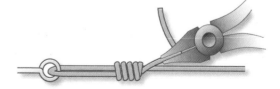

# The most essential leaders

*A LEADER IS A LENGTH OF LINE or wire attached to the end of your fishing line. It's almost always stronger than the line itself. Without a leader, the section of your fishing line most in danger of snapping or being damaged is that section closest to the hook. A damaged line that doesn't part may do so when the next fish tests it, or the one after that. For this reason we attach a leader, a stronger piece of line or wire, to the end of our fishing line.*

You may be asking yourself why not just use a stronger line in the first place. Well, instead of admonishing you for forgetting the First Golden Rule of Fishing – "Less is better, if it can get the job done" – I will supply you with a few of the countless reasons why not. The lighter the line (that is, the lower the test) you use:

1 The less visible your line

2 The more line you can put on your spool

3 The farther you can cast and the quicker it will sink

4 The better the action of your baits

5 The more challenging the fight with a fish

Now aren't you embarrassed that you asked?

■ **Give yourself** *more of a challenge and the fish more of a chance. Use lighter line.*

In Chapter 20 I'll thoroughly cover all the different leader materials. Right now, to keep it simple, I'll discuss the only two types of leaders necessary to get you started fishing – monofilament and single-strand wire.

## Monofilament leaders

Monofilament is and should be your leader material of choice. At comparable strengths, it's less visible to fish than any other leader material. It's also flexible, which enables a natural presentation of both artificial and real baits. Pure and simple, monofilament means more strikes.

There are countless ways to rig a mono leader. I recommend you begin as illustrated below. Here the hook is attached with an improved clinch knot. The loop on the opposite end of the leader is a surgeon's loop.

■ **You can attach your leader** *to a snap swivel using a surgeon's loop.*

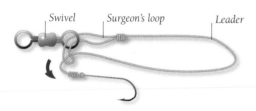

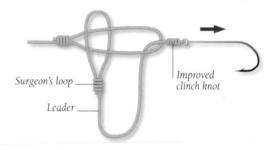

■ **Tie a surgeon's loop** *in your leader, thread part of it through a swivel (with no snap), then pull the hook and leader through that part of the loop.*

■ **Loop to loop:** *Tie a surgeon's loop at the end of your leader, and another at the end of your line. Pass the line loop through the leader loop, take the hook through the line loop, and pull tight to secure.*

You then attach the leader to your line using a snap swivel, standard swivel, or a loop in the end of your fishing line, as shown above. Of course, you can dispense with the time-saving end loop in your leader, tying the leader directly to a swivel with an improved clinch knot. You can also dispense with the swivel, tying your leader directly to your line with a surgeon's knot.

There's one very big drawback to monofilament leaders. Razor-toothed fish such as pike, barracuda, or wahoo can slice through them so quickly that you may not know you've been victimized until you retrieve your line. Amazingly, a 1-pound barracuda can make quick work of a monofilament leader strong enough to haul in a thousand-pound marlin. Other fish can grind mono with their teeth, or damage it with their gills or fins.

# Single-strand wire leaders

Single-strand wire can usually stand up to even the sharpest teeth. By single-strand wire, I'm referring to stainless steel, which is not always the case. In your case, I recommend it should be. Single-strand comes in two colors, natural stainless steel and coffee color. The advantage of the coffee color is that it absorbs more light and is less visible to fish. A disadvantage of it is that, after moderate use, the coffee color wears off, leaving you right back where you started. A disadvantage of single-strand wire, in general, is that both fish and fishermen tend to kink it. Any kink makes it susceptible to snapping in two.

In Chapter 20 I'll discuss alternate leader materials that do not possess these disadvantages, but they have disadvantages of their own. In the meantime, when you're dealing with toothy critters, stick to single-strand wire.

*Never, never straighten kinked single-strand wire. No matter how carefully this is done, the result is a substantially weakened wire. Replace all kinked single-strand wire.*

You attach your hook to single-strand wire, and single-strand to your line with a haywire twist. Actually, this haywire twist is a little more than a standard haywire twist, but the fish can't tell the difference, so I'll continue to keep it simple by ignoring this fact. Unfortunately, our haywire twist is not so simple to learn. Fortunately, once mastered, there is something quite enjoyable about making it.

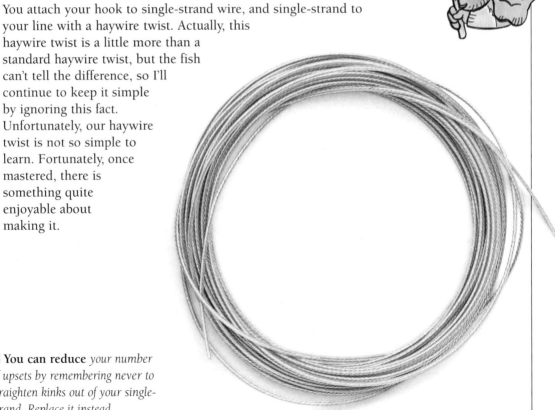

■ **You can reduce** *your number of upsets by remembering never to straighten kinks out of your single-strand. Replace it instead.*

■ **Barracuda are 46 percent teeth.** *If those teeth can reach your leader, you'd better make sure it's wire, not monofilament.*

## The haywire twist

This is a tough one, but here goes:

**1** Pass the tag end and a few inches of the wire through the eye. Bend it back approximately parallel to the standing wire.

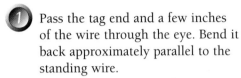

**2** Cross the standing wire and the tag end into an "X," keeping them apart with your finger.

RIGHT

WRONG

**3** Keep the two wires at equal angles from their parallel states. This is the key to neat spirals.

**4** Make five spiral twists, like those in a coat hanger.

**5** As you finish the last spiral twist, allow the standing wire to return to its previous angle (none at all), and increase the angle of the tag end to 90 degrees.

**6** With the tag end, make four neat, tight barrel wraps around the standing wire.

**7** Make a 90-degree bend in the tag end about a finger width from the standing wire. This gives you a "crank," with a shaft and a handle.

**8** Look down so the crank's shaft points directly at you. The handle should appear to be at a 90-degree angle to the standing wire. Picture the crank turning forward until the shaft is parallel to and adjacent to the standing wire. Turn the crank in this direction, and the tag end should break off cleanly from the haywire twist.

COMPLETED HAYWIRE TWIST

*If problems occur*

Despite the clarity and conciseness of the preceding instructions, the tag end may not break off close to the standing line. You don't want to leave enough tag end to catch and tangle your line while casting, collect seaweed or debris while retrieving or trolling, or draw your blood when handling.

To solve this problem you have two choices – snipping off the tag end with a wire cutter or completely remaking the haywire twist. If you choose the wire cutter route, you won't be able to snip the tag end as close to the standing wire as the crank should have. More important, the wire end left will be much sharper, perhaps razor sharp, compared to the wire end that remains after the successful use of a crank. A sharper end is all the more dangerous to your line and your hands.

Obviously, the proper thing to do is snip off the defective haywire twist and make a new one. The problem with this solution is that your second haywire twist may be just as defective, and so may the third, fourth, and so on. You can find yourself failing time after time to break off the tag end correctly. Even after rereading these instructions, you may not be able to figure out what you're doing wrong. My advice is for you to keep rereading the instructions and to keep trying. Just do your best. Use your wire cutters only when you have to. Eventually, you'll get the hang of it, time after effortless time. Interestingly (and frustratingly) enough, you may then have no idea what you're now doing right.

## A simple summary

✔ Rinse and apply a rust inhibitor to your reel seat both before and after exposing it to the elements.

✔ Check to make sure your reel seat is tight before and during each day of fishing.

✔ Monofilament has memory, which needs to be erased as much as possible before you put new line on your reel. Use hot water and wind tightly.

✔ Remember to always moisten a monofilament knot before you pull it tight.

✔ Monofilament should be your first choice as leader material. Use single-strand wire only if you're dealing with toothy critters.

✔ Never straighten kinked single-strand wire. You should replace it instead.

# Chapter 8

# Learning to Cast

SPINNING TACKLE, as I may have mentioned, is the most popular fishing gear in the world. One of the two main reasons for this, which I may have also mentioned, is the ease with which you can learn to cast. Long distances are attainable and disastrous backlashes are infrequent. However, competence does require some practice.

*In this chapter...*
- ✓ *How to practice*
- ✓ *The sidearm cast*
- ✓ *The overhand cast*
- ✓ *Feathering*
- ✓ *Distance is overrated*
- ✓ *Aim for accuracy*

LEARNING TO CAST REQUIRES A SAFE DISTANCE BETWEEN YOU AND ANY POTENTIAL CASUALTIES

# How to practice

MANY BOOKS ON FISHING *contain detailed instructions on exactly how to cast – where to place your feet, where to start your rod, how far back to bring it, when to start forward, and so on. The K.I.S.S. Guide to Fishing is one of these. However, I ask you not to accept any rigid, written-in-stone way to cast as the only way. There's no patent on the exact way. Some equally successful methods are markedly different.*

**INTERNET**

**www.shakespeare-fishing.com**

*This manufacturer's web site contains casting tips for spinning, baitcasting, and fly-fishing. It also has, among many other things, maintenance tips for both rods and reels.*

Consistency in casting results is, of course, enhanced by consistency in execution. Strive to cast the exact same way every time. However, strive as you may, you're not going to come close. Casting upstream, your right leg may be slightly higher, downstream your left. On top of a boulder, you may not be able to spread your feet as far apart as you can on a lake shore. In a boat, you may have to cast sitting down, or straddling a seat, or with one foot much higher than the other. If your target is under some low-hanging tree limbs, you'll have to lower the trajectory of your cast. If you're under a tree limb or a bridge, you may have to cast sidearm, or even underhand, but you can still aim for a smooth, graceful, balanced motion.

## Making a start

Start practicing with little more than a flick of the wrist. At first, distance should not be a prime consideration. What you're looking for is smoothness and timing. Once you have the wrist motion down, when the plug starts flying effortlessly from your rod, you can add some speed and a little more arm. Keep on adding, but slowly. Whenever you finish your cast off balance, you're trying too hard.

Start out casting with a ***practice plug***. Its weight should be within the range of plug sizes recommended for your rod (as written on the shaft or in the accompanying literature).

**DEFINITION**

*A **practice plug** is a hard-rubber or soft-plastic weight, usually shaped something like a bank sinker (see Chapter 17). As a murder weapon, it leaves a lot to be desired, even in the hands of an expert. Still, it can do very serious damage to people's eyes or other delicate parts, including yours, so be careful with it.*

Start by hanging the practice plug about 8 to 18 inches from your rod tip. If you're right-handed, you'll cast with your right hand and reel with your left. Take a comfortable, balanced grip on the rod with the reel-foot shaft either between your middle and third fingers or between your third and fourth fingers. If neither grip feels balanced and your reel seat is adjustable, move the reel forward or backward as you please. In any case, your thumb should lay extended atop and pointing down the rod.

■ **Point your thumb** *down the rod shaft, and point your rod where you want to cast your bait.*

# The sidearm cast

*YOU'LL USE THE SIDEARM CAST far less often than the overhand cast. Still, there are a number of reasons for learning it before the overhand:*

1. You will be more relaxed because, with a sidearm cast, there is less chance of hitting yourself in the face

2. The sidearm is a necessary cast when you stand beneath low-hanging trees, and in numerous other situations

3. It gives your bait a lower trajectory. This allows a softer entrance, one less likely to spook the fish

■ **Although you won't always** *be casting from beneath a low-hanging tree, it's important that you know what to do in such situations.*

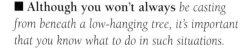

# PRACTICING YOUR SIDEARM CAST

Before you start, pick a distinct target. Make it a close one, no more than 20 yards away. If you're casting into water, any stationary object will do. On land, a pie plate or something similar is fine. A moving target makes corrections harder and should be avoided.

### 1 See the clock face

*Face your target. Picture yourself standing on a huge clock face, you at the center and your target in line with the marking for 12 o'clock. Assuming you're right-handed, as we'll do from now on, point your left foot at the target, a little forward of your right foot.*

### 2 Draw back the rod . . .

*Catch the line on the pad of the first joint of your index finger, and open the bail. Hold the rod near waist level, also pointed at your target. Casually, keeping your elbow near your body, draw your rod back to approximately 3 o'clock.*

Do not hold the line in the crease between the first and second joint of your index finger. It can get caught there.

### 3 . . . And cast

*Give a loose, slightly elevated, forward flick of the wrist, at the same time extending your arm, until the rod is back at 12 o'clock. Oh yes, along the way I recommend that you straighten your finger to release the line.*

Do not make a common novice mistake – hooking the line with your index finger, then forgetting to open the bail. Your terminal tackle can swing back and injure someone, most likely you. Also, the line can break, costing you a plug.

## Is your rod fully loaded?

Once you have gotten to grips with the sidearm cast, try this: As you cast, pay special attention to what happens to your rod tip around 3 o'clock. You should notice that the bend in the rod tip switches from forward to backward when the rod stops moving backward, and the plug crosses behind the rod. As your swing reverses, now moving toward the target, the rod tip snaps forward. Ideally, this should happen when and where in the swing you want to release the line.

*During the forward swing of the cast, the resistance of the plug bends the rod back (loads it like a spring). The forward force generated when the rod tip straightens (unloads), combined with the forward momentum you give to the rod, propels the plug forward.*

## It's not about force

If your rod tip had been as stiff as a broomstick while casting, the plug still would have shot forward. However, it would not have traveled anywhere near as far and as fast. The important thing to realize is that casting doesn't depend upon brute force. Not only that – in learning to cast, brute force has no place. Only when and if you get into long-distance casting, such as surf casting, will your strength and speed really come into play. Even then, you'll use your strength and speed mainly to load your rod so it can cast the plug.

*During your first day of casting practice, after you've gotten off a few mediocre-to-fair casts, take the practice plug in your hand, open the bail, and point the rod where you want the plug to go. Then, with all your strength, throw it there by hand. If the plug goes half as far as on your best cast, you have one hell of an arm.*

## Timing is the key

For now, timing is far more important than strength or speed. The two most critical moments during a cast are the moment you start the rod forward and the moment you release the line from your finger. The latter primarily affects the direction of your cast. It does not concern us now. The former – the moment you start to flick your wrist forward – determines how well you're loading your rod. This does concern us now. When you stop the rod's backward motion, you feel additional pressure on the rod pulling it further backward. This is the practice plug pulling the line taut behind you. You swing the rod forward, forcing the tip to bend back further. This loads the rod with the force that's going to help propel the plug forward.

Now, if you wait an instant too long, you'll feel that backward pressure lessening. This means the practice plug is on its way forward and the rod is unloading. The rod should have already been moving forward, loading itself even more. Instead, it partially unloaded. That unloaded force is lost to the plug, and the cast will be shorter for lack of it. You'll know so ahead of time, when you feel this lessening of pressure.

You can also start the rod forward too soon, before it is fully loaded. Determining when you didn't wait long enough is a little more difficult. You meet too little resistance, then suddenly too much. This tells you that the plug was still moving backward.

*The force expended by the forward movement of the rod to switch the plug's momentum forward, plus the force never loaded onto the rod, are both lost to the plug. This loss shows up in less casting distance.*

## Timing is a matter of feel

Feel comes from practice. Try casting a few times, gently, not for distance: 10 or 15 yards is fine. The only thing you're interested in is timing – judging those two critical moments when you flick your wrist forward and when you let the line slip from your finger. If the plug lands straight in front of you, then you released your line at the right instant. If it lands to the left you waited too long; to your right, not long enough. Practice a few dozen casts, but only for timing.

*You can add a little distance at the end of your casts by keeping your rod tip pointed at the line leaving it instead of at your bait. Following your bait, which sinks faster than your line, increases friction between line and line guides.*

# The overhand cast

*YOU'LL USE THE OVERHAND CAST far more than any other. It's the easiest to aim. Combined with the feathering technique I'll take up shortly, it is the most accurate way to cast. It also allows you to apply some muscle, enabling greater distance. Don't worry about getting your starting and vertical angles exactly right. There are no exactly right angles. You're striving for a smooth, clean motion and exact timing.*

# PRACTICING YOUR OVERHAND CAST

Popular because of its accuracy and potential achievable distance, the overhand cast is important to learn. Follow the steps below and make sure you get plenty of practice – this is the cast you'll use most often.

**1** Line up the plug

*Adjust the line so the plug hangs 8 to 18 inches from the rod tip.*

**2** Take the line

*Open the bail, catching the line with the first joint of your index finger.*

**3** Look ahead

*Face your target, the foot beneath your casting arm slightly forward.*

**4** Lift the rod

*Point the rod forward, approximately 60 degrees from the vertical (if the vertical is 12 o'clock, the rod starts at about 2 o'clock).*

**5** Bring it back

*Draw back the rod (by bending your elbow) slightly past the vertical until the tip is fully loaded (bent backward to the maximum).*

**6** Lower and flick

*Lower your forearm, and at the same time, give a sharp flick of your wrist.*

**7** Let it go

*Release the line as the rod returns to its approximate starting position.*

Rod is fully loaded

Rod returns to original position

STEP 1          STEP 5          STEP 7

An ideal overhand cast has a low, long arc. If there's ever a reason for having your plug go practically straight up and down like a bottle rocket, I can't think of it. When this happens, you're releasing the line (from your finger) a mite too soon. The result is the same, though the trajectory is as short as can be, if you release late enough. Your bait will again splash down right in front of you.

*If you're looking for some extra distance and have the wind to your back, then casting your plug a bit higher than usual is a good idea. If you have the wind in your face and you want to lose less distance, cast as low as possible, perhaps even sidearm.*

# Feathering

TAKE A LOOK *at the picture below. I would tell you to notice the position of the index finger if I thought there was a chance you hadn't already done so, and that you weren't already wondering what's going on here. Well, this educated index finger is* **feathering** *the cast.*

> **DEFINITION**
>
> **Feathering** *is slowing the line's escape from the spool by gently trapping it between finger and spool rim.*

Feathering is done for a number of reasons. Let's say you're trying to land your plug at the edge of a lily pad that lies against the opposite bank of a canal. Now, if the lily pad were farther away from the bank, you could cast over it and retrieve your plug right by it. If you overcast this particular lily pad, your plug is going to end up in the cattails, and will likely stay there. In fact, you do overcast. Luckily, you see what's coming in time. Laying your finger gently on the spool rim slows the release of your line and shortens your cast just enough to make it a perfect one.

■ **Feathering not only shortens** *an overcast, it also softens your bait's landing and minimizes slack.*

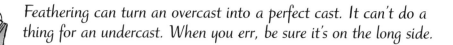

*Feathering can turn an overcast into a perfect cast. It can't do a thing for an undercast. When you err, be sure it's on the long side.*

Sometimes your terminal tackle will spin or your line will overtake it upon landing, causing a tangle. Feathering will straighten out your line, keeping your terminal tackle foremost. Slowing your plug down also results in a softer landing and less of a splash. This can prove worthwhile around easily spooked fish.

Let's say you cast a floating plug without feathering. It pulls line from the spool as it goes. When the plug hits the water, it stops. However, nothing stops your line. A little of it continues to fly from the spool. You now have extra line lying slack in the water. This is usually no big thing, but some lunker bass down below might find the extra line suspicious. Also, in order to start working your plug, you have to first reel in the slack line. There's a way to prevent this small problem. Right before your bait hits the water, press your index finger against the spool lip just hard enough to stop the line without jerking back the plug.

## When not to feather

There's at least one time when you should not stop the line. If the opposite canal bank is very steep, you may want your sinking bait to go straight down and hit bottom right up against it. In this case, you certainly don't feather. Let the slack line leave the spool, and if necessary, strip off additional line.

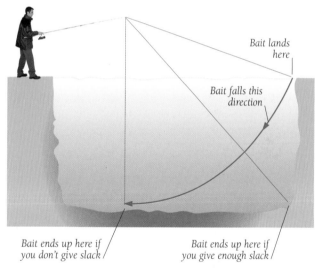

*Bait lands here*

*Bait falls this direction*

*Bait ends up here if you don't give slack*

*Bait ends up here if you give enough slack*

A similar but unrelated matter concerns bottom fishing in a strong current. You let out line figuring it will stop going off the spool when your bait hits bottom. Instead, your line keeps going out. Your bait now sits on the bottom, while the current empties your spool. If you had watched closely as your line left the spool, you would have seen a slight pause between the time your bait hit bottom and when the current started taking out line. Better yet, if you had used your finger as if feathering, you might have picked up by feel a pause and a subsequent difference in line speed and pull. You didn't do either, now you have to reel in all the slack, trying to detect the first feel of your bait so as not to lift it off the bottom.

# Distance is overrated

BEFORE I GET INTO THIS SUBJECT *and give you an example, I want to say something. Do not practice casting for distance, not now, perhaps never. Distance is likely to come by itself – with better timing and technique. Besides, distance is overrated.*

Let's say you're standing on shore. Three large boulders sit offshore in front of you. They are 10 yards apart, with the second 10 yards farther out than the first, and the third 10 yards farther out than the second. You cast your plug in front of the closest. Nothing. You cast a half dozen more times. Still nothing. You move down the shore, opposite the second boulder. A dozen casts in front of it, and still no strike.

Well, there's one more boulder left, the farthest one. You move down the shore opposite it. A beautiful cast leaves your plug 3 yards short. You try again, putting a little more muscle into it. This cast leaves you 10 yards short. That's not the way it's supposed to work. You try a dozen more times. Only once do you come close to the distance of your first cast. Irritated, you become obsessed with reaching the boulder, so obsessed that it may not even occur to you to try a lighter line or a heavier bait. A dozen more casts, and your plug lands everywhere except on target.

## Is there a fish there?

If only you could reach that boulder. There's a fish there for sure. A monster. What makes you so sure? The boulder is the same as the other two, only a few yards farther out. Maybe none of them hold any fish. Maybe they all have fish, but the fish don't like your bait. Or maybe the fish are just not biting. No, you keep casting, sure that the one boulder out of reach is the one surrounded by fish. Well, the only reason you're so sure is because you can't cast far enough to reach it.

<u>The Fourth Golden Rule of Fishing</u>: "No matter how far you can cast, the best-looking spot is almost sure to be just out of range." Concentrate on casting accuracy, not on distance.

## Trivia...

*To illustrate more forcefully the principle of hitting a target by keeping your eyes on it, allow me for a moment to ditch the fishing gear for ski equipment. You're flying down a slope with plenty of white space between you and the trees. Suddenly you notice one lone tree standing out at a slight distance from the rest. Still, this tree is way off to the side. There's no chance it can be a problem. However, oddly, it seems to be becoming a problem. You begin to sweat, unable to take your eyes off that tree. The next thing you know, you're cartwheeling head over heels through the snow, in a barely successful attempt to miss it. Well, if you had been able to keep from staring at it, you wouldn't have come near that tree. Look where you want to go, not where you don't want to go.*

# Aim for accuracy

*ACCURACY SHOULD BE YOUR MAIN OBJECTIVE* when you're *learning to cast. It depends first upon your ability to cast straight in line with a target. It also depends upon your range – your ability to control the distance of your cast. Range is largely a matter of touch. Work on your aim and, at the same time, range may take care of itself.*

Do not try to aim an overhand cast by lining up the rod between your eyes and the target. Your rod should stay to the side of your head, not directly in front of your face. Strive for a smooth, uniform motion. Every time you achieve it, immediately try to duplicate it. Don't try too hard or get irritated. You need to relax.

*If you want to hit a target, keep your eyes glued to that target during the entire cast.*

## A simple summary

✓ The Fourth Golden Rule of Fishing: "No matter how far you can cast, the best-looking spot is almost sure to be just out of range." Concentrate on casting accuracy, not on distance.

✓ Keep your health and legal costs low. Practice your casting with a practice plug, and at a safe distance from other people.

✓ You must master the sidearm cast. Often it's the only cast possible.

✓ You can't beat the overhand cast for accuracy, and in its surf-casting variation, you can't beat it for distance.

✓ If your overhand cast is too low, you're releasing the line too late. If it's too high, you're releasing too early.

✓ Feathering can turn an overcast into a perfect cast.

✓ Cast low into the wind, high with it.

# Chapter 9

# Fisherman Meets Fish

T HE FIRST FEW TIMES fisherman meets fish, one thing above all others is likely to occur – mistakes. And you can bet the farm most of these mistakes will be made by the fisherman. Don't worry, and not just because it won't do you any good. Accept the fact, and just concentrate on never making the same mistake twice, or, if you need more slack, three times. There will be moments when you'll think that you'll never learn how to catch fish. Take this as a sign you're thinking too much. If you learn to avoid repeating your mistakes, eventually you have to run out of ways to lose fish. If this isn't learning how to catch them, it's plenty close enough.

## In this chapter...

✓ Pregame
✓ Presenting the bait
✓ Detecting nibbles
✓ Setting the hook
✓ Playing the fish

# Pregame

*PREGAME IS THE PERIOD BETWEEN the moment you reach the fishing spot and the moment you wet your line. The first part of this period is usually spent deciding where exactly to wet your line first, but let's postpone that topic until Chapter 12.*

## Don't spook the fish

As you approach your chosen fishing spot, try not to draw the fish's attention. You don't want to make a lot of noise. Nor do you want to cast your shadow over any place there might be fish. This is what birds do, and most fish do their best to avoid birds. You can let your bait cause some excitement, if it's a popping plug or some other type that's supposed to do so. Just make sure that you, the fisherman, don't make a commotion.

## Setting your drag

Unfortunately, there's no magic formula for setting a drag. Different baits and strategies require different drag settings. Your setting for bottom fishing will more than likely be different from your setting for trolling. Your target fish should also be taken into consideration. A species that will stay on the surface and head for the horizon can be given more line than one that will head straight down toward a rocky hole. Even a bottom-hugging species can get a lighter drag if you're catching it on a safe, sandy bottom as opposed to a rocky or refuse-strewn one.

I'll throw out a number just to get you started. Set your drag at roughly 30 percent of the line's breaking strength. I give you this number knowing damn well that you will probably set your drag at twice that strength, and also that you will often get away with it. In any case, modify your drag settings through experience.

*Keep in mind that more fish are lost because of tight drags than loose ones.*

You can try setting your drags by feel, but chances are you do not yet have the feel, or will any time soon. There's a simple way to get an accurate drag setting. Say you're using 15-pound test and want to set your drag at 5 pounds. Tie a 5-pound sugar bag to the end of your line. Tighten your drag enough to lift the bag off the ground. Slowly, in small increments, loosen the drag until the bag falls. The drag is now set at 5 pounds. Of course, carrying around bags of sugar can be a pain, especially when setting the drag on your 80-pound test outfit. There's a more convenient way to set a drag – short, but not so sweet. It involves the use of a spring scale, often referred to as a Chatillon scale.

*If you can get a spring scale, but not one with a sliding indicator, to save the drag setting, you can make your own indicator ring with a plastic electrical tie. Tighten it enough to keep it from sliding by itself, yet loose enough to move up and down the scale.*

## Not looking for fish

The secret for spotting fish is not looking for fish. Look instead for a fin, a tail, a wake, a little cloud of mud, a shadow on the bottom . . . anything that stands out. Look with your bail open and your reel ready to cast. Once you spot a fish, you do not want to take your eyes off it. You'll spot more fish by scanning the water methodically, moving from near to far, as opposed to letting your eyes just dart around.

*A pair of polarized sunglasses that filter out the water's surface glare is a very big help in spotting fish. Reasonably priced sunglasses are easy to find. The more reasonably priced they are, the more reason to choose a plastic frame. The lower-priced metal frames tend to leave odd green lines on your face.*

# Presenting the bait

*IF YOU SPOT A FISH, never cast at it. A stationary bait, one that you're going to let sit, should be cast in front of a fish. Don't place it any closer than necessary for the fish to notice it. If the fish doesn't notice it, you can reel it in and cast again, this time a little closer. If you hit that fish on the nose with your bait, you won't get a second chance. A moving bait, one that has to be retrieved, should be cast in front of and well past a fish. Again, when you reel it in, the bait should not come any closer to the fish than necessary.*

Many other different ways of presenting many different baits are covered in Part Four, cleverly entitled "Baits." I recommend you put off reading it until you get some fishing under your belt. In the meantime, watch other fishermen. Do what you see works for them. If that doesn't work, try doing what you are told works, especially by the staff at your tackle store.

# Detecting nibbles

*IF ANYTHING WORKS, you'll get some bites or hits. Sometimes these bites will be vicious enough to be called strikes. Sometimes they'll just be nibbles. If the latter is the case, you want to be sure to notice them. The more sensitive your rod tip, the easier this will be. Just remember, the more sensitive the tip, the less help it will be in setting a hook (which I'll cover shortly). A rod with a sensitive tip better have some backbone beneath that tip.*

There's a better way to detect nibbles, especially in the dark, a way that doesn't require the concentration necessary to keep your eyes glued to a rod tip. Extend your index finger down against the line, and use your sense of feel. If your index finger can't reach the line, reel in just enough for the bail to bring the line to the top of the spool. The tauter the line, the more distinct the nibbles will feel.

While you're waiting for a bite, I suggest you keep the bail closed. After you've gained some experience, you can leave it open under some circumstances. Doing so allows the fish room to run and some time to swallow your bait. As of now, if you want to give some slack on a bite, just lower your rod and point it at the fish. This necessitates holding your rod close to the vertical as you wait for that bite.

■ **If you hold** *your index finger lightly against your line, you'll feel nibbles you wouldn't notice by watching your rod tip.*

*Whenever you close your bail or start to reel, glance down at your spool. Make sure the line is going on evenly, and that there are no loose loops sticking out from the spool. If there are, pull off the faulty coils and start again.*

# Setting the hook

AS WITH A NUMBER OF OTHER SKILLS in this chapter, there's no one right way to **set a hook**. Different species of fish take baits differently. Even fish of the same species, at different times or places, will behave differently.

## When to set the hook

Some fish will mouth a bait and spit it out, perhaps because they don't like the bait or perhaps because they feel the hook. With these fish, it's of course advisable to try setting the hook at the first and slightest sign of a bite. With other fish you should wait until they start to run with your bait. Sometimes you should even wait until a few seconds after a fish stops running, thus giving it time to swallow the bait.

*Needlefish and houndfish, when rigged whole, are excellent and extremely durable trolling baits for sailfish and marlin. On the bottom, they can get you very large grouper, among other things.*

## How to set the hook

Starting out, I recommend that you don't apply any pressure until the fish does, exceeding this pressure only slightly. If this doesn't hook the fish, next time try a moderate jerk of your rod at the first nibble. If this too fails, keep increasing the time you wait before setting the hook, and also the muscle you put into it. Whenever you're not satisfied with the ratio of hookups to hits, also experiment with hook size, type, and placement in the bait.

*Never try setting the hook until you're sure there's no slack in your line. Slack reduces or completely eliminates the force you're trying to transfer to the hook point.*

> **DEFINITION**
>
> *To **set a hook** means to force its point into the fish's flesh where it can find hold. The fish can do this to itself by biting down on the hook barb or applying pressure to the line. The fisherman can set the hook by applying pressure to the line with a backward jerk of his or her rod.*

> ## Trivia...
>
> *It took me a long, long time before I realized that I was wasting my life trying to set hooks in the narrow, bony mouths of needlefish and houndfish. Now I just set a live bait fish under a bobber, place my rod in a rod holder, and wait until my rod bends double. At the other extreme are species such as sheepshead. These bandits are so proficient at stealing bait, all the experts agree it's advisable to set the hook a quarter to a half second before you feel the bite.*

# Methods of setting the hook

On these pages I will describe two different ways of setting the hook: the vertical method and the sideways method. You should remember in both cases that you must first point your rod at the fish; this is to maximize the distance you can jerk back your rod. Also consider the amount of line between yourself and the hook. Monofilament stretches. The more line out, the more stretch. A jerk of a your rod that would rip a fish's lips off at 10 yards might not even be felt at 100 yards. Adjust the force you apply to the amount of line out.

*Do not set the hook more than once, or reset it during the fight. Set it hard enough on the first try.*

Before I go into how to set the hook, I just want to say that there's one thing I often see that makes me wince every time. Some fishermen set the hook by jerking the rod back three or four times, and then reset it a time or two during the fight. Though some excellent fishermen disagree, I feel this is more likely to enlarge the hole the hook has made than to bury the hook deeper. The looser the hook, the more likely the fish will throw it.

There are two basic ways to set a hook, and you need to learn both of them. You will, no problem.

STEP 1

## The vertical method

The most common way to set a hook is vertically.

1. Start with the rod pointed in the approximate direction of your bait.

2. Jerk the rod straight back to a near vertical position.

The reel can end up wherever you choose – in front of your face, to the side of your head, or over your head. In fact, if the hook pulls out, the reel can end up stuck to your face. If your bait was close to the surface, it can also fly back and end up stuck to your face. It is because of these two possibilities, that I recommend, unless your bait is down and deep, that you start out setting your hooks a less common way.

STEP 2

### The sideways method

Setting your hook with a sideways motion is not only safer, it can also be more effective. We're not talking about some karate move that needs to be executed in the same exact way every time. This is not brain surgery either.

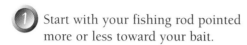 Start with your fishing rod pointed more or less toward your bait.

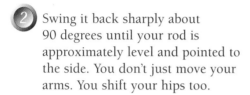 Swing it back sharply about 90 degrees until your rod is approximately level and pointed to the side. You don't just move your arms. You shift your hips too.

Setting a hook sideways allows you, if necessary, to apply more penetrating force to the hook than would be possible setting it vertically. Also, if you're using a top water bait and don't hook the fish, there's less chance you'll pull this bait out of the water. If it stays in the water, or only hops out for a short distance, the fish may strike again, even harder.

STEP 1

STEP 2

**INTERNET**

www.insidesportfishing.com/Encyclopedia/Articles/1041.asp

*This page of the Inside Sportfishing web site gives in-depth directions on how to set the hook.*

*The most critical aspect of setting the hook is starting with the sharpest possible hook in the first place.*

# Playing the fish

PLAYING A FISH CORRECTLY *means putting the correct amount of pressure on it. Put too little pressure on a fish, and you give it too much line; you'll also give it too much time to throw the hook or find some other way to escape. Put too much pressure on a fish and you may rip the hook out or break the line. Put the correct amount of pressure on a fish and you'll most likely wear it out and capture it in the optimum amount of time.*

Basically, playing a fish depends upon how you set and adjust the drag, and how you handle your rod and reel. The novice should avoid at almost all cost adjusting the drag during the fight. No skill better separates the expert from the rest of the pack.

## Second-to-last resort

There's a technique for feathering the drag that allows you to temporarily increase it without adjusting the drag knob. The novice should also avoid this as the second-to-last resort. Still, you have to learn sometime. When a fish is stripping your reel of line, the rotor and bail remain in place while the spool spins on its axis. You can slow the fish's run by cupping your thumb and index finger around the front rim of the spool and applying the appropriate amount of pressure.

■ **Once you've mastered** *the basics of rod and reel handling, you'll want to learn how to feather a drag.*

*When feathering a drag, never touch the moving line. It will cut you like a razor.*

Before you resort to feathering the drag, make sure you're holding your rod back far enough to put a nice bend in it. This in itself will increase the drag by increasing friction on your line.

# Drag increases by itself

Before I explain about drag increasing by itself, you first should commit to memory the following important point:

*As line leaves your spool, the drag increases without any adjustment.*

At the same drag setting, the more line that a fish strips from your spool, the harder it is for it to strip more line. Think of your spool as the round handle on a garden hose valve. Opening and closing the valve is almost effortless. Now remove the screw at the center of the handle that holds it in place. Remove the handle. You're left with the square end of the valve stem. Grasp the stem between two fingers and open the valve. You can't, because you have very little leverage. Replace the handle and the valve works easily again. Replace the original handle with one half its diameter. Now you can open the valve, but doing so is about twice as hard as with the original handle. Get a handle twice as large as the original, and you'll be able to open the valve with only half the force. In fact, this oversized handle may make turning the valve too easy. If you're not careful, you may snap off the valve stem.

## How the spool works

A spinning reel's spool works the same way as a valve handle, except you turn it by pulling off line. When full, it turns easily, like the garden hose valve with its original handle. When the fish strips the spool halfway down, this is similar to replacing the valve handle with one half its size (and half its leverage). The fish then has to work about twice as hard to turn the spool. This is equivalent to double the original drag setting when the reel was full.

*When the spool is down to half the diameter of its full state, the fish has taken far more than half the line. This is true because the coils of line are far longer at the top of a full spool than those at its middle. Also, the shaft at the center of the spool takes up space that could have been filled by line.*

## Don't turn the handle!

Keep in mind that when a fish is taking out line, you keep the pressure on by keeping a good bend in your rod. Turning the reel's handle gains you nothing because the drag is already slipping. In fact, don't turn the handle even if the fish is stationary. If you're not gaining line by drawing the fish closer, turning the reel's handle merely twists your line.

*Twisting your line makes it more likely to tangle and, after a point, weakens it.*

■ **The sight of your fish** *jumping out of the water is always exciting. Just remember, it's also a warning. In air, your fish is not only heavier, it's quicker too.*

## Lessening the drag

One case where lessening the drag would be advisable is when that drag is set tight and your fish jumps from the water. In the air, it's not only heavier, it's free of water resistance and quicker. Unfortunately, there's no practical way to lessen the drag during this frantic moment. What you can do is "bow" to the fish. This means give it some slack by bending forward and extending your rod even further.

## Cast your mind back

Remember when I suggested an initial drag setting of around 30 percent of your line's test strength? This probably seemed surprisingly low to you. It shouldn't any more. A 30-percent setting increases to 60 percent if a fish runs out enough line to lower your spool's line level by half. When this happens with an initial drag setting of 50 percent, your actual drag setting reaches your line's breaking strength, if your line doesn't break first. You better slack off on your drag first.

*Choosing your initial drag setting involves a paradox. The lower the setting, the more line the fish has to remove from your spool to reach any specific drag tension. However, the lower the initial setting, the easier for the fish to run out line and increase your actual drag setting.*

# A simple summary

✓ Until you gain experience, avoid adjusting your drag during the fight.

✓ Setting your hook with a sideways motion is safer and has other advantages over doing so with a vertical motion.

✓ The most critical aspect of setting the hook is starting with the sharpest possible hook in the first place.

✓ When and how to set the hook depends upon species of fish, bait, fishing equipment, conditions, and location.

✓ Remember: You must remove all slack from your line before you set a hook.

✓ As a fish pulls line from your spool, the drag is continuously increasing by itself, without any adjustment.

# Chapter 10

# The End Game

THE END GAME begins when the fish is played out and ready to take. Its object is to do just that. The end game can't be rushed. The fisherman must think ahead and be ready for surprises. Losing a fish is always disappointing. During the end game, it can be disheartening.

In this chapter...
- ✓ Hands on, hands off
- ✓ Netting a fish
- ✓ Gaffing a fish
- ✓ Using a tailer
- ✓ Releasing a fish unharmed
- ✓ Preserving your catch

GREAT FISHERMEN AND GREAT PHOTOGRAPHERS ARE ALL TOO RARE. SO WHAT?

# Hands on, hands off

ONE OF THE BEST WAYS *for a fisherman to impress people with his or her machismo (if she can have machismo) is by removing a fish from the water with nothing more than a bare hand. However, in the wrong hands, this little stunt is one of the best ways to look like an idiot.*

The following pictures and their captions explain some of the ways in which fish can be removed from the water:

■ **Tuna,** *largemouth bass, and many other species can be lifted by inserting your index and second finger through its gill opening.*

■ **The rooster fish** *can often be lifted gently out of the water with one hand under its belly and the other gripping its tail. Bonefish often require no more than one hand cradling its belly.*

■ **Other varieties,** *such as tarpon (left) and largemouth bass, can be grasped by the lower jaw alone, with your thumb and index finger.*

Please note that the first of the three methods shown here can severely injure a fish, and should never be done if you intend to release it. Furthermore, try this trick on numerous other fish – including the bass's saltwater cousin, the grouper – and you may end up on your knees, feeling as if you stuck your fingers inside an inside-out porcupine, and begging the fish to release you.

At the extremes, there are fish with lethally poisonous spines and fish that will lie immobilized in your hand if held the right way. The trick is knowing which fish can be held how, and which should not be held at all. The best way to learn is not from a book. The best way is to let other people do the lifting, and to learn from their expertise or embarrassment.

# Netting a fish

*NETTING YOUR FISH is not only your last opportunity to lose it, it's also your best opportunity. There are countless ways to foul up this little operation. With time and persistence, I'm sure that you will experience most of them. I have. However, if you'd just as soon pass up these humbling experiences, allow me to suggest that you always remember to do one little thing – take your time.*

Don't try to net a fish until both you and the fish are ready. The area must be clear, the net in reach, the amount of line between rod tip and fish just right, and, most important, the fish must be ready. If there's too much line out, you won't be able to direct the fish to where you want it, nor will you be able to prevent it from going where you don't want it. The fish is ready when it's played out and no longer *green*. Signs of this are listlessness, poor posture (a marked leaning to one side), and swimming in small circles.

> **DEFINITION**
>
> A **green** *fish is not yet played out (worn out) enough to be safely unhooked or taken from the water. It's still too active to land.*

If possible, you don't want the fish to see the net except from the inside. This means gently slipping the net into the water behind the fish. I say "gently" because fish are very sensitive to vibrations. For this same reason, it's also better to ease the fish backward, toward a stationary net. This is somewhat easier if the net is downstream or down current from the fish. Wait until as much of the fish as possible is over the net before making your final move. The scooping motion of the net should be as vertical as possible. Avoid any contact between fish and net for as long a possible. The deeper you can place the net, the leveler you can hold it. The leveler the net, the larger the available opening. The larger the opening, the quicker and more vertical the scoop can be. The larger the fish in comparison to the net opening, the more critical the prepositioning of the net.

If necessary, you can net the fish from in front. However, this requires you to hold its head farther out of the water. The added strain can snap the line or yank the hook.

■ **This fisherman** *apparently sees no need to keep the net out of view behind the fish. In a minute, he may.*

# Gaffing a fish

GAFFS ARE USED PRIMARILY ON BOATS *fishing in saltwater. Longer-handled models have proved useful to anglers fishing from high jetties and piers. The three most common are the standard gaff, the lip gaff, and the flying gaff. They are necessary because a fish weighs more when lifted out of the water than when in the water. The weight difference may be more than enough to break the line or leader, or to rip loose the hook.*

A fish weighs less in water because of the buoyancy of water. If you are skeptical of this fact, there is an easy way you can prove it to yourself. Hang on to the side of a swimming pool. Then gently push off and relax. Unless you're among those few percentage points of the population labeled "sinkers," you will float quite effortlessly on your back.

Now try this experiment again, only this time empty the swimming pool first. If you float this time, there's something very seriously wrong with you and I suggest you see your doctor. If you fall, the increase in your speed of descent through air as compared to that through water should be very apparent. If not, your accelerated impact with the bottom of the pool certainly will be. Even if you're a sinker, you should notice the difference between falling through air as opposed to falling through water. You should also better understand why a fishing line that can support a fish in water may not be strong enough to support it in air.

*The Fifth Golden Rule of Fishing:* "Gaffs can be just as deadly to fishermen as to fish. Keep gaff tips covered until just before use."

Treat gaffs with respect. In the wrong hands, these fisherman's aids can aid in the demise of the fisherman. Rough seas and a wet deck can facilitate this process. Even when the tip is covered, if gaff meets fisherman with enough force, it can end up piercing both its tip cover and the fisherman.

*Proper use of a gaff should not be learned from a book, but rather firsthand from an expert.*

The following paragraphs are meant merely to give you an overview of the subject.

## Lip gaffs

The lip gaff is the only gaff that, if used correctly, does no serious harm to fish or fisherman. This fact makes possible the eventual release of the fish, and is usually the angler's reason for using a lip gaff in the first place. It holds the fish's head steady while the angler removes the hook. A lip gaff is almost indispensable for releasing a 200-pound tarpon.

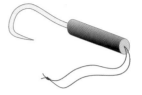

LIP GAFF

*Though some would argue they are dispensable, an unhooking device or a pliers certainly adds a significant margin of safety when using a lip gaff. If you're looking for a sure way to sweat off some pounds, try sharing the same hook with a large fish for a few moments.*

## Standard gaffs

The standard gaff is used only when the fisherman intends to keep the fish. No method of use is either patented or foolproof. This gaff, when used incorrectly, which is quite often, is also an excellent aid in the release of fish. Banging your trophy over the head, aside from being unsportsmanlike, tends to anger and revive it. If you anger a fish enough, it's likely to break your line and swim away.

■ **The gaff man** *should position himself as close as possible to the fish. He should also make sure the fish is gaffed properly – one strike is better than several weak ones.*

The point of the gaff should pierce the fish's head or shoulder. The reason for this is the same reason you don't catch a tiger by its tail – control. An angry wahoo or barracuda, gaffed in the middle of its back, can spin on the gaff hook like a compass needle, choosing whichever angler looks tastier.

*Experienced gaff men keep their gaffs razor-sharp.*

### The importance of timing

Gaff men need the patience to wait for the right moment, the knowledge to spot it, and the skill not to waste it. They almost always bring the hook down from above. This method presents a few challenges. If the fish sees the gaff coming, instinct will tell it to dive or swim away. The gaff better be moving fast enough to prevent the fish from doing either. When the gaff comes from behind, the fish sees it later and has less time to react. You don't want the gaff hitting the line, or getting hit by it. This could easily result in a cut line, a tangle, or both. If the fish does have time to move, it won't be straight backward. That is another reason why the gaff should come in from behind the fishing line.

The novice is prone to make a number of mistakes when wielding a gaff. First of all, he or she will go for the wrong gaff, usually the most humongous one around. The larger the gaff, the more unwieldy. It's possible to swat a fly with a two-by-four, but a fly swatter greatly improves one's odds. At the very least, it requires less sweat. Also, the larger the hook point, the more force is needed to penetrate a fish. I'm not sure exactly why, but it seems to me that the larger the hook's *gap* in relation to fish size, the likelier you are to miss the fish. The appropriate gaff need only be strong enough, with a safety margin, to lift your fish through the air. Excess size works against the fisherman. Another novice mistake is to strike too soon, before the fish is close enough or still enough. Failing to position the hook point is one more. Careful aim does you no good at all if you have the hook point facing the wrong way. Always grasp the gaff with the same grip, and with the hook point at the same angle.

> **DEFINITION**
>
> *The **gap** of a hook is the distance between the shaft and the point.*

*A good way to stay aware of your gaff's hook position is by gripping the gaff with your index finger pointing down the shaft on the exact opposite side from the hook point.*

Keeping your finger straight out takes some getting used to, but it quickly becomes second nature. You can also save yourself the trouble of looking down the shaft to line up the hook by painting a line along the grip opposite the hook point.

A correctly positioned hook won't help if you wait until the gaff is over the fish before starting to aim it. A big hook hovering above does not tend to relax a fish and keep it in one place. One last mistake is to divide what should be one continuous gaffing motion into two herky-jerky ones. The novice will often bring the hook down upon the fish, trying to impale it with one motion, then jerk it up into the boat with the other. An experienced gaff man will instead use one smooth, sweeping motion. He or she will stretch the gaff hook over and beyond the fish, hooking it while at the same time lifting it out of the water and into the boat.

*The thinner the hook end of a gaff's shaft, the less water resistance it creates. This attribute makes it easier both to slice a gaff through the water and hold it in place in a current.*

## Flying gaffs

The flying gaff is a modification of the standard gaff. It was developed for landing larger fish. A standard gaff shaft more or less serves the purpose of the rope in a tug of war. When that tug of war is between a 200-pound gaff man and a thousand-pound marlin or tuna, the fish better be close to belly up before the tug of war starts. Otherwise the gaff man is in real trouble. He has to hold onto the gaff. The fish doesn't have to hold onto anything. If the gaff man lets go, he can not only lose the gaff and the fish, he can get beaten over the head by his own gaff handle. It would not surprise me if the inventor of the flying gaff had some large bumps on his noggin.

The flying gaff is larger and stronger than the standard gaff. Its hook is attached to the shaft with a release device. The release will not activate until the hook hits the fish with more than enough force to bury itself. Now free from the shaft, the hook is still secured to the boat by a rope (often tied around the base of the fighting chair). The gaff man was holding this rope alongside the gaff shaft. He can now drop the shaft into the boat, while keeping hold of the rope and pulling it taut. Any slack in the rope will allow the fish to throw the gaff hook. Now the pressure is off the fishing line. When the fish tires, it can be pulled to the boat by the gaff rope.

■ **Your charter boat** *should have all the equipment you need to land large fish. If not, find one that does.*

# Using a tailer

A TAILER IS A DEVICE *usually used to release a fish unharmed. With it, the fisherman can lift the fish into his or her boat to remove the hook. Anyone who has ever seen a fisherman lean over the side of a boat, more out than in, with or without an "inside man" holding his legs, in a rough sea, trying to unhook his favorite lure from a large fish's mouth, without also hooking himself . . . anyone who has ever witnessed this salt-sprayed tableau truly understands the need for a tailer.*

You want to end up with the tailer loop around the base of the fish's tail. As insurance against missing completely, it's a good idea to trigger the tailer farther up the fish's body. Jerk the tailer upward, and hold it high and taut. The loop should slip down easily enough and tighten around the fish's tail.

Unfortunately, a tailer won't work with all species of fish. It won't even slow down the soft-tailed varieties. There are species you can grasp behind the head, but if this were the way a tailer should be used it would not be called a tailer.

■ **You'd have trouble** *landing a large fish over the side of a boat like this, so make sure there's a tailer handy in case you need one.*

*Never use a tailer on a toothy critter unless you're certain whether and where it can be grasped. If you think ten is the desirable number of toes, do not, I repeat not (with emphasis on the "not"), ever try using a tailer to lift a barracuda by its tail, not (again, notice the "not") unless you are wearing your steel-toe boat shoes.*

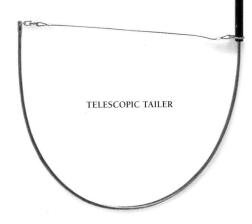

TELESCOPIC TAILER

# Releasing a fish unharmed

FISH ARE A DEPLETABLE RESOURCE, *and we're doing an excellent job of depleting them. All fishermen have a stake in halting this destructive trend. Life is short. We want to spend more of it catching fish and less of it searching for them. Still, this pales to irrelevance alongside the fact that we love to fish – as much for the relaxation as for the excitement. Fishing is an experience best shared. It's up to us to insure that there will always be fish to share for those who come after us. This requires resisting the temptation to take more fish from our waters than we need. It also requires lending our support to people and organizations that are trying to protect our natural resources.*

**INTERNET**

**www.cmc-ocean.org**

*If you want to get involved in marine conservation, the Center for Marine Conservation will tell you exactly how to go about it.*

<u>The Sixth Golden Rule of Fishing</u>: *"All unneeded fish should be returned to the water unharmed."*

## Reviving a fish

There's no point in releasing a fish only to have it die or immediately fall prey to another fish. If your catch is exhausted, you must first revive it. Understand that the problem facing a worn-out fish is twofold – lack of oxygen and an excess of lactic acid. The buildup of the latter is caused by exertion. If it hasn't gone too far, it will fix itself. In the meantime, all you can do is address the lack of oxygen.

A fish absorbs oxygen by passing water through its gills. This proves difficult if the fish hasn't the strength to swim. You can help by gently moving the fish back and forth in the water until you feel its strength return. If possible, release the fish in a place you can grab it again if it goes belly up.

■ **If necessary,** *revive your fish before you release it.*

## Piercing the swim bladder

When you bring a fish up from the depths, its abdomen sometimes expands like a balloon. Actually, it's the fish's swim bladder that's full of air. This is the organ that allows it to keep the same buoyancy at different depths. If you release the fish in that condition, it may float on the surface until eaten by another fish. You can help prevent this problem by not raising a fish too fast. Otherwise, puncturing the swim bladder is necessary. You need the needle part of a hypodermic needle, preferably large. If you can't acquire one, get a needle for filling basketballs and footballs. Grind down the tip at an angle to give it a sharp point. If you can't get either of the above, use a sharp hook point instead. Slip the tool under a scale and into the swim bladder until it deflates. Then revive the fish and release it. Different species of fish may need to be punctured in different places. Try to find someone knowledgeable enough to tell you which species should be pierced in which places.

## Barbless hooks

Admittedly, it's far more trouble to remove a lure from a live, unharmed fish than from a dead one. One solution to this problem is to remove all but one of the hooks from a double or triple hook lure. However, this can throw the lure off balance. A better solution is barbless hooks. You can file down the barbs or you can flatten them down with a pliers. Sure, you'll lose a few fish, but fewer than you think. The added challenge will more than make up for them. Just remember the Third Golden Rule of Fishing: "Keep your line tight." This rule is the key to fishing competence. Using barbless hooks is the best way to practice it. Furthermore, the ease and speed with which you can release fish will leave more time for catching them.

Generally, as far as sportsmanship, challenge, and enjoyment are concerned, the lighter the tackle you use the better. There is one exception. The lighter the tackle, the longer the fight, the more worn out the fish. You can so exhaust a fish you will not be able to revive it. Learn from experience how light you can go for different species.

## Handle with care

A fish should be handled as little and as gently as possible. The slimy coating that makes a fish hard to hold also protects it against disease. For this reason you must remove as little of it as possible. Wearing gloves aids in this, but make sure they're wet. Also, you can take a gentler, more relaxed grip on the fish if you remove the hook with a pliers or a de-hooking device instead of your fingers.

*Never remove a hook if this may cause serious injury to the fish. Cut the line or leader as close to it as possible.*

If you can, leave the fish in water when removing the hook. Large fish are especially susceptible to injury. In air, as opposed to water, their weight alone can

■ **Handle a fish gently** *if you intend to release it. Be sure to wet your hand first if you are not wearing a wet glove.*

damage and destroy their own vital organs. Never drag a large fish over a narrow gunwale or otherwise leave it without support. Even lifting a small fish by its lower jaw, using only your fingers, can cause injury. When it's necessary to take an active fish from the water to remove the hook, it sometimes helps to hold it upside down, eyes covered with a wet towel.

*Undeniably, it is better for the fish to remain in the water while you're removing the hook. However, just as undeniably, it's better for the fisherman to avoid falling in.*

# Preserving your catch

*ALWAYS CARRY A COOLER WITH YOU.*
*If you can't, try to keep your fish alive as long as possible. That means placing them in a container and changing the water often. If you don't have a container, place your fish on a **stringer** and return them to the water.*

> **DEFINITION**
>
> A **stringer** is merely a heavy cord with a short stick attached to one end and a ring to the other. Fish are strung onto it by pushing the stick through a gill opening and out of the mouth. When all the fish are on the rope, the stick is passed through the loop to make sure they stay on it.

Many dark-fleshed fish should be bled as soon as they're caught to improve their flavor. Bleeding can be done by cutting a ring around the fish's tail or by inserting a knife in one gill opening and out the other, then cutting downward to completely sever the throat.

Later, when the fish has been filleted or steaked, more of the blood can be removed. Coat the meat with kosher salt for at least 15 minutes, then rinse off the salt before cooking.

*Fish, especially cleaned fish, most especially saltwater fish, deteriorate more quickly when left in contact with freshwater.*

If there is water in your cooler, the fish should be separated from it by a layer of plastic or burlap. If cleaned, the fish should be placed in plastic bags. Once home, cleaned fish should be refrigerated and frozen as soon as possible. If frozen, the meat should be wrapped in thin, clinging plastic without air pockets to prevent freezer burn. If thicker plastic is deemed necessary, place it around the thin plastic.

■ **A sturdy cooler** *can double as a seat and a workbench.*

*Freeze drinkable water in plastic bottles. This gives you ice and drinking water in half the space, with no water leaking on the fish.*

## A simple summary

✔ The Fifth Golden Rule of Fishing: "Gaffs can be just as deadly to fishermen as to fish. Keep gaff tips covered until just before use."

✔ The Sixth Golden Rule of Fishing: "All unneeded fish should be returned to the water unharmed."

✔ Learn which species can be taken by hand, by net, by gaff, or by tailer.

✔ Bring the fish to the net.

✔ A fish weighs more in air than water. Don't lift one by line or leader unless they provide a wide margin of safety.

✔ It's preferable that a fish remains in the water while you're removing the hook. However, it's more important for the fisherman to avoid falling overboard.

✔ Be patient and wait for the right moment to use the gaff.

✔ Always gaff a fish in the head or shoulder so you can control it, especially the part with teeth.

✔ Gaffing should be done in one smooth motion.

✔ You can help revive a fish by moving it back and forth in the water.

✔ Cutting your fishing line with a gaff doesn't qualify as a valid release. It's considered a lost fish.

# PART TWO

TIME OF DAY IS AN IMPORTANT CONSIDERATION

# Chapter 11

# When to Fish

THE QUESTION IS "When should I go fishing?" To answer it, consider all the factors discussed in this chapter. Keep in mind that none of these factors works in a vacuum. They cancel each other out in one instance, and have a cumulative effect in another. You must remember the factors that contributed to each day of fishing, making it a success or a failure. If you're able to keep a written log with all the details of a day's fishing, do so. If not, remember as best you can.

In this chapter...

✓ The best time to fish
✓ Water temperature
✓ Changes in weather
✓ Changes in currents
✓ Changes in food supply
✓ Applying what you know

# The best time to fish

*BEING ABLE TO TELL TIME has proven itself a great asset in the business world. It's also a skill the serious fisherman should strive to master. In addition to clock time, even the half-serious fisherman should remain conscious of some other ways to measure the passage of time. Time of year is an obvious one. While the numerical days of the month are irrelevant, the phases of the moon they were based upon are extremely important. These phases, in turn, are responsible for another equally valid division of time – the changing of the tides.*

## Time of day

Time of day is an extremely important factor. Almost all fishermen agree – as do I – that the best times to fish for most species are dawn and dusk. I also feel these are the two most beautiful times of day to do many things, fishing being just one of them. If fishermen had to choose between dusk and dawn, most would choose to fish at dawn. That puts me in the minority, and not merely because I'm getting too old to stay up that late. One reason I prefer dusk is the pleasant anticipation I experience during the hours preceding it – anticipation that the fishing is going to get better. At dawn, I often find myself thinking that I better catch a fish now because it's downhill from here on out. Even when fishing is good, there's the feeling that, as the sun rises higher, it will tail off.

*The Seventh Golden Rule of Fishing:* "*Whenever you cover a lot of ground searching for fish – be it by trolling, circling a lake, walking a river bank, or driving from pond to pond – return to the most productive or promising spot for dusk.*"

There's no time of day when fishing is not worth a try. Any experienced fisherman has stories of high-noon action with trophy fish. Still, you'd better learn the times of day each particular species bites best, and also the hours when you are knocking your head against the bulkhead targeting it. Don't misunderstand me. Just because you never catch a fish during certain hours doesn't necessarily mean they don't bite during those hours. It does mean, as far as you're concerned, they might as well be fasting. Still, don't give up. During particular hours, the fish you're targeting may be in deeper or shallower water. They may also be in the same water, only at a different depth in the water column. Take a few minutes to check out these possibilities, and any others that occur to you.

■ **You can usually depend** *upon dawn and dusk for the best fishing. You can depend upon them even more for the most pleasant views.*

Many fishing writers before me have emphasized the importance of time of day. However, they never emphasize enough something that greatly enhances the value of this advice. Let's say you catch a trophy fish at 5 o'clock. You decide to go back the next day, and to be ready and in place by 4 o'clock. Daylight saving time goes into effect that night, so you go at 5 o'clock DST instead, and catch an even bigger fish at 6 o'clock DST. You want to remember, perhaps even write down, the best hour to fish. Should you remember 5 o'clock or 6? Three months later, in the dead of winter, you decide to go at 5. The problem is, when you open the door to leave, it's dark already. Six months later, in the heat of summer, you still haven't figured things out. You arrive at 5 o'clock, don't catch a fish until 7, and there's a good hour of daylight remaining. Clock time misled you.

*Time till sundown and time after sunrise are better guides to the best hours of fishing than clock time.*

## Time of the year

Time of the year is also a factor. If you want to catch salmon, you'd better know the season. It doesn't pay to look for them in the ocean when they're already up river. There are some great marlin fishing grounds on this planet that are a waste of time 10 months a year. If you want to catch one of those trophy fish following the huge annual mullet run down the east coast of the United States, then you'd better

■ **Getting knocked over** *by a jumping salmon is a good sign that they are in the area!*

know what month those mullet are likely to arrive. The same for the squid off California. Last but not least, if you want to go ice fishing, you'll be in for one wet, shivering surprise if you show up even a day or two too early or late. Keep in mind that I'm talking about changes in seasons, not changes in dates. The seasons are not known for their punctuality.

## Tides

Pay special attention to tides when you're fishing river mouths. An outgoing tide carries all kinds of succulent delicacies, and even some things that fish will eat. An interesting phenomenon is the grouping of species along an estuary according to freshwater tolerance. These groupings, of course, move back and forth with changes in salinity.

■ **The view of a coast** *at low tide can show you the best places to present your baits at high tide.*

Some fish are known to follow the rising tide up onto the shallow, table-like bonefish flats. Other fish wait off the deep edge of these flats for the falling tide and all the tasty morsels carried out by it. Whenever I fish from an ocean shore, I personally try to catch the 2 hours encompassing high tide. If you like high and low tides, you should like them even more during a full moon. That's when they're highest and lowest.

## Phases of the moon

The phases of the moon affect more than just the tides. Night fishing seems to improve during a full moon. Bright moonlight aids fish in their search for food. You too will see a lot better on these nights. If you plan to go fishing at night, that's when you should try to arrange it. I go a step further. I avoid fishing the daylight hours of a full moon. To me, the fishing seems slightly slower then.

*If you ever find it necessary to thread line through your rod's line guides in the dark (and you will), first double up the last few inches of your line. The added stiffness will make this job easier.*

Don't misunderstand me. I'm not telling you never to go night fishing when there's no moon. I've caught some amazing fish during the dark of the moon, at the wrong hour, on the wrong tide, in the wrong season. What I'm saying is that you should take advantage of a full moon if you can.

■ **The glow of a full moon** *aids fish in their search for food, fishermen in their search for fish, and both in their search for romance.*

# Water temperature

AN EVEN MORE IMPORTANT FACTOR *than time of day is water temperature. Every species of fish has a range of water temperatures it prefers. If you want to find the fish, find its preferred range. If you can't find its temperature range, don't waste your time trying to catch this species.*

When it comes to measuring water temperature, a sensitive big toe can be a real advantage. However, unless you're very long-legged, this advantage is limited to gauging surface temperature. Water temperature almost always varies with depth. If the surface temperature is out of your species' preferred range, a *temperature probe* will prove helpful. It can be a discrete unit or attached to a *downrigger*. Once you find the temperature range you're seeking, you lower your baits to that depth. Keep in mind that during the day this range and the fish it contains can move higher or lower for numerous reasons.

*You can make your own temperature probe by tying a weather thermometer to a marked line.*

When lowering a temperature probe, you will sometimes notice a constant temperature or a slow, gradual change in temperature that ends in an abrupt change. This indicates a *thermocline*, and fishing its borders is definitely worth the effort. Fish often gather along these temperature changes.

> **DEFINITION**
>
> A **temperature probe** is a thermometer lowered into the water on a cable that transfers its readings to the surface, where they can be read by the fisherman. A **downrigger** is a device that lowers your trolling lures or baits to a specific depth and keeps them there.

> **DEFINITION**
>
> A **thermocline** is the meeting of broad layers of water of substantially differing temperatures. The water above the thermocline is called the epilimnion, while that below is the hypolimnion.

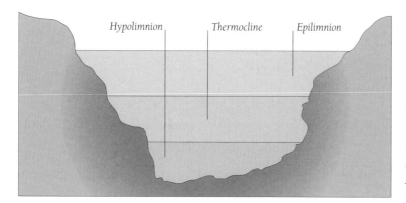

Hypolimnion    Thermocline    Epilimnion

■ **An abrupt change** in water temperature indicates a thermocline. Time to get your rod and reel out – fish love hanging out near these temperature changes.

141

# Changes in weather

*TEMPORARY CHANGES in weather can have extraordinary effects upon fishing. The problem is that there are so many possible changes and they can have countless different results in different fishing spots. The only way to take advantage of weather conditions is to learn and remember what they mean and where.*

## Rain

A heavy rain up a river can mean a runoff of pollutants and algae into a bay. This will drive fish away from the river's mouth and into deeper water. If the runoff is clean and full of tasty little creatures, it can rinse out the estuary and attract fish closer to the river's mouth. Other factors, such as a low saline content, can drive away the more sensitive fish but have no effect on snook, ladyfish, and more adaptable species. A heavy rain directly over a bay may dilute and improve the more polluted water that lines the shore. Fish that had been feeding farther out will work in closer. A heavy rain after a dry spell seems to improve lake fishing, but a few weeks of rain, depending on the lake, can hurt the fishing. Perhaps this is because of fertilizer or some other runoff.

■ **A bright, sunny day** *can do wonders for your mood, but so can an overcast day when it brings you better fishing.*

## Wind

Wind speed and direction are also very important. A strong breeze from a certain direction can warn you to expect sailfish; from another direction, it may tell you to forget about them. Fish seem to change their habits just ahead of a front, knowing more than they could possibly know.

## Sun

Bright sunlight can affect all fishing. It does seem to have more of an effect on freshwater than on saltwater, especially the deep-water variety. Freshwater fish are more likely to find shade or go deeper. If shade is sparse, the fish may concentrate under it, to your advantage. Where there's no shade, I personally have had better luck fishing freshwater on slightly overcast to very overcast days. Unfortunately, so have the mosquitoes that sucked me dry.

# Changes in currents

CURRENTS ARE AN EXTREMELY IMPORTANT FACTOR. *They not only change the behavior of fish, they change the behavior of fishermen. If the current is too strong, your live bait may not stay where you want it to or it may look unnatural. You might have to change the way you're hooking it or the amount of weight you're using (see Chapter 18). Perhaps you will have to forget about that particular type of fishing, or fishing altogether.*

**INTERNET**

**www.cyberangler.com**

*At this site, among other interesting things, you can find your local tides and weather forecasts.*

A slowing current may cause the fish in a channel to gather in the narrower, faster sections. Too much current may cause them to do the opposite, or perhaps find larger cover or deeper holes in which to lie in wait (see Chapter 12).

# Changes in food supply

KNOW WHAT THE FISH ARE EATING. *Sometimes you can see it from a distance, as when mayflies are swarming. In this case, you do as fly fishermen do: "Match the hatch." This means find a bait as similar as possible to what the fish are dining on. If you can't see what they're eating, which is, unfortunately, usually the case, cut open a fish's belly. More unfortunately, this involves one of life's little ironies. The time you want most to look inside a fish's stomach is when you can't catch a fish.*

*To know and match the hatch, see what the spiders are catching in their webs.*

■ **The baits used in fly-fishing** *are designed to resemble, among other things, the flies and insects that the fish eat.*

Never assume, when you see fish in an eating frenzy, that they wouldn't be interested in your little old bait, no matter how different. I've thrown ravenous flounder up on a beach, then returned to find dozens of minnows spit out on the sand. A marlin caught on a measly 3-pound tuna can have two 40-pound dorado in its stomach. How hungry could it have been? Hunger alone does not explain why fish strike a bait . . . not by a long shot.

*Never assume a fish has to be hungry to eat.*

■ **Even the insects with the best grips** *sometimes end up in the water. Learn to look for fish wherever you see insects.*

# Applying what you know

*ALL THE VARIABLES I'VE DISCUSSED* can come into play, determining *which fish are where, and how anxious they'll be to hit your bait. They are cues to take and clues to ponder, some more important than others. Only time and experience will enable you to take full advantage of the benefits they offer you.*

## Change leads to change

Don't forget these variables never work in isolation. For example, when you have a change of tide at river mouth, you have a change in the speed of the current, and sometimes even the direction. This triggers changes in salinity, water temperature, and food supply. If this happens during a full moon, the tides and their effects are going to be more extreme. The time of year will accentuate or dampen changes in such things as water temperature. Changes in time of day and weather can also come into play. It's up to you, the fisherman, to determine the relative importance of all these factors, figuring out and remembering how they influenced, for good or ill, each day's fishing. File away with them the knowledge that there are a few fish out there that like to break all the rules. Be thankful for that.

## A simple summary

✓ The Seventh Golden Rule of Fishing: "Whenever you cover a lot of ground searching for fish – be it by trolling, circling a lake, walking a river bank, or driving from pond to pond – return to the most productive or promising spot for dusk."

✓ Dawn and dusk are the choice times to fish.

✓ Time till sundown and time after sunrise are better guides to the best hours of fishing than clock time.

✓ Learn the water temperature ranges of the fish you target, and target them only within these ranges.

✓ Target thermocline borders.

✓ Learn how time of day, time of year, tides, phases of the moon, weather changes, and currents affect the species you target.

# Chapter 12

# Reading the Water

READING A BODY OF WATER means reading the clues it offers as to where fish are most likely to be. This takes practice. You see a clue, such as a fallen, half-submerged tree. You present your bait according to that clue, casting close to the tree. Even if you don't catch a fish, you still cast near trees the next few times you see them. If you don't catch any fish, you'll start ignoring this clue. However, if you catch a fish or two, you start seeing more than fallen trees – you "see" the fish lurking within them.

*In this chapter...*

✓ *The ambush*

✓ *Finding fish in a stream*

✓ *Finding fish in a lake*

✓ *Finding fish along an ocean shore*

✓ *Finding fish in open water*

✓ *Finding trophy fish*

THE FEWER FISH YOU ARE CATCHING, THE MORE NEED AND TIME YOU HAVE TO READ THE WATER

# The ambush

IN ORDER TO BECOME *a decent fisherman, you must learn how to read the water. You can't read the water unless you keep in mind an obvious little fact – one that never would have occurred to you except for your good fortune in reading the K.I.S.S. Guide to Fishing. This fact is that humans didn't invent the ambush. Not only that. As some of us are unfortunate enough to know, if humans have a claim to fame with regards to the ambush, it's the ingenious ways we've found to blow them. But that's going a little deeper than necessary into this subject.*

The Eighth Golden Rule of Fishing: *"To read water you must understand the ambush. To find your target fish, find its ambush site."*

Though you are the prime predator, you're not doing the ambushing. The fish is the ambusher, laying in wait for its prey. Your bait must play that prey. How well it does so, determines your success at blowing the fish's ambush, and whether you earn yourself a fish release or a fish dinner.

## BODIES OF WATER

Take a look at the three objects below. Each object represents one of three bodies of water I'll discuss in this chapter. Believe it or not, what we have here are a stream, a lake, and an ocean shore, all taken to a simplified extreme.

Now, where in these habitats would a hungry fish of above-average intelligence lay its ambush? Where could it lie in wait unnoticed? Allow me to save you some thought. Nowhere. There's no cover for an ambush in any of these three forms.

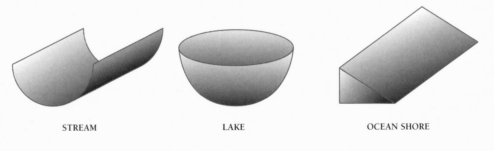

STREAM        LAKE        OCEAN SHORE

# Finding fish in a stream

COMPARE OUR SIMPLIFIED STREAM *to the (at least slightly) more realistic one on this page. Here we have myriad places for fish to lay in ambush – myriad places for us to present our baits disguised as prey. We find these places by recognizing how our realistic stream deviates from our simplified stream. Almost all these deviations, in varying degrees of suitability, are ambush sites. What makes them so? Three important factors: structure, objects, and current. If you want to be able to read the water, pay close attention to these factors.*

As you can see from the illustration at right, finding fish in a stream turns out to be a snap. There must be dozens of them here. By the way, we're going to use this stream to represent a river or a canal too. For instance, that boulder sticking out of the middle of the stream, in a river it would be a small island. In a canal it would be a dumped washing machine or Ford Fairlane. To make our exploration of this stream more relaxing, we'll go with the flow – in this case, the current. That means from north to south. Note that the fish we're looking for, when holding stationary in the current, usually face that current.

## Location 1

The first ambush site we come across is a small boulder on the east bank of our stream. Sure enough, we have a fish there, protected from the current and waiting in ambush. Small fish swimming with the current are safe as long as they hug the bank. Our ambusher would run aground and scrape his lower jaw long before he could reach them.

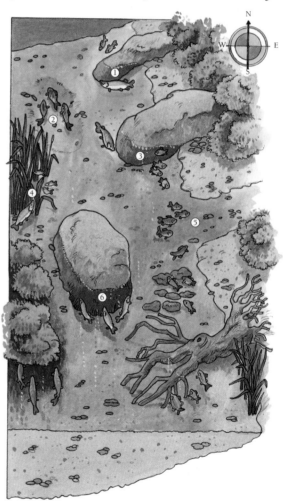

■ **Looking at a stream,** *you won't see many fish, if any. However, if you know what to look for, you can see where fish are most likely to be.*

However, in order to get by the rock, the little fellows have to travel in much deeper water. They get practically all the way around that boulder, ready to make a dash for the bank, when what do they see directly between them and the skinny water? That's right, our ambusher. Well, if you want to blow his ambush, I suggest you cast your bait near the bank, just upstream of the boulder. Retrieve it or let it drift right by him. If you're working a lure, you might give it an extra, nervous little twitch when you think it's in front of our friend's snout.

_The Ninth Golden Rule of Fishing:_ "When you cast your bait to a spot where you think there may be a fish, cast it as if you're 100 percent positive there is a fish." The more you put into a cast, the more you're likely to get out of it.

## Location 2

Our next ambush site is farther out in the stream. As the current rushes by, we have a three-fish ambush in a depression deep enough to keep them below both the current and the line of sight of anything swimming near the bottom. It's fortunate for them that fish don't have necks. These boys would have some stiff ones. They spend the day looking up, waiting for something tasty to drift or swim by overhead. The experience is probably similar to watching the Home Shopping Network lying flat on your stomach in front of the TV. If you want to offer your bait to these sedentary shoppers, I suggest you get it down deep.

## Location 3

Along the east bank, we find our next object of interest – a huge boulder. The small area between the down-current end of the boulder and the shore is one of those still, contemplative pools where little fish can catch their breaths (if that's what they catch). They can also find tasty insects and little animals there trying to avoid getting swept away by the current. Notice a larger fish about to turn the corner and join them. It's looking for lunch and this will not be the first time it has found a meal in this spot. A good cast on your part, and you can take it home for lunch.

■ **Where you see a boulder,** _a fish sees cover for an ambush. If you want to see a fish, make your bait look like easy prey._

## Location 4

We have to cross to the west bank for our next spot – a clump of reeds. Not only are there plenty of little fish between these reeds, there are insects crawling all over them. Sometimes the insects get careless and wet. A one-fish ambush waits for them just downstream, and also for any little fish that ventures too far from the reeds.

## Location 5

Notice the many fish waiting by the mouth of the tributary as it enters the stream. It's sure to carry something good for them to eat.

■ **Reeds usually mean insects,** *small fish, and larger fish that find both of them appetizing.*

The faster a stream flows, the more morsels it's likely to carry. This would also be true of a *conduit*. If fish are around, some of them are likely to be around any strong current. They will also be avoiding as much of this current as possible, holding behind objects large and small, close to bottom or the banks.

> **DEFINITION**
>
> A **conduit**, *in this book and around the Everglades, where I grew up, is a huge pipe laid under a road or dike that connects a canal to a wetland or to a wet something else.*

## Location 6

Next we have a huge boulder sticking out of the middle of the stream. It's providing excellent cover for three hungry fish. Just downstream on the west bank we have a big shady tree that fish find appealing. The sunnier the day, the more appealing they find its shade. Also appealing are the insects and other edibles that keep falling from the tree. Directly across stream we have some rocks providing cover for some smaller ambushers. This cover is nothing compared to the cover provided by the top half of that fallen tree. Fish of all sizes call it home.

*I am not sure why fish like shade, but the fact that it makes them less visible probably has a lot to do with it. For sure, this affinity predates the thinning of the ozone layer. In any case, wherever you see shade, in a mountain stream or in the Gulf Stream, look for fish.*

Notice that most of the fish in our stream are along the bank. If they're not using it for cover, they're hunting along it. Some are doing both. This is contrary to a common misconception of the novice fisherman – the largest fish are in the deepest water.

# Finding fish in a lake

*WE CAN SEE from the pictures on this page that a lake can have many characteristics in common with a stream, even disregarding the obvious ones such as wetness. Lake fish take advantage of tributaries, shade trees, and half-submerged dead trees in similar ways to their stream-bred cousins. Reed beds and other patches of vegetation not only provide refuge for smaller fish, they also provide lairs and ambush sites for the larger species that prey upon them.*

Bottom structure is also very important. Naked bottom offers little cover or food for fish, with the exception of those few species that have adapted to it. Monotonous bottom, such as a vast area of level sand, is less likely to attract fish. Look for small, submerged islands of vegetation among wide areas of sand. First, explore the outer edges of these patches with your bait. Afterward, crisscross them. Also, present your baits near any anomalies such as trenches, depressions, springs, underwater mounds, boulders, or old stoves.

*A clearly defined point of land sticking out into any body of water is worth at least a few casts.*

If you want to find fish in a lake, you should gain some understanding of thermoclines (see Chapter 11). Many fish and good fishermen are attracted to the edges of these abrupt changes in temperature. When you locate a thermocline, by all means possible and halfway reasonable, present your baits at its borders.

**SHADE TREE**

**SUBMERGED TREE**

**VEGETATION**

■ **Present your bait** *any place your prey is likely to wait for or search for its prey. In other words, look for places that can provide cover for your prey or for your prey's prey.*

# Finding fish along an ocean shore

TAKE ANOTHER LOOK *at our oversimplified ocean shore on page 148, because now we're going to cover some of nature's embellishments that could make it look like the ocean shores we know. Each and every one of these provides a fish habitat or a fish hunting ground.*

*The Tenth Golden Rule of Fishing: "When searching for fish, try a few casts at anything that catches your eye." It may have caught some fish's eye also, and it only costs a few casts to find out.*

## Boulders catch your eye

Wherever you see a group of small boulders just off of the beach, keep in mind that there are surely insects and little animals living on them. Below the high water mark, there are barnacles and maybe sea worms too. Fish, living and hiding in the crevices, eat all of these. They also eat any morsels uncovered when the waves stir up the sand around the boulders. Larger resident fish eat the smaller, finding cover for their ambushes between the boulders, or else in their shade. Other, even larger fish patrol by when higher tides allow.

■ **Huge offshore boulders** *provide not only cover and sustenance, they also offer protection when the surf is rough. That's the time to cast your baits at calm, protected niches.*

## Check out the vegetation and coral

Grass beds supply cover and sustenance to conchs and other shellfish. Some of these have kinks in their armor – kinks known to patrolling predators. Certain species of small fish also inhabit the grasses, and so do their predators. The prime predator is you, the fisherman, and these predators are your prey.

Mangroves grow right to the edge of a shore because they are expanding that shore. Trapping sand between their roots, they build up the beach and give themselves more room to grow. The labyrinthine protection of their roots provides cover for countless small fish.

Shallow flats are of special interest. During rising tides, fish come out of the depths to glide over these flats looking for crabs and shrimp. For the falling tide, other fish show up just off the deep edge of these flats. They wait in anticipation, ready to feed on what the retreating waters bring with them.

■ **Some fish are attracted to vegetation** *because of the food and cover it provides. Others are attracted to vegetation because of the fish it provides.*

*If a flat or any shallow water looks promising, try to see it at low tide. Chances are you'll spot some fish-attracting structure or holes that aren't visible at higher tides.*

Sea fans and small coral patches often dot the flats. They provide all kinds of ingenious cover and rich sustenance for fish and other marine life. If it's alive, you can bet something larger visits often in hopes of eating it. A patch of coral is like an oasis – the more barren the surrounding land, the busier the oasis. When you're looking for fish, never pass by an isolated coral patch. The more isolated, the more enticing it should be.

## Walls, ledges, and trenches

A drop-off means a wall, and a wall is the closest thing to Main Street you will find in the ocean. A wall often causes an upwelling of nutrients. It provides hold for coral and plants, and hiding places for little animals and the fish that eat them. If you know a cruising predator is in the area, and you want to catch it, the best place to sit in wait is over a wall.

A ledge (a 1- or 2-foot drop-off) is a good place to find fish. An even better place is a trench. Caves or overhangs in the sides of a trench make the finding of fish even more likely.

## Sandbars

Where you have two or more sandbars, you have **sloughs** between them. Fish like sloughs. They lay low and protected in these channels. Cast your bait to them there.

> **DEFINITION**
>
> **Sloughs**, *pronounced "slews," are long, narrow depressions or channels between sandbars.*

*Even if you can only see one sandbar, by watching the waves you may be able to tell whether there is a second sandbar with an interesting slough in between them.*

Swells peak or break on an outside sandbar. If there were no other sandbars on the inside of it, the swells would quickly diminish after crossing it. Then, as they approach the beach, they would gradually build again before breaking on the shore. However, where there's a second sandbar with a slough preceding it, the swells start to diminish, but quickly build again before peaking over the inside sandbar. They then diminish once more before building once again and breaking on the shore.

# Undertows

**BEFORE WE LEAVE THE SHORE,** *there's one more place we should mention. It's not a permanent place. In fact, it's a phenomenon that can occur just about anywhere along a sandy beach. An* **undertow** *is always an interesting (if not necessarily productive) target. It's also a dangerous place to fish.*

> **DEFINITION**
>
> *An* **undertow** *is a flash current running from or near a beach, out toward the open sea.*

## HOW AN UNDERTOW IS FORMED

In order to better understand what undertows are, it's worth first knowing what conditions lead to undertows being formed.

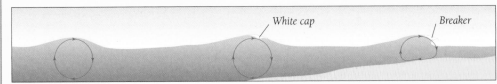

White cap    Breaker

■ **Starting out as swells,** *which move like wheels, waves can be turned into white caps by the wind and into breakers by beaches. The latter happens when the wheel hits the ocean bottom.*

Sandbar forming

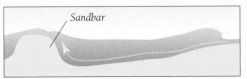

Sandbar

■ **When breakers** *hit a beach, they fall back taking sand with them. This sand builds sandbars.*

■ **As the sandbar grows,** *swells or breakers still pour over it on their way to the beach. But outgoing water, having spent its force on the shore, has a hard time getting past oncoming breakers and over the sandbar.*

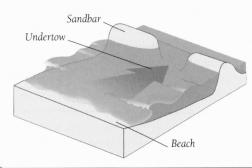

Sandbar

Undertow

Beach

■ **Water trapped** *between beach and sandbar exerts pressure on the sandbar until it bursts at a weak point. Water rushes through this break, out toward the ocean, in a narrow, powerful current – an undertow.*

You can spot an undertow from the beach. There will be a dip in the swells or breakers passing above the gap in the sandbar. The current rushing out through the break, which is the undertow, carries some tasty morsels with it. If there are fish around, it's a good bet they're waiting for a meal just outside the break in the sandbar. It pays to send your bait out to them.

## The dangers of an undertow

If you can't get your bait into the undertow from the beach, do not go wading. That will be your first mistake. You'll find yourself inching out, and a gradual increase in wave size may catch you unaware. You can lose your balance.

*Never get your feet wet fishing an undertow — they drown people, including fishermen.*

Instead of trying to gain your feet, you may try to swim. This will be mistake number two. The undertow will carry you toward the break in the sandbar.

You will refuse to let go of your favorite fishing outfit. Mistake number three. The current will sweep you out into the ocean. Suddenly the rod and reel won't seem so important anymore, and you'll finally let go of it.

With both hands free and your confidence returning, you try to swim against the undertow and back through the break in the sandbar. Mistake number four – your last and perhaps fatal one. Without help from someone else, you, the fisherman, are bait.

*An undertow is misnamed. It does not take you under, it takes you out. Don't ever try to swim against an undertow. Swim perpendicular to it, parallel to the beach. Sure, at first you will be pushed farther out, but you will also be moving along the beach. Soon you will escape the undertow, and be able to swim straight back to the beach.*

## Fishing an undertow

If you can cast a sinking bait through the break in the sandbar, you're home free. If you can't, cast a floater as far as you can, and see if the current will take it out. A floating bait can get lost in the *sloppy* water, but give it a try.

There are ways to fish an undertow when it's out of casting range. Probably the best is to place a bobber above a natural or live bait, then cast it as far as you can. If you reach any part of the undertow, the current will carry your bait right through the break in the sandbar.

> **DEFINITION**
>
> *The term* **sloppy**, *when applied to water, means rough and covered with white caps or foam.*

Don't let your line come taut, or your live bait will start doing the sidestroke on the surface. Since the water will probably be sloppy, use your biggest bobber.

*If you can't see your largest bobber, tie a balloon to your swivel. Blow it up as large as you like, as long as it's not so big that the wind will catch it and blow your bait off course.*

## Plan B

Along a shore, all of these different places that I've mentioned are worth a cast or three. Any abrupt changes in shape or depth are worth a few. Sometimes nothing works. Sometimes nothing works until you try something else. Keep trying.

<u>*The Eleventh Golden Rule of Fishing:*</u> *"If you can't get the fish to bite on what you brought, try using what's there to catch what's there — a frog off a lily pad, a grasshopper from the bank, a piece of barnacle off a boulder, a piece of shellfish on a grass patch, a crab on a flat, or any bait fish you can catch."*

## USE WHATEVER YOU'VE GOT!

A friend of mine lived on a sailboat. At anchor, he used to keep a baited hand line off the stern in case a free meal swam by. One day he went for supplies, leaving on the boat a friend who knew nothing about fishing. His friend had no idea what the noise was when the fish alarm went off. The guy ran to the stern to see the beer bottles and cans tied to the hand line banging on the deck. It took a good, long moment, but he finally figured out what was going on.

The fish not only put up a good fight, it won. It also turned this first-time fisherman into a fisherman for life. He rushed to check the galley fridge, but it was empty. Knowing nothing about fishing, he took a paper towel and sopped up the liquid from some dirty plates. He then ran and stuck this on the hook. When my friend approached in the dinghy, he was met by shouts, "Did you bring any bait?" This in itself was funny enough, but when my friend heard what this clown had put on the hook, he almost fell overboard. He was still laughing his butt off when the alarm went wild again. The fish they brought in was an 8-pound grouper.

# Finding fish in open water

OUR AMBUSH METAPHOR *works for some open-water fishing spots but not for others. Of course it applies to deep-water reefs. It works fine for any change in structure, such as ocean-floor mounds and depressions, both huge and small. It also applies well to trenches, ledges, and walls. Shipwrecks can support entire ecosystems. If these spots are not marked with buoys, you have to find them with* Loran, GPS, *or a* Fishfinder. *Remember, it's a huge ocean, and its fish are nowhere near evenly distributed.*

**DEFINITION**

Loran *and* GPS, *using radio waves and satellite signals respectively, give you your geographic position. A* Fishfinder *uses sonar to give you a picture of the bottom, plus any fish between it and you.*

**INTERNET**

www.ufish.com/
latlontds/loran.htm

*This US web page offers links to sites containing some Loran and GPS coordinates.*

However, in open water, the predator that is your prey often patrols its domain like a fighter pilot patrols the skies. Still, your bait must still pose as prey. Again, the key to catching fish is to explore just about anything on the wide, wide ocean that catches your eye.

*Never waste time fishing blind, unless you have no choice.*

## Look for change

Any change in anything should be explored. A change in water color can be a bonanza. Along the United States' East Coast, any place the deep, royal-blue Gulf Stream meets lighter inshore water is worth a very serious look. Fishermen call such borders an *edge*. Fish are attracted to these anomalies. Trolling or drifting along them makes far more sense than blindly leaving things up to chance. However, don't expect these edges to be straight lines. They often transform into curls and eddies.

**DEFINITION**

*An* **edge** *is a dividing line between two currents, water temperatures, bottom contours, or any of the many other changes that attract fish.*

■ **The more an ocean** *looks the same, the more important it is to find something – anything – different.*

If, scanning the ocean, everything looks the same, then you don't have a clue. Anything different you see is a clue. Let's say all the wave tops look uniform except in one elongated area where the seas look choppier. You determine that this area is not moving with the wind, and therefore not caused by it. What you probably have is a *rip current*, or a "rip." Again, for different reasons, fish are attracted to such departures from the normal or ordinary. In any case, doesn't it make more sense to try fishing in this area instead of the vast, uniform remainder of the ocean? The borders of this type of anomaly are also often referred to as an edge.

Another type of edge exists where two temperatures meet. Of course, this often occurs where two currents meet, but not necessarily. Sometimes it occurs without visible clues. Monitoring water temperature can prove very rewarding.

> **DEFINITION**
>
> A **rip current** is the meeting of two currents. They can both be surface currents, or one can be an upwelling or vertical current caused by a huge bottom formation.

## Watch the birdies

On the open ocean there are clues more obvious than edges. Birds are a tremendous help when they are feeding. You spy a flock of birds diving time after time into the water. You run for the spot to see what's going on. Sometimes you find the water boiling, thousands of small fish jumping from it while the birds dive down ravenously upon them. A bird's shadow should send them deep. Why doesn't it? Then you see the larger fish that have chased the small ones to the surface. Even if you don't see them, they're there. Otherwise, the small fish would instinctively dive down away from the birds. It's the big fish chasing the small fish that you want to catch. There are times you can plow through the water right up to them, but those times are rare. A far more advisable approach is an oblique one, just close enough to troll by or cast your bait to the edges of the melee. Better yet, aim your boat downstream of it, and let the melee come to you.

> **Trivia...**
>
> Sometimes you'll approach diving birds to discover they're not diving into a school of bait fish, but rather into a garbage slick. Don't waste much time, but spend a little. Game fish have been known to do a little slumming.

■ **For sea birds,** *fishing is not a sport: it's a matter of survival. Follow them long enough and they will lead you to fish.*

## Look for seaweed

Seaweed provides sustenance and cover for myriad forms of sea life. This sea life attracts larger fish, which are sustenance to even larger fish. Huge, solid patches of seaweed are bonanzas for the fishermen who fish their edges. Long lines of scattered seaweed can also be trolled along and cast to productively.

## Check the trash

Some valuable clues can hit you right in the hull and cost you your valuable boat – a tree log, a sheet of plywood, and any other kind of *flotsam*.

> **DEFINITION**
>
> **Flotsam** *is floating refuse or debris.*

*Small fish are attracted to just about anything that floats, for the algae growing on it or the shade it offers. Larger fish are attracted by the little fish, and also by the shade.*

It's always surprising how many fish you will spot under flotsam. This is further proof of our Tenth Golden Rule of Fishing – "When searching for fish, try a few casts at anything that catches your eye."

# Finding trophy fish

*FINDING TROPHY FISH depends upon numerous variables, and one of them is luck. Your knowledge and experience are, of course, important. Access to virgin fishing grounds can't hurt. There is a correlation, with exceptions, between size of bait and size of catch. Larger members of the same species will also hit types of bait that their smaller relatives won't touch. Ask any bass fisherman.*

When you target trophy fish, you're ignoring the large majority of the fish in that species. Therefore, you will catch fewer fish. Unfortunately, this brings us to a paradox. The more fish of a species you catch, the more likely you are to catch a trophy specimen. This paradox should be enough to get us back to our current subject – reading the water. There is an aspect of this that applies to catching trophy fish.

Trophy fish of any species are survivors. If they're not prime predators – for example, those fish at the top of the food chain, such as marlin and muskies – then they have to worry as much about being eaten as eating.

<u>The Twelfth Golden Rule of Fishing</u>: *"Trophy fish of almost any species are likely to be in the best place to get food without becoming food."*

The size alone of trophy fish entitles them to first choice of the ambush sites. I'm sorry I can't be more specific, but I don't need to be. If you keep the Twelfth Golden Rule of Fishing in mind whenever you're reading the water, you will, eventually, catch trophy fish.

■ **Marlin rarely come to you** – *you have to find them. Past experience helps, but you still have to read the water.*

# A simple summary

✔ The Eighth Golden Rule of Fishing: "To read water you must understand the ambush. To find your target fish, find its ambush site."

✔ The Ninth Golden Rule of Fishing: "When you cast your bait to a spot where you think there may be a fish, cast it as if you're 100 percent positive there is a fish." The more you put into a cast, the more you're likely to get out of it.

✔ The Tenth Golden Rule of Fishing: "When searching for fish, try a few casts at anything that catches your eye." It may have caught some fish's eye also, and it only costs a few casts to find out.

✔ The Eleventh Golden Rule of Fishing: "If you can't get the fish to bite on what you brought, try using what's there to catch what's there – a frog off a lily pad, a grasshopper from the bank, a piece of barnacle off a boulder, a piece of shellfish on a grass patch, a crab on a flat, or any bait fish you can catch."

✔ The Twelfth Golden Rule of Fishing: "Trophy fish of any species are likely to be in the best place to get food without becoming food."

✔ Three important factors that contribute to making a good ambush site are structure, objects, and current.

✔ Fish holding stationary in a current usually face that current.

✔ Fish like shade.

✔ Never leave a thermocline untried.

✔ You can fish an undertow, but only from the shore. Remember, though, that it's dangerous.

✔ An edge, or any change in anything, should be explored.

# Chapter 13

# Chumming

I STARTED CHUMMING when I was a little kid, before I'd ever even heard the word. To find mullet and blue gills in a nearby canal, we'd walk along the bank tossing out quarter slices of bread every 10 yards or so. As soon as the fish began ripping up a piece of bread, we'd cast our bobbers and dough balls beyond it, then reel them up close. Many a careless fish ended up taking the bread with the hook in it.

## In this chapter…

✓ Why chum?

✓ When to chum?

✓ Necessary equipment

✓ Old family recipes

✓ Preparing chum

✓ Creating a chum slick

✓ Fishing a chum slick

FISH-CLEANING TABLES ARE A GREAT SOURCE OF CHUM

# Why chum?

*BEFORE WE DISCUSS WHY WE CHUM, first let's look at that rare combination of conditions that makes chumming unnecessary:*

1. You know where the fish are

2. You're sure they're going to stay there

3. You can reach them with your bait

4. They're biting

If all of the preceding conditions do exist, you should:

1. Consider yourself quite fortunate

2. Immediately get in touch with me

However, when one of the aforementioned conditions is absent, chumming is worth a try. If you don't know where the fish are, you don't know where to place your bait. Casting blindly, it might be quite a while before you hit the right spot. Chumming may bring fish close enough to be visible. If not, you can still cast into the *chum slick*, hoping it has attracted fish. They are more likely to be there than anywhere else.

If you know or think there are fish out of your reach, a chum slick stretching from you to them can draw them closer. If fish are already within your reach, but you fear they will drift off, it pays to chum them. If you can reach them, but they're not biting, then some chum may improve their appetites. Regardless of whether or not their bellies are full, I doubt anything triggers a fish's feeding instinct quicker than the sight of other fish eating.

> **DEFINITION**
>
> A **chum slick** *is a continuous area of water containing chum, stretching from the source of that chum to its farthest reaches.*

■ **Let's hope this chum** *whet the fishes' appetites more than it seems to have whet this fisherman's.*

# When to chum?

*CHUMMING SHOULD BE TRIED just about any time you're not catching fish, or when you're afraid the fish you're catching will move on. Unless you can reach the fish with both your chum and your bait, you need a current to carry your chum to the fish and lead them to your bait. There's no way this can happen if your chum slick has breaks in it. You must chum continuously. Even when you do so, extremely rough water can break up your slick and make chumming futile.*

There's no reason that chumming should be restricted to boats. Chumming from streams, bridges, seawalls, lakeshores, beaches, or rocky seashores can all be worthwhile. However, there are problems with these places, especially with crowded bridges. If you're both the only angler chumming and the only one catching fish on a crowded bridge, this could cause some envy, even resentment. Two of the many ways your fellow fishermen might react are worth noting. You may notice everyone on the bridge slowly moving closer to you. Soon you could find yourself gasping for breath at the center of a tight knot of fishermen, all of them attempting to share your chum slick and the fish it contains. A worse, though far less likely possibility, is that an envious fellow fisherman, possibly after sharks, will decide to use you as chum. The successful fisherman should strive to avoid getting tossed off a bridge into his or her own chum slick.

*Never chum where people are swimming, and if you ever find yourself in a chum slick, remove yourself with all possible speed short of panic. This means swimming perpendicular to the current, never with or against it.*

When the fish aren't biting or have stopped biting, a little impromptu chumming won't do any harm and may do some good. For example, you're on a lakeshore using worms as bait. A worm without a hook in it might be a little more enticing. Throw one out. Watch it sink as far as you can. When that worm is out of sight, throw in another one. Try a few more. You may learn something. If you see a fish check out a worm and back off, a change of bait might be advisable.

If a fish takes a worm, try rigging your worms more naturally, perhaps with a smaller hook. Even if you see nothing, a few freebies may give the fish an appetite to take your baited hook. Cast to the spot where you're chumming. Try this same procedure with any bait you're using and any bait you have that you're not using. You don't want to leave that dying shrimp or shiner (a bait fish) in your bait bucket. Throw it toward your baited hook. It may do some good.

# Necessary equipment

THOUGH SOME STORE-BOUGHT *chum dispensers show fine forethought and workmanship, there is no reason you can't make an acceptable one yourself. All you need is some PVC pipe and fittings, a lead weight, and some nuts and bolts. The amount of chum you want to use determines the size of the pipe. The size of the chum and how fast you want to distribute it determines the size of the holes you will drill into that pipe.*

In saltwater, you often need something larger. Many people wire two plastic crates together or make large, wire-mesh cylinders. I much prefer a nylon mesh bag, slightly smaller than a pillow case. You can buy them just about any place you can buy chum, or you can sew them yourself. They take up practically no space – a feature much appreciated in car and boat. Also, in rough seas, you don't have to worry about them marking your hull.

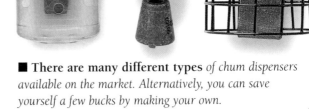

■ **There are many different types** *of chum dispensers available on the market. Alternatively, you can save yourself a few bucks by making your own.*

*A chum you can toss out by hand does not require a dispenser.*

## Bringing fish into view

If you're using a sinking chum and can't see the bottom, throw it to a likely place, then cast a similarly baited hook to the same spot. If you have the advantage of seeing the bottom, toss your chum only as far as you can observe it. If no fish approach in a reasonable time, toss some chum beyond where you can see, but adjacent to the chum you can see. The idea is to attract fish to the unseen chum in the hope they will keep eating until they are close enough for you to see. While you wait, there's no reason not to cast blindly to any spot that appears promising.

# MAKE YOUR OWN CHUM DISPENSER

Why spend money on a chum dispenser when it's so easy to make your own? As a special gift to you for buying this book, I will share with you the way I make mine. Just follow the simple instructions below.

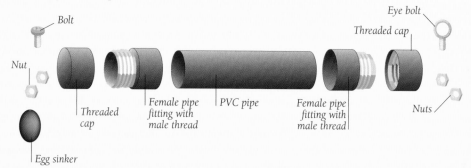

*Bolt*

*Eye bolt*

*Threaded cap*

*Nut*

*Threaded cap*

*Female pipe fitting with male thread*

*PVC pipe*

*Female pipe fitting with male thread*

*Nuts*

*Egg sinker*

### 1  Attach the fittings

*Glue the fittings with the male threads to the pipe.*

### 2  Make the holes

*Drill holes in the sinker and the centers of each cap big enough for the bolts. The chum holes in the pipe must be larger.*

### 3  Assemble the dispenser

*Attach the sinker to the inside of one cap, and the eye bolt to the outside of the other. Screw a second nut on both bolts to lock down the first nut.*

# Old family recipes

THERE'S NO END TO THE STRANGE INGREDIENTS *you can use in chum, not to mention their infinite possible combinations. Here is a short list: ground-up, cut-up, and/or pulverized bait fish; what remains after cleaning food fish; chunks of any fish; dog food and cat food, both canned and dry; sardines, menhaden (mossbunker), or any other oily fish – the oilier the better; shellfish or their discarded parts; corn and peas (seed, canned, and frozen); live bait (injured accidentally and purposely); bread and dough; cereal, cornmeal, and oatmeal; pasta of all varieties and colors . . . and so on.*

*There is little danger of including something in your chum that will drive fish away. However, finding the chum ingredients a particular species prefers is worth quite a bit of trial-and-error experimentation.*

To get back to our original question, use anything that works as chum. Experiment with whatever you have. Learn what works, and what doesn't, for each individual species of fish. Learn what ingredients are essential and what you can do without. In any case, this trip's leftover bait is usually the first ingredient in the next trip's chum.

■ **The ingredients in chum** *are far from exotic. You can find them in your pantry and in your garbage.*

# Preparing chum

**THE SIMPLEST WAY TO PREPARE CHUM** *is by throwing pieces of fish, shellfish, and other ingredients into a bucket, and then pounding them into a paste with the fat end of a baseball bat (or caveman club). I'll pass over this method for two reasons among many. First, there are easier ways to go. Second, this method is not only one of the best arguments against the use of chum, it's also one of the best for restricting your bait to the artificial variety.*

I much prefer the use of a knife and cleaver to a baseball bat. This brings up the question, "How large should you cut the pieces?" The answer is all sizes. The reason is to increase the size of your chum slick. Generally, the smaller the pieces, the slower they sink. In theory, if all the pieces of chum are the same ingredient cut the same size, they will sink together. So, as the current carries away your chum slick, it will fall in the water column, taking the shape, roughly – very roughly – of a descending cylinder. However, if your chum is made up of different-size pieces of different ingredients, and if this chum contains fish oil or floating particles that will remain on the surface, then your chum slick will cover more of the water column and look more like a falling curtain. The larger your chum slick, the more likely it is to find and attract fish. Use the cleaver on the hard-to-cut chunks, leaving them larger. Use the knife on the easy-to-cut chunks, cutting them as small as you desire.

SLICK WITH
SAME-SIZE CHUM

SLICK WITH
DIFFERENT-SIZE CHUM

A much easier and better way to make chum is to grind most of your more solid ingredients in a meat grinder. I do recommend that you later mix in some cut chunks of different sizes. Stir the chum to get a fairly even mix.

If bread is one of your ingredients, soak and soften it in cool water first. Squeeze out this water if you plan on molding your chum into solid balls that will slowly disintegrate. If you want a broad slick, add some water to your chum. A good trick for increasing the height of your slick in the water column is to mix in some sand. It sinks quickly and also adds sparkle.

*One of my favorite chum ingredients is a can of sardines, oil and all. In fact, if you ever see fresh sardines for sale, buy and freeze them in small packages. Whole sardines are excellent bait.*

# Creating a chum slick

**THERE ARE TWO BASIC METHODS** *to create a chum slick. One involves the use of "fresh" or defrosted chum, which I'll refer to as soft chum. The other method uses a frozen block of chum.*

## SOFT CHUM VS FROZEN CHUM

Soft chum is often spread as it is made, directly from a meat grinder set up at the transom of a boat. Additional ingredients and larger chunks can be tossed into the slick thus created. Soft chum can also be scooped out of a bucket and tossed into the water at regular intervals. Frozen chum is much easier to handle. You put it in a mesh bag and lower it into the water.

| The pros of soft chum | The cons of soft chum |
| --- | --- |
| Soft chum is fresher. | Fish are not freshness freaks when it comes to chum. |
| You can add whatever you have handy to soft chum. | You can do the same with frozen chum. |
| You can make soft chum according to your own personal recipe. | You can do the same when you make and freeze your own chum. Even when you buy a frozen block, you can add you own homemade frozen block, or spice up your slick by scooping out some fresh chum. |
| If there's a member of your party who is best kept occupied, he or she can ladle out the soft chum. | That member of your party may be you. |
| Soft chum, because of its appearance and smell, tends to induce boating party members to contribute their own chum to the slick. | One of those party members may be you, doubled-up and heaving your contribution over the transom. |
| You can fine-tune your slick, adding just the right amount of chum. | One fisherman has to remain completely occupied with the slick. A break in it is worse than no slick, drawing the fish away from you. You must then start an entirely new slick to compete with your old one. |

As far as I'm concerned, soft chum is not worth the trouble. Its most serious drawback is the difficulty in keeping the chum slick continuous. This requires a very single-minded person. Those ever-present distractions, such as hungry fish, nature's call, or the beer cooler, can make an hour's chumming worthless. There's also the mess and smell of the chum itself, plus the mess, smell, and incapacitation of fishermen heaving their guts out.

## Frozen chum

Frozen chum has very little odor until unfrozen. By then, it's in a mesh bag hanging submerged in the water. The appetizing scent is thus saved for the fish. As the frozen block defrosts, you're assured of a continuous chum slick. Frozen chum is also much easier to place anywhere in the water column, including on the bottom. All you need is a long enough rope.

Make sure the mesh of your chum bag is large enough to release the chum. It pays to have different mesh sizes for different chum or target fish. If you have to stretch your chum, a smaller mesh size will make it last longer. Always have a few chunks in your chum bag larger than its mesh. That way, even when the rest of the chum is gone, fish may still be attracted to the scent emanating from the bag. Those remaining chunks may give you the extra few minutes needed to refill the bag before your slick breaks completely. If you don't have larger chunks, you can place some chum in a smaller mesh bag and put that bag into or alongside the larger mesh bag.

■ **A chum bag** *keeps chum and its nauseating aroma out of your boat and in the water.*

*Warning! Do not attempt the preparation of chum in your home kitchen without prior agreement from your spouse. Not only is this proven grounds for divorce, in some states it qualifies as spousal abuse.*

# Fishing a chum slick

FISHING A CHUM SLICK is not just *freelining*. You want your bait to act exactly like the chum that surrounds it. Not only must it travel at the same speed as the chum, it must also drop the same distance in the water column. Even if you leave your bail open and allow the current to take out line, the small amount of resistance from the spool lip and line guides will retard the movement of your bait. You must continually strip the line from your reel before it comes taut. In fact, sometimes it is necessary to strip this line from your rod tip.

> **DEFINITION**
>
> **Freelining** means leaving your reel's bail open in order to give your bait freedom to swim or to be taken by the current or by a fish.

If you intend to use soft chum from a boat, feed sardines to the members of your party first. Not only does this increase the likelihood that they will add their own personal contribution to the slick, it also improves the fish-attracting quality of the chum they will contribute.

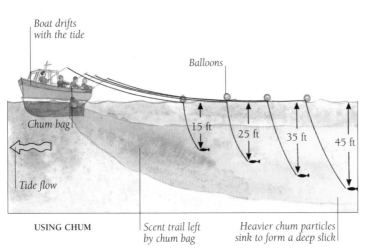

Boat drifts with the tide

Balloons

Chum bag

15 ft

25 ft

35 ft

45 ft

Tide flow

**USING CHUM**

Scent trail left by chum bag

Heavier chum particles sink to form a deep slick

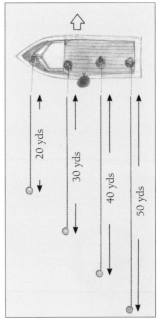

20 yds

30 yds

40 yds

50 yds

**SPACING THE BAITS**

■ **If you can't** keep your baits in the chum slick, you are far better off without a chum slick.

## The right bait

Your bait will not stay in the slick if it's much larger than the pieces of chum. If you have to use a larger bait, it will pay you to chunk some similar pieces of bait into the slick. Also, use the smallest hook possible, so its weight won't drag your bait down.

There's no reason why you can't use artificial baits in a chum slick. Having trouble keeping real and/or live baits where you want them is a very good reason to switch to artificials. You can drift some artificials as if they are part of the slick, and you can work others as if they're feeding on the slick. When using artificials, it's even more important to draw the fish as close to you as possible

## Aiming your chum

Assume you're anchored over a very small reef that's loaded with fish. The first problem is that they won't take your bait unless it's on 6-pound test or less. The second problem is that as soon as they do take it, they snap your line on some coral. You decide to chum them away from the coral to eliminate the second problem. Well, if you hang out your chum bag while anchored directly over the reef, by the time its slick reaches the bottom the current will have carried it off the reef. Now you could lower your chum bag until it is just above the reef. However, getting your bait near it can prove difficult. A better solution is to anchor up current of the reef. Of course, this involves another problem: How far up current? Still, this is your problem, not mine. Good luck with it.

You can aim your chum on a river or off a bridge almost as well as from a boat. This involves figuring out the current and where you have to place the source of your slick.

■ **Chumming off a bridge** *requires that you know where to place your chum so that the current will take it where you want it to go.*

Not only will a slick attract fish, the fish it attracts can attract much larger fish. When you catch one of the smaller fish, try sending it right back out attached to a hook. If the water is rough, a balloon may be easier to keep an eye on than a bobber. When the wind is blowing across the current, do not blow up your balloon any larger than need be. Seeing the balloon is of little value if the wind has blown it out of the slick.

## Never overchum

Overchumming defeats the purpose of chumming. The idea is to attract fish to your bait. If possible, your bait should be kept close enough to watch. Also, you want to keep the fight as close as possible, and to make the fish pay for every inch of line. If you overchum, fish can position themselves way back in the slick, perhaps beyond your bait, and eat at their leisure. In addition, you want the fish to fight recklessly over the chum. The more chum, the less reckless the fish. Also, the more chunks of bait to choose from, the worse odds a fish will choose the one hiding your hook. Finally, you don't want your target fish to be stuffed to the gills or suffering a bellyache by the time your bait arrives.

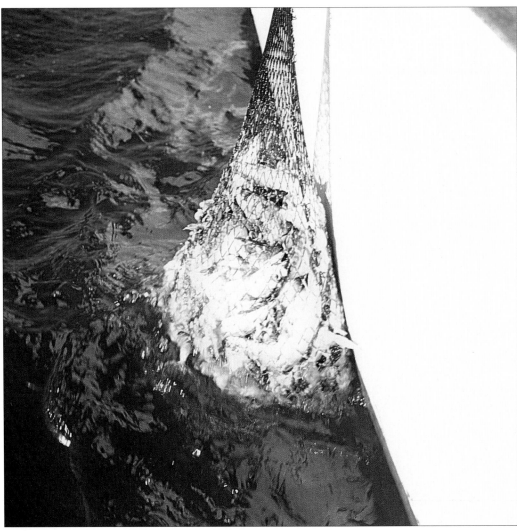

■ **The purpose of chum** *is to attract and hold fish, not to satisfy their appetites.*

## Final thoughts

Chumming requires skill and knowledge. Still, don't attempt to elevate it to an exact science or an artistic endeavor. You're chumming in order to fish, not vice versa. Chumming will give you a distinct advantage. Yet, it's basically just a dirty job that no one is forcing you to do.

*Never let your bait get out of the slick. Not only will your chum do you no good, it will actually do you harm by drawing fish away from your bait.*

# A simple summary

✔ Chumming is used to attract fish to, and hold fish near, your bait.

✔ Chumming should be tried just about any time you're not catching fish or when you're afraid the fish you're catching will move on.

✔ If you ever end up swimming in your own chum slick, remove yourself with all possible speed short of panic. This means swimming perpendicular to the current, not with or against it.

✔ Finding the chum ingredients preferred by each particular species of fish is worth quite a bit of trial-and-error experimentation.

✔ A break in a chum slick is far worse than no slick at all, since the break draws the fish away from you. The solution is to immediately start an entirely new chum slick to compete with your old one.

✔ Aim your chum by judging the current. Know where you want your chum slick to go, and where it has to enter the water to get there.

✔ Overchumming defeats the purpose of chumming.

# Chapter 14

# Trolling from Place to Place

TROLLING IS PERHAPS the most underutilized method of fishing. This is true not only in terms of the fish that could be caught, but also in terms of the knowledge that could be gained. Trolling is not just for catching big game fish. In the right place, the right bait can catch you anything from quarter-pound bream, to freshwater bass of any size, to snapper and grouper, to marlin and giant tuna.

## In this chapter...

✓ When and where to troll

✓ What you need to troll

✓ Trolling spreads

✓ Lure distance, speed, and depth

✓ Keeping your lines untangled

✓ Trolling tricks

✓ Optional equipment

IF YOU DON'T KNOW WHERE THE FISH ARE, YOU CAN COVER A LOT OF WATER TROLLING

# When and where to troll

*SAY YOU INTEND to fish an area by boat, be it lake, river, coastal shore, or open sea. Like perhaps nine out of ten fishermen, you anchor or start drifting at the first promising spot. If that place doesn't pan out, you try another. At the end of the day, you haven't even come close to covering much of the water.*

## When to troll

Whenever you arrive at a new spot or one where you must cover a large area to locate the fish, doesn't it make sense to first explore the entire area, then start fishing at the most promising spot? You know it does, but you just can't wait to get your lines wet. Well, why not wet them by trolling the entire area, stopping at a place to fish only if you first get a strike there?

Scouting an area by trolling can not only produce fish along the way, it can give you information about the fish that inhabit or do not inhabit that place. Trolling can tell you where they are in relation to depth, water temperature, and structure. It will give you hints about what baits will be most effective and how they should be presented.

## Where to troll

Let's say you arrive at a lake you've never fished before. A novice might think that the most and largest fish would be in the deepest part of the lake. This is possible, but unlikely. To find fish, first look for structure. Clear water or a Fishfinder can help you check the bottom. Yet you don't need either to find the most structure. Just look along the shore.

■ **When you're faced** *with a lot of water and you don't know where the fish are, trolling is the way to go. If you don't troll, you could be in for a long, hard day.*

# What you need to troll

ONE THING YOU DON'T NEED is level-wind trolling tackle. As long as you use line of 30-pound test or less, spinning gear is a good second choice. And in those few cases where a quick retrieve is paramount, spinning gear is superior.

Learn the appropriate bend in your rods for different baits at different speeds. Too much bend may mean your bait is fouled with weeds or a plastic bag. Too little bend can mean that you no longer have any bait.

Unfortunately, unless you know a trick that I don't, one of the things you do need to troll is a boat. Still, it doesn't have to be a 30-foot Sportsfisherman. It doesn't even have to have a motor. A rowboat or a canoe can be good enough.

Do not, under any circumstances, try to learn both fishing and boatmanship at the same time. Make sure you perfect one of these skills before attempting the other. Fighting a fish can be one hell of a distraction, enough of one to leave you fighting for your life. If you're foolish enough to disregard this warning, please don't be foolish enough to do so in water more than waist-deep.

■ **One person can troll** *from a canoe or rowboat, but a crew of two makes things easier.*

# Trolling baits

This is the next thing you need. You can't just thread a hunk of mullet on your hook as if you were bottom fishing. A great casting lure is not necessarily suitable for trolling either.

## Live bait

Live fish can make excellent trolling bait and is often the bait of choice. Using it does involve two overriding problems. Live bait must be rigged so as to act alive, stay alive, and hook your prey. Some simple and effective rigs are illustrated in Chapter 22. You also must troll them at speeds that lend these baits an enticing action without killing them.

■ **Most fishermen know** *that mullet makes great bait, but few of them know that it also makes great eating when grilled over charcoal.*

## Natural bait

Natural baits require much less care in handling than live baits. Still, the more care you take in their preservation and rigging, the more fish you will catch. Generally, real baits should be trolled at speeds between those ideal for live baits and artificials. However, some naturals can be trolled at speeds high enough to mix with artificial baits, while others can be pulled slow enough to mix with live baits. You'll learn how to rig them in Chapter 21.

## Artificial bait

Artificial baits can make trolling a pleasure. You don't have to worry about keeping them fresh, not to mention alive. More important, they can be rigged ready to go in your spare time, not your fishing time. Rigging artificials is not the dirty job rigging real baits can be. You can never depend upon getting high-quality live or real baits. Also, even if you plan on using real baits, artificials are a convenient backup.

A large fish is likelier to hit an undersize lure than a small fish is to hit an oversize one. Larger lures will catch you larger fish, but they're likely to decrease your strikes. If you know the size lure you want to use, fine, use it. If you can't decide between two sizes, you're usually better off with the smaller one. Whenever possible, troll one bait that stands out as larger from the rest and another that stands out as smaller. Sloppy water is one reason to move up a size to more visible lures.

# Trolling spreads

*IF YOU WANT TO TROLL more than one bait, you're going to have to learn how to arrange your spread. You place your lures so as to maximize their effectiveness in catching fish and minimize the likelihood of tangled lines. A good fisherman can troll five lines without a problem. An expert can troll nine, but rarely would. The more lines you troll, the closer attention you have to pay to them and the more restricted your boat maneuvering. Depending upon the experience of the crew, the fish you're after, and the conditions, there's always a point at which the addition of another line to the spread takes more away from the fishing experience than it adds. The last thing you want to see when you look back at your spread is your baits weaving a monofilament rug.*

### DEFINITION

*Your **spread** is the arrangement, or pattern, of your trolling baits. It encompasses not only their position laterally behind the boat, but also vertically in the water column.*

## Bait choice and placement

If you're trolling for one particular species, say largemouth bass or tuna, you'll know fairly well from which lures to choose. If you're only trolling one or two lines, that pretty much decides your spread. However, if you're fruitlessly trolling four or five artificial lures, you may want to replace one or all with something very different. Until you know which baits are hot and which are not, give the fish a real choice. Also, until you know where the fish are in the water column, you want to troll your lures at different depths.

## A two-bait spread

In the picture below, two friends are fishing two lines from a canoe. The *starboard* bait is a deep-running lure or a weighted live or natural bait. The *port* bait is a surface lure or an unweighted live or natural bait. As you can see from the side view, you would have a hard time tangling lines even if you tried.

### DEFINITION

*When you're facing forward in a boat, the **port** side of that boat is to your left and the **starboard** side is to your right. No matter which direction you turn to face, the port and starboard sides of the boat do not change.*

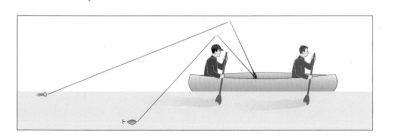

With this simple spread you've covered the two extremes in the water column. You can get the deep-running bait even deeper by fishing it farther back. Then you'll also have to run the surface bait farther back to avoid tangles. The farther back you run these or any other lures, the more likely they will tangle. Still, by adjusting the line lengths carefully, and keeping an eye out, you can help prevent this.

*The farther back you place a sinking bait, the deeper it will run — up to a point. There is a limit to how deep you can get a bait, because for every inch of line you let out, you add to the water resistance of the line as a whole. When this resistance overcomes the weight and shape of the bait, the lure will sink no farther. However, if you choose, you can then lessen resistance and get the lure lower by decreasing your trolling speed.*

## Surface baits for trolling

There are many, many surface-trolling baits from which you can choose. The plastic-lipped floating plug is very effective in both freshwater and saltwater. The live bait fish must be trolled at exactly the right speed if you wish to keep it at the surface and also keep it alive and swimming naturally. The skill with which you rig it is critical (see Chapter 22).

**WILLIAMSON SKIRTED STRAIGHT RUNNER**

**PLASTIC-LIPPED FLOATING PLUG**

**WILLIAMSON SKIRTED CHUGGER**

The durability of the strip-and-tail rig gives you a range of possible speeds much larger than that of live baits. If prepared correctly, you should be able to run it just as fast as many plugs. I cover its preparation in Chapter 21. Skirted lures can range in size from a few inches to well over a foot. They're designed for saltwater. The blunter variety, sometimes called a "chugger," twists with an enticing, water-spraying action while occasionally making short, shallow dives.

The chugger's minimum effective trolling speed is about 5 knots. This would require some very strenuous canoeing, and probably a coxswain with a whip in his hand. Its pointier cousin is a straight runner that can be pulled over three times that speed. Do not try this unless your boat has a motor.

### Using them correctly

Surface lures can catch fish while doing things they're not designed to do. However, they will catch a hell of a lot more fish if you have them doing what they are designed to do. The best place to position most surface lures is on the front face of a wave in your boat's wake. These lures should appear as if surfing. Fortunately, such placement allows you the best possible view of them.

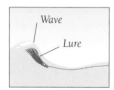

LURE POSITION

## Deep baits for trolling

Many baits run deep enough to use on the starboard rod in your canoe. The odd-looking crankbait (*below*) is designed for freshwater, but it will catch fish in saltwater too. If that's where you plan to use it, switch to some stronger hooks if necessary. This lure's optimum and maximum speeds are the lowest of the lures pictured below. The metal-lipped lure (see Chapter 23), though also a countdown casting plug, can be trolled much faster than a canoe can be paddled. It will swim fairly deep, depending upon your speed and how far back you run it. The Australian-type trolling plug (see Chapter 23) will run even faster and deeper. The Japanese feather is strictly a trolling lure. Up to a point, the slower and farther back you run it, the deeper it will go. Our old friend the strip-and-tail rig can be weighted ahead of the leader to run deep.

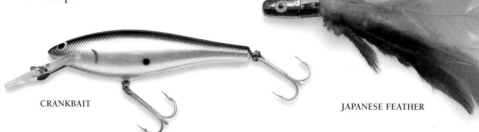

CRANKBAIT

JAPANESE FEATHER

## A nine-bait spread

Now you know how to troll two whole lines without getting them tangled, why not jump to nine? Even if you never troll that many, or half that many, the next few paragraphs offer you numerous tricks that will make even a three- or four-lure spread easier and more productive.

This boat (*right*) is a 30-foot Sportsfisherman. Let's start with the baits set just off the transom corners. Bait 1 is a surface-running skirted bait. Notice that its line doesn't run straight from rod tip to lure; it runs through a release device attached to the lower part of the rod. I'll discuss these devices later in the chapter. Right now it's only necessary to know that they lower the angle of the line pulling the bait. This allows you to run a bait closer to the transom, with more separation and less chance of entanglement between it and the baits behind. Otherwise, this bait would continually jump out of the water. If you can't keep your lures in the water, they won't do you any good. Notice that we don't need a release for bait 2. It's a deep-running Australian-type lure that can be placed quite close in without causing it to jump out of the water.

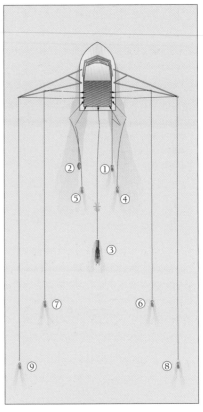

NINE-BAIT SPREAD

The largest lure is the center one, bait 3. The funny-looking thing causing all the commotion in front of it is a bird, which I'll cover shortly. Bait 3 can be a king-size version of a skirted lure. In theory, this lure appears as if it's both chasing the bird and the smaller lures in front of it (baits 4 and 5), and leading the smaller lures behind it (baits 6 and 7). I doubt game fish are aware of this theory, but they have been known to hit all nine lures in this spread.

Notice that this pattern has baits 6 and 7 running from halfway up the *outriggers*. If you're using natural or live baits that you want swallowed, then it's advantageous, though not mandatory, to run them from an outrigger to provide some *drop-back*.

The trailing baits, baits 8 and 9, are the farthest apart, being run off the tips of the outriggers. This is advisable because the longer the lines, the greater the danger of tangles. The fact these baits may be out of sight compounds this problem, along with the mess you're left with if and when you finally realize a problem exists.

## Other spread options

Again, the spread illustrated on the previous page is just one of many patterns that enable the trolling of nine lines. For example, baits 8 and 9 could be trolled much farther forward, even halfway between baits 1 and 2 and baits 4 and 5. This would be preferable if the tuna were hitting these closer baits. Even if they're also hitting baits 8 and 9, why start the fight with any more line off your reel than necessary. You would only want baits 8 and 9 so far back if, for instance, they were aimed at a different species, such as wahoo, or if you were not getting any hits, especially on a dead-calm day. The thinking behind this would be that the farther back the baits, say Japanese feathers or weighted bait fish, the deeper they would run and the less chance the boat would spook your prey.

# Lure distance, speed, and depth

THE DISTANCE BACK YOU SET A LURE *and the speed you pull it greatly influence the lure's action (behavior). Speed and distance also influence another very important variable – lure depth.*

## How far back?

No trolling lure comes with an inherent distance that it must be run behind a boat. When I first started trolling, I noticed that my longest lines were my best producers. This wasn't surprising where deep-running lures were concerned. Running them long meant running them deeper. However, even my surface baits seemed to produce better long. Well, my lines got longer and longer, and I did better and better. Not surprisingly, my lines got longer still. Looking back, I'm sure that the skills and knowledge I was gaining played a far more important role than the length of my lines.

*The closer the strike, the closer the fight and the better your chance of winning it. Every inch of line between you and the fish enhances its chances. All things being equal, you want to troll your lures as close to the transom and to the surface as possible.*

As my lines got longer, I had to work harder. The farther back your baits are, the more trouble it takes to let them out and reel them in.

You also have to be more careful about tangles, both in handling the lines themselves and in maneuvering the boat. Sometimes I took it easy, bringing my lines in a little. The fish didn't seem to mind, so over the years my lines got shorter and shorter. I saw more strikes, and was able to react more quickly to them.

These days I keep my spreads as tight and close in as possible. Sometimes I start out with a line or two long, at least until I have that first fish in the boat. Yet, reeling in those long lines, I start remembering all the fish, from little tuna to beautiful marlin, that have hit lures trolled within feet of my transom. As soon as my short lines start producing, my long lines get short.

*On those dead-calm, glass-surface days when the fish will not bite, my favorite tactic is to put out my deep-running lures and get them as far back and deep as they will go.*

## How fast?

The baits you run determine the speeds you troll, or vice versa. Live baits must be trolled the slowest and artificials the fastest, with natural baits in the middle. If there's any excellent combination of live and artificial baits that can be trolled together, I have yet to find it. Still, I sometimes mix them when scouting water without a specific target fish in mind. This means trolling the artificials at less than optimum speed, the live baits at more than optimum, or both. However, there are many natural bait rigs that can be trolled slow enough to mix with live baits, and others that can be trolled fast enough to mix with artificials.

Live baits, as I may have mentioned, must be trolled slow enough to keep them alive. That said, there are only two other criteria for judging trolling speed. The first is appearance. Does the current trolling speed give your baits a realistic, enticing action? Baits can look injured, but to fish they must look like prey. Spray and bubble trails are great. So is skimming the surface. Jumping out of the water is not. Switch to a bait that will stay wet at the current speed, or else lower your speed. With experience, you'll learn how to look at a lure's action and determine whether to speed up or slow down.

Rowing or paddling speeds are too slow to get an enticing action out of most trolling lures. In this case, try trolling some casting lures. Don't be surprised when some casting jig or other with no inherent action turns out to be a dynamite trolling lure.

RUBBER SANDEEL

■ **If your speed** *is very limited and the fish are ignoring your trolling lures, troll some casting lures.*

SPOON

## Are you catching anything?

The second criterion for judging trolling speed is productivity. If you are not catching fish, the problem may be your baits or the lack of fish in your area. Before you change your baits or location, try the simpler alternative of changing your trolling speed. Even if your speed has proven productive at other times, change it anyway. A sudden jump in speed may be just the stimulus to change fish from bystanders to strikers. Likewise, a drop in speed may cause your baits to drop. This drop, even if only a matter of inches, may entice a strike.

*The proper speed for each bait is not an exact number. It's a range. If you don't like the action of a bait or it's not producing, the first change you make should be the easiest — a change in trolling speed.*

## TUNA FOR LUNCH

Don't make the mistake of thinking that there's only one exact trolling speed for a particular time, place, and lure spread, and that you have to find it or you won't catch any fish. Once, during a successful charter, I had my inexperienced fishing party worn out by noon. The boat of a friend of mine was a mile off my port side, dead even with us. I had noticed the same thing twice before in the previous hour. He must have seen how well we were doing and was matching our speed. This friend, too proud to ask me for trolling tips, rarely caught anything except the occasional plastic bag.

I decided to revive my party with a quiet lunch and have some fun with my friend at the same time. I kept raising and lowering my speed to see how long it would take him to catch on. Fifteen minutes later he was still dead even with us. My party had yet to revive, so I reeled my spread right in against the transom, took one engine out of gear and lowered the other to idle. The current facing me was now moving faster than my boat, but this didn't stop my friend from staying even as we both moved backward. My fishing party was probably wondering about the amused expression on my face when a rod suddenly bent double and changed that expression to one of surprise. A beautiful tuna had scarfed up a barely moving lure just 3 feet off my transom. As one of my fishermen tried to tame it, I kept looking over at my friend, still dead even, hoping he had his binoculars on us.

# Trolling depth

If you know the depth of the fish you're after, get your sinking baits down as close to that depth as possible. If you know the depth of a thermocline, check out that depth. If you know the depth of structures such as trenches, holes, underwater peaks, and so on, get your sinking baits down to them.

If you have no substantial clues about the location of fish in the water column, then cover the entire column as best as you can. That means at least one bait on the surface, one as deep as possible, and your other baits in between. This can be done in two ways or in a combination of the two.

## Method 1

The first way is to use different baits that seek different depths at the same trolling speed. This illustration shows three different lures in a vertical spread. The surface lure running from the rod on the port side of the boat is a skirted lure. The deepest lure, running from the center of the transom, is an Australian-type plug. The lure running from the starboard side is a metal-lipped countdown plug. It's being trolled farthest back from the boat in order to get it down in the water column halfway between the other two lures.

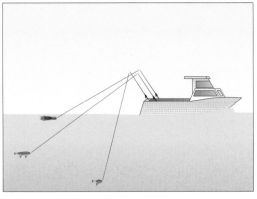

METHOD 1

## Method 2

You could also distribute your lures in the water column by using the same sinking lure at different distances from your boat. The farther back, the deeper it should sink (up to a point), as illustrated by these Japanese feathers. This method usually requires substantial separation between lines to prevent their crossing.

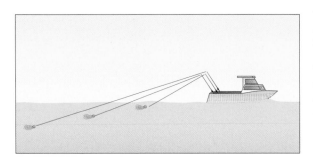

METHOD 2

If you care to use natural or live baits, you can also add trolling weights. Using a variety of weights, you can distribute your baits vertically. Using equal weights, you could vary their depths according to their distances from your boat.

# Keeping your lines untangled

*THERE'S NO REASON you should ever get your lines tangled if you keep a perfectly straight course, never troll in a wind, and don't catch any fish. Allow me to warn you that if you do keep a perfectly straight course you'll eventually hit land, unless you hit another boat first. If you wait for windless days to troll, you're not going to do much trolling. If you don't catch fish, there is no point in trolling. If you troll a lot of lines, every once in a while they are sure to tangle. However, by following a few rules, these tangles can be kept to a minimum.*

## Changing course while trolling

Some trolling spreads are tangle-proof. This is usually accomplished by limiting the number of baits, their type, and their placement. Conversely, when a fisherman maximizes the possibilities of his or her spread, he or she most likely increases the danger of tangled lines. It's a trade-off.

When you make a turn trolling, lines of equal length pulling identical lures will take the same time to straighten out again behind your boat. This means that if you keep your turns wide, your lines are not likely to tangle. However, these turns are often paid for in forfeited time. Problems arise when you're pulling markedly different baits, or any baits at unequal distances back. The longer the distance, the longer it takes a bait to reposition itself directly behind your boat. Look at the diagrams on this page.

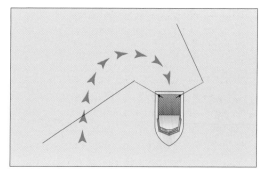

TURN TO STARBOARD

The boat on top has just made a 180-degree turn to starboard. Notice that the shorter of its two trolling lines has almost straightened behind it already. The boat on the bottom has made a 180-degree turn to port, and the shorter of its two trolling lines is also almost directly behind it. Notice that, for some reason, this boat's lines are crossed and ready to tangle.

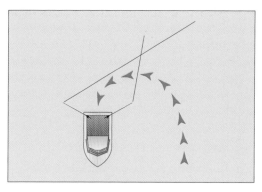

TURN TO PORT

_The Thirteenth Golden Rule of Fishing: "When trolling, unless your lines are tangle-proof, always turn to the side of your longest line."_

The shorter the line, the faster it swings back behind the boat. It will always swing to the outside of the turn. If it is the line on the outside of the turn, and the longer line is on the inside of the turn, then your lines should not cross.

If all of your turns are going to be in the same direction, say to the right, then you can keep your right line longest and your left line shortest. However, usually you will be turning in different directions. If necessary, you can adjust the lengths of your lines before each turn.

_A helpful, though bothersome, way to keep track of the length of line you have out is to mark it every 5 or 10 yards with a marking pen. To keep from having to measure again, remark before the originals fade completely. Don't make aggregate marks at say 50 or 100 yards. These will become meaningless as you strip away worn line._

## When the wind blows

The wind is no problem when you're heading into it, and little problem if it's coming from behind. The problems occur when it's blowing across your lines. The solution is easy – travel with the wind or against it. However, this isn't always possible. Even when it is, you'll still have to brave a crosswind on your turns. Very often, say to follow a shoreline or an underwater ledge, you'll want to set your trolling course at an angle to the wind. Still, the real test comes on the turns. You'll find that, by always turning into the wind, its force upon the lines will help you straighten them and keep them under control. When encountering a strong crosswind, it's always important not to make these turns too wide. Only experience will teach you how wide is too wide.

> **DEFINITION**
>
> The **leeward** side is the side farthest from the source of the wind. The windward side is the side closest to the wind.

Windy days can also make it difficult to troll lines of different tests and materials. Lines that are the most susceptible to getting blown across the spread should be moved to the _leeward_ side of that spread. Lines that are too susceptible should be replaced.

_Often you can remove much of the wind-caused bow in a line by attaching a lure with more drag._

# Trolling tricks

*IF YOU'RE NOT GETTING STRIKES, vary your speed to vary the depth and action of your baits. Vary the length of your lines to vary depth. Even try a zigzag pattern every once in a while. If none of these tricks work, change some of the baits, if not all of them.*

<u>The Fourteenth Golden Rule of Fishing:</u> "If the fish are not biting, whatever you do, do not not do anything."

A change in direction, if there is any wind or current, may change your lure action for the better. In fact, by turning, you change the speed and likely the depth of your baits. Notice in the illustration shown here that the bait on the outside of a turn covers a larger arc (more water) than the one on the inside. It does so in the same period of time, so the outside bait must be moving faster.

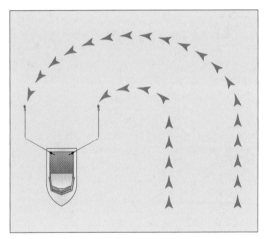

BAIT ACTION DURING TURNS

*If you are not confident about your trolling speed, make a few turns. If an outside bait gets a hit, then, when you straighten out, raise your trolling speed a notch. If an inside bait gets the hit, lower it a little.*

Warning: The reason you get a hit on a turn may not be because of the change in bait speed. The inside lure on a turn not only slows, it also likely drops. The vertical drop, or the subsequent rise, not the drop in speed, may have enticed the strike. In this case you can get your baits deeper not only by decreasing speed, but also by dropping them farther back, weighting them, or changing them. You can also keep everything the same, and just start making a lot of turns.

*Never cut your speed immediately upon a hookup. Give the other fish a chance, and you may be rewarded with a multiple hookup.*

When you get a strike, the first rod you grab is not necessarily the one with the fish on it. If another rod is in the way, get it out of the way. For example, in the picture on page 186, someone should be responsible for getting line 3 out of the way and out of the water as soon as there's a hookup on any other rod. Usually the baits that have to be retrieved, should be retrieved in order, closest first. The angler and the helmsman must work together. Keeping the boat moving forward until the other lines are brought in helps to keep them straight and untangled. It also keeps the baits moving to enable multiple hits. There is no more exciting sound than fish after fish stripping line from your reels.

*The Fifteenth Golden Rule of Fishing: "The best place to find fish is where you just found a fish." When you get a strike, keep going back to the same spot until you stop getting strikes.*

# Optional equipment

BEFORE I GET TO OPTIONAL EQUIPMENT, *let me remind you that swivels are rarely optional. When trolling, use good ones. If good ones don't prove good enough, use the best. Ball-bearing swivels are expensive, but money saved on swivels is often wasted on new line. Twisted line can cause more than tangles and lost fishing time. It can also cost you a trophy fish.*

## Rod holders

Unless you have enough hands with nothing better to do, you'll need some rod holders. If you stay away from saltwater and large fish, you can get away with the clamp-on type. If you have enough boat for them, quality chrome on brass flush-mount rod holders can handle any fish. In plastic, they won't last long unless you keep your fishing light. If you troll from a small boat, you can use PVC pipe and fittings to make your own serviceable rack of rod holders to slip onto the transom. The more makeshift your rod holders, the greater the need for a safety line on your rods.

## Outriggers

Outriggers allow you to troll more lines with fewer tangles. The drop-back they provide gives fish a chance to swallow your natural or live baits.

■ **When the action gets hot and heavy,** *you'll need rod holders and help, not fishermen standing around with rods in their hands.*

## Downriggers

Nothing gives you more control over the depth of trolled baits than downriggers. They're a phenomenal but awkward-to-use fishing tool. If you want to get even more complicated, you can troll more than one line from each downrigger by adding another release clip. Keep things simple until you get some experience.

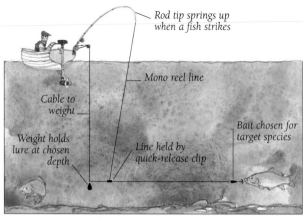

*Rod tip springs up when a fish strikes*

*Mono reel line*

*Cable to weight*

*Weight holds lure at chosen depth*

*Line held by quick-release clip*

*Bait chosen for target species*

■ **Although not easy to use,** *downriggers give you a huge amount of control over the depth of the baits you are trolling.*

## Teasers

Teasers are huge, hookless, saltwater lures. They create a commotion to attract fish to your spread and the hooked baits in it. I recommend them, in particular the bowling-pin type, for tuna and marlin, and the mirrored type for sailfish. You run them directly off the transom, or from the lower part of an outrigger. They should be positioned on the face of the first or second wave of your boat wake. Run one a few times and check it for teeth and bill marks. You'll be surprised, probably enough to run a lure or two just behind it.

## Birds

Birds, which are also hookless, get their name from their appearance. Their job, which they do quite well, is to create enough commotion to attract every fish within their area code. They put out more spray than a head-first water skier. I like to run one in the middle of my spread, my largest lure attached behind it. Perhaps this appears to fish as if the lure is chasing the bird, and that the smaller lures in front are trying to escape. Whatever the reason, fish are incited to hit all the lures in the spread, not just the one attached to the bird.

There's no doubt in my mind that birds are a big advantage when fishing for tuna, and a worthwhile one when you're after marlin. I do suspect, though, that they frighten off some fish – sometimes sailfish, for one. However, depending upon where and how you use a bird, you may conclude differently.

<u>The Sixteenth Golden Rule of Fishing</u>: *"The most important technique in trolling is to keep your lines in the water." When they aren't, all the other techniques are worthless.*

# A simple summary

✔ The Thirteenth Golden Rule of Fishing: "When trolling, unless your lines are tangle-proof, always turn to the side of your longest line."

✔ The Fourteenth Golden Rule of Fishing: "If the fish aren't biting, whatever you do, do not not do anything."

✔ The Fifteenth Golden Rule of Fishing: "The best place to find fish is where you just found a fish." When you get a strike, keep going back to the same spot until you stop getting strikes.

✔ The Sixteenth Golden Rule of Fishing: "The most important technique in trolling is to keep your lines in the water." When they aren't, all the other techniques are worthless.

✔ Learn the appropriate bend in your rods for different baits at different speeds. Too much bend may mean you've hooked some weeds. Too little can mean you no longer have any bait.

✔ The types of baits you troll pretty much determine your trolling speed, or vice versa.

✔ The ideal speeds for live and artificial baits don't overlap. Avoid trolling both in the same spread.

✔ Troll your lures as close to you and to the surface as possible.

✔ On those dead-calm, glass-surface days when the fish will not bite, put out your deepest running lures and get them as far back and as deep as they will go.

✔ The farther back you place a sinking bait, the deeper it will run – up to a point.

✔ When trolling in a crosswind, try to make your turns into the wind.

✔ If you're not confident about your trolling speed, make a few turns. If an outside bait gets a hit, then, when you straighten out, raise your trolling speed a notch. If an inside bait gets the hit, lower it a little.

# PART THREE

LINE UP ALL YOUR ESSENTIALS

# Chapter 15

# Line

WHEN DISCUSSING FISHING LINE, we must consider the following qualities: tensile strength, shock strength, durability, abrasion resistance, diameter, limpness, stretch, and visibility. Tensile strength is the amount of gradually increased force that a fishing line can withstand. It is also a line's test rating. Shock strength is the amount of sudden, abrupt force it can withstand. Tensile and shock strength, measured in kilos or pounds, can be markedly different values for the same line. Equally important, the tying of knots in a line can change one or both values to surprising degrees. Knot strength is the measure of a particular type of knot's effect upon line strength. If a knot halves the line's strength, that knot is said to have a knot strength of 50 percent.

## In this chapter...
- ✓ Monofilament
- ✓ Dacron
- ✓ Multifilament lines

# Monofilament

*MONOS IS GREEK FOR "ONE." Not coincidentally, monofilament is single-strand nylon line – often referred to as "mono." Monofilament, by a very large margin, outsells all other lines combined. More important, it is by far the line best suited for spinning tackle. There is no cogent reason for putting any other type of line on a spinning reel. For this reason, we shall devote most of this chapter to monofilament before looking briefly at Dacron and multifilament.*

## Stretch

One quality that distinguishes mono from other lines is more stretch – anywhere from 10 to 30 percent. Now, line stretch is quite a shock absorber, and it comes in very handy if your drag is set too tight, but it does have its disadvantages, too. If there is a dainty nibbler on the other end of your line, mono can absorb faint hits. A picky eater may just nibble your hook clean before you even suspect it is there. Also, even if you do feel a bite, the hook-setting force you apply dissipates as it travels down the mono.

■ **Monofilament's stretch** *dampens the indications of a bite. The best way to detect them is by keeping your finger on the line.*

*Keep in mind, the more line there is between you and your fish, the more stretch there will be. Therefore, you must apply more force to set the hook. Conversely, the closer you reel in that fish, the less shock absorption – and the less room for error – there is, and the more careful you must be.*

### Casting and retrieving

Stretch will not prove a problem when you're casting and retrieving. When trolling, the speed of the boat can help you set the hook. However, *deep jigging* or deep bottom fishing can prove difficult. Still, merely because such fishing can be done better with braided line on conventional reels, doesn't mean it can't be done well with mono on spinning tackle.

---

**DEFINITION**

**Deep jigging** *is working a lure with sharp jerks of the rod in deep water.*

---

Despite its appearance, monofilament does absorb some water. When wet, its stretch increases. Wet mono also has lower tensile, shock, and knot strength. In addition, wetness facilitates the loosening of knots. This is not a problem if your knots are tied tight enough in the first place. In any case, if there's a way to keep your line dry and still catch fish, I'm unaware of it.

## Contraction

There is one more disadvantage to stretch that should be mentioned. Let's say you're fighting a trophy fish and it's stretching your line to the limit. The line going on your spool is under far more tension than the line beneath it – an unnatural condition. Once on the spool, this line strives to contract. Slowly, it manages to do just that. Millimeter by millimeter, it relaxes and stretches the line beneath it, thus increasing line tension on and on down toward the spool.

Some day you may witness the result of the contraction of mono tighter and tighter around the spool. A fisherman will be fighting a prize fish, which in turn will be fighting for its freedom. Suddenly there will be a loud, god-awful CRACK, sometimes followed by an exploding sound, some ricochets, and a BOING or two. When you and everyone else get off the deck and out from behind the coolers, you will see the fisherman staring dumbfounded at what is left of his reel, usually a level-wind. The spool will be in at least two pieces, deformed and askew, the only thing holding it together being the line. If the mono was really feeling its oats, one side of the reel will be blown off to who knows where. If you're not the fisherman or owner of the reel, I guarantee, in your relief at still being alive, you will find this sight hilarious. However, if you are the now catatonic fisherman, you will be more than ready for at least a month at Shady Rest Convalescent Home.

Exploding spools are not something the owner of a quality spinning reel has to worry about. However, when mono first came into wide use, it was something for everyone to worry about. Many old spools, particularly on level-wind reels, weren't strong enough. Even today, spools made of inferior metals or plastics are no match for the pressure that mono can put on them.

■ **Today's quality spools** *are more than a match for all the contraction pressure mono can apply to them.*

## Color

Now I'll get to the topic that you might have assumed was the subject of this section of choosing the right mono – color. I have my preferred colors, even my favorite color. What I don't have is any real proof that they are better than any other colors. Stretch and limpness are far more important qualities. So I will leave color up to you.

*If you have more than one preferred color, it's helpful to buy different line tests in different colors. You will then be able to distinguish your line tests at a glance.*

■ **Using color** *to identify lines of various test ratings can be a time-saver.*

## Protecting your line

Monofilament is very durable and doesn't rot like linen and the other natural fibers that preceded it. However, it does eventually deteriorate with time and exposure to the elements. Do not leave it in the sun unnecessarily. You can store it wet, but try to rinse off as much saltwater as possible.

■ **Always wash** *your line roller after use. After use in saltwater, apply a rust inhibitor to its hidden surfaces.*

Abrasion resistance is a strong point of mono. Still, you need to exercise proper care. Rinse your line guides, bail, and the bail's line roller thoroughly after each use. If that use was in saltwater, do more. Apply a rust inhibitor, getting as little as possible on the line. Make sure your line roller is not frozen. If it wasn't supposed to roll, it wouldn't be called a roller. Check all parts that come in contact with the line for corrosion, scratches, or chips that can damage it and cost you fish.

Before every day's fishing, cut off any cloudy mono at the end of your line. Then examine, by eye and by running it between two fingers, the first 30 or so feet of what remains. Chances are you will find more nicks with your fingers than with your eyes.

*Do not discard even small lengths of old monofilament into the water where it can entrap and kill birds, fish, and other animals.*

# Dacron

**DACRON, LIKE MONOFILAMENT,** *is a synthetic line. Like mono, it is resistant to sunlight and saltwater – in fact, slightly more so. Unlike mono, it is a braid of tiny fibers instead of one single strand. This means much less stretch than mono, say, less than 5 percent versus more than 20 percent. Less stretch makes it easier to set a hook, and also gives Dacron extra sensitivity to better alert you when to set a hook. Dacron line also has practically no memory. This, combined with its extreme limpness, means fewer backlash problems than with monofilament when used on conventional (level-wind) reels.*

Dacron is not what you want on your spinning reel. It is too limp and, when casting, does not spring off the spool like mono. Once off the spool, its braided surface creates more friction when moving through the line guides. This same surface chafes more easily than mono. Of greater import, Dacron is more visible to fish than monofilament.

*You can get the added sensitivity and hook-setting force of Dacron, and also the lower visibility of mono, merely by adding a monofilament leader to a Dacron running line.*

# Multifilament lines

**MULTIFILAMENT LINES DIFFER** *among themselves more than monofilament lines do. Still, we can make some generalizations, the first being that there is no cogent reason for putting multifilament on a spinning reel. Stick to mono.*

*Multifilaments are gel-spun polyethylene or Kevlar fishing lines. Polyethylene is used to make cheap ski rope. Kevlar is used to make bulletproof vests. Gel-spinning does not sound like anything the home handyman should attempt on his living-room rug.*

Multifilaments are braided lines exhibiting extra limpness and practically no memory or stretch. This last quality makes them as sensitive as Dacron. Their abrasion resistance is far superior to Dacron.

# TYING MULTIFILAMENTS

Multifilament lines are much stronger than monofilament lines of matching diameters. Still, be suspicious of their pound-test ratings. A 30-pound test line the same diameter as 6-pound mono sounds great, but multifilaments' weak knot strength may cut this figure in half. Stick to double-line knots such as the Palomar to attach a hook or swivel and the spider hitch to double the end of your line.

## Palomar knot

1. Double up 4 inches of line and pass it through the hook eye.

2. Tie an overhand knot in the loop.

3. Pass the whole hook through the loop while pulling the line taut.

4. Pull the tag end until the knot is snug, and then trim it.

## Spider hitch

1. Double up your line and make a small loop in it.

2. Take five turns around your thumb (and small loop), then pass the long loop through the small one.

3. Pull steadily on the long loop so the wraps leave the thumb one at a time, in order.

4. Pull the tag end to snug down the knot. Trim the tag end.

## Knot minuses

Although the spider hitch (*see box, left*) performs well under steady pressure, under sudden pressure it is much inferior to the harder-to-tie Bimini twist. Also, don't attempt to tie the spider hitch in lines over 30-pound test. You will find all knots harder to cinch tight with multifilaments as compared with mono. Multifilaments just don't slide as easily when tying, and they slip more easily once tied. Another drawback is price – around three times that of mono. Not only that – since its diameter is thinner, you will need more of it to fill your spool.

*Save money on multifilaments by buying just the length you need, then tie it to enough backing line of Dacron or mono to fill the spool.*

## Multifilament pluses

Still, these thin lines do have some real advantages. You can load more yards of the same-test line onto your reel. You can also load the same amount or more yards of a higher test. In this case, make sure your rod and reel are rated strong enough. If not, you can break the rod or overwhelm the drag. You also have to set that drag much lighter than for equivalent-test mono. No stretch means no shock absorption, and therefore no safety factor.

**INTERNET**

**www.maxima-lines.com**

*This line manufacturer's web site contains helpful instructions for tying a number of knots, including the Bimini twist.*

# A simple summary

✔ There is no cogent reason to put any line other than monofilament on your spinning reel.

✔ The stretch in mono line is proportional to the distance between you and the fish.

✔ When you have a lot of line out, mono acts as a shock absorber.

This makes it harder to set the hook, but also harder for the fish to break your line.

✔ When the fish is close and line stretch reduced, a mistake by you is more likely to cause a break in your line.

# Chapter 16

# *Hooks*

THE FIRST FISH HOOKS were invented 20,000 years ago, give or take a year or two. They were made out of wood and bone and weren't much to brag about. Despite this, from what I've heard, the fishing back in those days was unbelievable. Since then, the development of the fish hook is the perfect example of a brilliantly simple idea that has gotten way out of hand. These days, there is a huge number of hook sizes and point, eye, and shank shapes available.

*In this chapter...*
- ✓ *Hook sizes*
- ✓ *Hook shanks*
- ✓ *Hook eyes*
- ✓ *Hook points*
- ✓ *Double and treble hooks*
- ✓ *Weedless hooks*

THIS SAILFISH IS HOOKED IN THE PERFECT PLACE FOR A QUICK, SAFE RELEASE

# Hook sizes

**TAKE A LOOK AT THE CHART BELOW** *for an idea of the various sizes that hooks can come in. Though the chart illustrates only hook sizes 20 to 5/0, hooks can range in size from at least 28 to 20/0. Twenty-eight is the smallest. The next largest size should be 26 because there are supposedly no odd whole-number sizes. Evidently, a few manufacturers never got the word or chose to ignore it. As the size numbers get smaller, the hooks get larger, until you reach the number 1. The next number is 1/0, pronounced "one-ought" by the purist, and "one-oh" by down-in-the-dirt fishermen such as you and me. The next size is 2/0, and so on (including odd numbers) as hook size increases.*

*Eye*

*Shaft*

*Gap*

*Point*

*Barb*

*Throat*

**PARTS OF A HOOK**

*Bend*

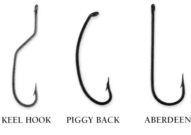

KEEL HOOK   PIGGY BACK   ABERDEEN   SPROAT

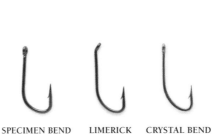

SPECIMEN BEND   LIMERICK   CRYSTAL BEND

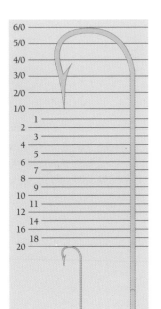

6/0
5/0
4/0
3/0
2/0
1/0
1
2
3
4
5
6
7
8
9
10
11
12
14
16
18
20

■ **Always use** *the smallest appropriate hook, regardless of style.*

**INTERNET**

**www.mustad.no**

*This hook manufacturer's web site has an interesting article on the history of the fish hook. The fact that it's one history lesson you will never be tested on makes it even more interesting. The site also contains some fish-hook illustrations suitable for framing.*

Don't waste your time looking for any logic behind this system. While its inventors may not have been complete idiots, they certainly had no talent for organization and were absolute disasters when it came to planning ahead. I would not take these size classifications too seriously either. Hook manufacturers don't. One's 3/0 hook in a particular style is not necessarily the exact same size as another's.

## Which hook to use?

Appropriate hook size depends upon the fish you're targeting and the bait you're using. Generally, in accordance with our First Golden Rule of Fishing, the right hook is the smallest one strong enough to get the job done. The smaller and lighter the hook, the less visible to the fish and the less likely to affect the appearance or action of your bait. The smaller the wire (shaft) diameter, the easier the barb will penetrate.

Sometimes you have to compromise on hook size because you want to use a specific size bait. Sometimes you have to compromise on choice of bait or its size, because you want to use a particular hook size. Sometimes you have to compromise on both. When the novice errs, it is usually the choice of too large a hook, too large a bait, or both.

## USING HOOKS TO SAVE FACE

If you ever do something particularly stupid in front of another fisherman, try working the following nonessential facts into your conversation as soon as possible. The less intelligent he or she is, the more knowledgeable you will appear.

1. A hook classified 3X Long has a shank as long as a hook three sizes larger

2. A hook classified 3X Short has a shank as short as a hook three sizes smaller

3. A hook classified 3X Stout has the diameter of a hook three sizes larger

4. A hook classified 3X Fine has the diameter of a hook three sizes smaller

5. A hook classified SS is "super strong" compared to a regular hook of that size

# Hook shanks

*THE SHANK OF A HOOK can tell you much about the supposed purpose of that hook. The shape of the shank and its length are obvious indications.*

## Shank and strength

The regular hook, in cross section (*right*), has a round shaft diameter, as if it were merely a wire bent into the shape of a hook, which in fact it is. The forged hook has a flattened shaft. This shape alone increases hook strength. It also usually indicates that the hook has undergone a more complex manufacturing process to strengthen the metal itself.

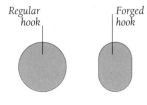

Regular hook     Forged hook

**HOOK CROSS SECTIONS**

## Shank length

Part of choosing the right hook is choosing the right shank length. Again, less is better, and the shank should be only as long as you need it. The short-shank live-bait hook is less visible to your target fish than a long-shank variety, yet the main reason it is the hook of choice is its lighter weight and the increased freedom it allows a live bait. When rigging a plastic worm or a ballyhoo (proper name balao), the shorter the hook, the better the bait's action. However, other factors come into play. You want your hook point where the fish is more likely to hit it, farther back in the bait. Additionally, in these two cases, the hook shaft is completely hidden by the bait anyway. If you are targeting a leader-shy, razor-toothed variety, a longer shank may be just enough to keep those teeth away from a preferably less visible monofilament leader. A longer-shanked hook is also easier to grab, and gives you more leverage when removing it.

**LONG SHANK**

**MEDIUM SHANK**

**SHORT SHANK**

### Rigging the bait

The complications that can arise when matching hook shank and bait can be illustrated with the strip and tail, explained in Chapter 21. The most natural way to rig this bait, the way to give it the most enticing action, is

## Trivia...

*I doubt the fact that hooks made with high-carbon steel are stronger than their cheaper counterparts would surprise you. However, the fact that they weigh less might.*

with a short-shank hook attached to a monofilament leader. This will work fine if your target fish has dull teeth and usually swallows the whole bait. If your target fish has teeth sharp enough to slice the monofilament, you'd better sacrifice some action and switch to a long-shank hook, or else to a wire leader. If your target fish is known to cut off baits behind the hook, then you should again go to a longer shank.

## Circle hooks

The circle hook has been around a long time. Yet its rapidly increasing popularity has made it something of a phenomenon. Perhaps I lack imagination, but to me this hook appears almost safe enough to use as a diaper pin. I would think that even the most suicidal fish would need a lot of determination to hang itself on this baby.

**CIRCLE HOOK**

**DEFINITION**

*Longliners are commercial fishermen who set out lines – often miles long – with thousands of hooks dangling from them. By the time they retrieve their lines, the fish they have no use for or are forbidden to harvest such as marlin, are already dead. Longliners are no friends to sport fish or sportfishermen.*

Obviously, I think wrong. Many *longliners* prefer circle hooks. Fish seem to have little trouble getting hooked on them, and a lot of trouble getting unhooked. Circle hooks are especially popular with catch-and-release fishermen. These hooks not only have an excellent hookup ratio, they usually lodge harmlessly in the corner of a fish's mouth. This is a great place to hook species such as tarpon and sailfish for a quick, safe release.

*Never try to set a circle hook. You'll only manage to yank it out of the fish's mouth. Circle hooks work best when the fish hooks itself by turning to run with the bait.*

## Sliced shanks

The hook to the right has slices in its shaft. These slices resemble barbs, which in fact they are. Their purpose is to keep your bait on your hook. They allow you to put more muscle into your casts without fear of your bait outdistancing your hook. They also make it more likely that if a fish takes your bait, it takes your hook along with it. These hooks are most often used with plastic worms. They can also help keep you from losing natural and live bait, if that bait is threaded far enough up the shaft to reach the slices.

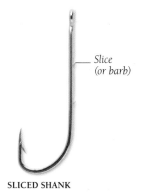

*Slice (or barb)*

**SLICED SHANK**

213

# Hook eyes

THE FIRST THING *I'll tell you about hook eyes is that there are more types of hook eyes than we have either the time or the patience to cover.*

## Flattened shanks

Our first hook eye is no eye at all – blind as a bat. It's a flatted (or flattened) shank, and it works fine. The knots used to attach them, all similar to a *snell*, are no more difficult to tie than the knots we've covered. Still, if there is an advantage to flatted shanks, I don't know it. Nor do I know of any reason to use them. You sure don't want to try attaching a snap swivel to one. This could take years.

**FLATTENED SHANK**

> **DEFINITION**
>
> A **snell** *is a barrel-wrap-type knot used to attach line to the top of a hook's shaft instead of to its eye. The line runs through the hook eye if this eye is turned up or down. This enables a straighter pull, which, as a matter of interest, defeats the supposed advantage of a turned-down eye – a superior penetration angle for setting the hook.*

## THE BALL EYE AND TANDEM HOOKS

The ball eye is your most common hook eye, and for a good reason. In the large majority of circumstances, it gets the job done. Before buying them, make sure the eye is completely closed or very close to it. If necessary, you may be able to finish the job with a pliers. These eyes enable you to open them slightly so as to rig hooks in tandem (*below*). This process will fatigue the metal enough to weaken it, but hopefully not enough to lose you a fish. Every once in a while, opening the eye will snap off the end. That's the price you pay.

**BALL EYE**

**BALL EYE OPENED**

**THREADING THE
SECOND HOOK**

**FINAL HOOK
ARRANGEMENT**

## The welded eye

The welded eye is merely a ball eye welded shut. This substantially strengthens the eye, but in a place where added strength is rarely necessary. It also protects monofilament in a place mono very rarely reaches. The welded eye is most advantageous when you are using wire, especially single-strand thin enough to work its way into the crack between the end of the eye and the hook shaft.

## The angled eye

The turned-down eye is intended to give the hook point a superior penetration angle. I'm sure it does, but I'm not sure the difference is significant. Many people *are* sure, including some very good fishermen. The supposed drawback is that it makes it harder for the fish to get at the barb. I also doubt the significance of this, on all but perhaps the smallest gaped, shortest shanked hooks. The turned-up eye leaves extra clearance for the fish to get at the barb. However, I am just as skeptical of the significance of this. Furthermore, if you believe a turned-down eye gives you better penetration than a standard in-line eye, then you have to believe that a turned-up eye gives you worse.

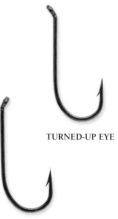

TURNED-UP EYE

TURNED-DOWN EYE

Another way of making tandem hooks is by using a pliers to flatten the barb of one hook so it will pass through the eye of the other. You then pry the barb open again with an old knife (not your precious fillet knife). Be very careful. The knife will sometimes slip. Both the barb and eye methods weaken hooks at the points where you bend them. If the barb fails, you can still bring in the fish if you keep your line tight. If the eye of the hook fails, the fish is lost. Still, it's difficult to get a bent barb back exactly the way you want it.

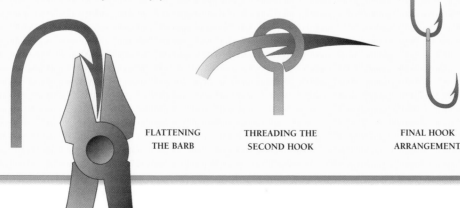

FLATTENING
THE BARB

THREADING THE
SECOND HOOK

FINAL HOOK
ARRANGEMENT

# Hook points

THERE ARE SO MANY *different types of hook points that even I wouldn't pretend to know the supposed purposes of a fraction of them. This page shows merely a few. I have a feeling that most of them were "perfected" in the harsher climates by fishermen trapped indoors. No doubt some of these points are better for certain types of fishing than the most popular styles. However, I refuse to believe that they are anywhere near significantly better. Thus, one of the few areas where I have successfully simplified my life is that of hook points. The hollow-point hook and its close relatives – the conical, the curved, and the knife-edged points – satisfy almost all my needs.*

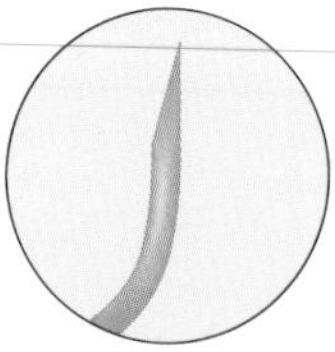

BARBLESS

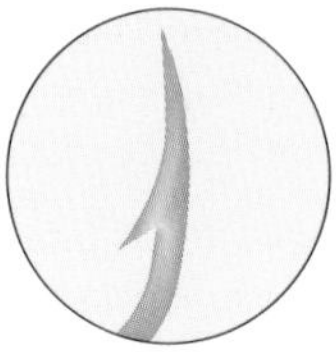

BEAKED

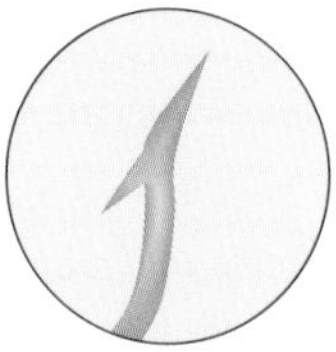

DUBLIN

FALKUS OUTBARB

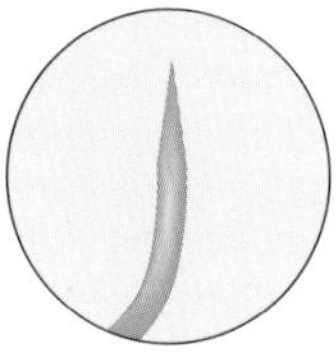

CONICAL

## Be sharp

If this book had been written in the 1970s, it would have contained the warning: "Sharpen all hooks before you use them." Today, you can not only buy hooks that don't need sharpening, you'll ruin some of these hooks if you try to sharpen them. There is a misconception that both of these facts are true because these hooks have been *chemically sharpened*. Actually, the sharpness results more from the cutting and honing process, and also the use of higher quality steel.

**DEFINITION**

A **chemically sharpened** *hook has been dipped in acid to remove metal burrs that hinder penetration.*

Still, the large majority of hooks on the market today needs to be sharpened before being used. Every accomplished fisherman must know when this has to be done and how to do it. Generally, the larger the hook, the more likely the need for sharpening. Cut points, as opposed to needle or conical points, are also more likely to need some work. However, don't ever rely upon generalities.

_The Seventeenth Golden Rule of Fishing:_ "_If you don't take time to check the sharpness of every hook you use, you're wasting fishing time._"

### A fish's best friend – dull hooks

If you think hooks out of the box are sharp enough, you're either a very inexperienced or a very lucky fisherman. The only explanation for such a misconception is that you've yet to lose a trophy fish on a hit or hook-set that should have been strong enough to bury the barb. Perhaps you convinced yourself that your talented fish "spit the hook." If you ever catch yourself using this phrase, a blindingly bright warning light should go off in your head. Fish are overrated spitters, and hooks are not easy to spit. They have a way of getting caught on the way out.

Most fish are hooked in the mouth, and large areas of their mouths are very, very hard. In some species they qualify as armor-plated. It takes a sharp point to penetrate this armor. Also, the tighter your drag during the strike or hook set, the greater the danger of your line breaking. The duller your hook, the tighter you must set your drag.

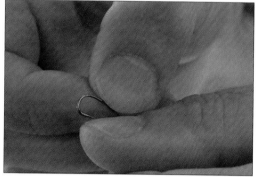

■ **Test the sharpness** _of a hook by resting the point on your thumbnail at about a 45-degree angle. Applying just enough pressure to keep the point in contact with the nail, slide the point forward. If it does not catch and stick in your nail, it's not sharp enough._

## Sharpening a hook

You can sharpen your hooks with a sharpening stone, a file, or both. The smaller the hook, the more likely a stone will do. Large hooks require a file. Files will rust unless you keep them covered with a rust inhibitor/fish repellent. Don't, unless keeping your files rust-free is more important to you than catching fish. Just make up your mind that files will not last, and try to do all your file work at home so at the fishing hole you can get away with stone touch-ups.

There is a lot a disagreement on the right way to sharpen a hook. Different point styles go in and out of fashion. Some supposedly don't penetrate well enough; others rip such large holes that the hooks work loose. Very small hooks often need no more than a few stone strokes to whet the very point. Large hooks may need to be transformed from point to barb.

### The diamond point

On the right, you can see a variation of the diamond-style point. Notice the concave inside edge that results. This gives the hook a "hollow point." I seem to like my points a little more hollow than most fishermen. The easiest way to get them that way is with a round file or the round side of a file that is flat on the opposite side. It's important that the file size matches the hook size. If you prefer a straight inside edge (a knife point), then you want to stick with a flat file.

DIAMOND POINT

*The length and width of the hook between point and barb is a trade-off. The shorter and narrower, the easier it will penetrate. The longer and wider, the better it will hold.*

## The offset hook point

Some long-forgotten fisherman came up with something else to do with a hook point aside from sharpening it. I would like to think this innovation was pure genius, but it might have resulted from an accident followed by observation. Still, our clever forgotten fisherman was sharp enough to notice that an **offset hook point** increases the chances of a hookup.

If you doubt the advantages of an offset point, try this experiment. Take a hook with an in-line point and lay it flat on a board. Cover it with the palm of your hand. Slowly, gently, using the slight pressure of your open palm, slide the hook back and forth around the board. The hook point will not imbed into the board. Unless you are extremely clumsy or unlucky, neither will it imbed into your palm. Now try this trick with an offset hook, *making sure that the point is pointing down toward the board.* It will not be more than a few seconds before the offset point sticks into the board. If the point instead imbeds into your palm, reread the point made in italics two sentences back.

> **DEFINITION**
>
> *An **offset hook point** is bent out of line with the hook's shaft. If a hook's point is offset, it won't lie flat on a flat surface.*

OFFSET LEFT
(KIRBED)

OFFSET RIGHT
(REVERSED)

The advantage of offset points is most evident when they're used with natural baits. They're more likely to catch and dig into a fish's mouth whether you set the hook or the fish sets it. This advantage is much slighter when trolling for species that jump on a bait and devour it. Also, when trolling or retrieving, you want an in-line point because they track truer, giving a lure or bait less reason to spin or take on an unnatural action.

## Barbless hooks

Some hooks can be bought barbless, but there is no point in looking for them when you can take any hook you want and file off the barb, or easier yet, just press it down with a pliers. Barbless hooks enable you to release a fish with the least possible damage. Almost as important is the ease with which you can do so, and the enjoyment this adds to your fishing. Another bonus is that the time saved unhooking fish can be devoted to catching more fish.

Fishing with barbless hooks will take more skill and cost you some fish. Yet it will cost far less than you think. All you have to do is remember the Third Golden Rule of Fishing: "Keep your line tight." Try it. You'll like it. So will the fish, at least more than the other kind of fishing. One person sure to be pleased is the next person to catch that fish. Let's hope he or she also does so with a barbless hook.

# Double and treble hooks

THE TREBLE HOOK *results from an attempt to build a better mouse trap, or more correctly, fish trap. It has its place, an important one, but a smaller place than most novice fishermen tend to think. I know of no case where a three-pointed hook is three times more effective than a single-pointed hook. In many instances, it's less effective. Wary nibblers are likelier to drop a natural bait if it is on a treble. For some baffling reason, this hook gives the fish a better chance for throwing it. Perhaps the treble's shape provides improved leverage, or keeps the barb from penetrating as deeply as a standard hook. The treble also seems more likely to* **foul hook** *a fish. Do not misunderstand me, in many situations the treble is the hook of choice. If this were not true, then the next few paragraphs would be unnecessary.*

## The stinger rig

The stinger in a stinger rig is usually a treble hook. There is a reason for this – superior results. This rig is a defense against kingfish and their like that specialize in cutting off your natural baits just behind the hook. If you're like me and just about every other fisherman, you'll at first assume this is just a matter of bad luck. It will take a few more cutoffs right behind the hook before you start moving the hook back in the bait.

> **DEFINITION**
>
> *To* **foul hook** *a fish means to hook it anywhere outside of its mouth. This may not bother you, but it bothers the IGFA. A foul-hooked fish cannot be submitted for a record. Ironically, foul hooking usually enables a fish to put up a better fight, especially if that hook is embedded near its tail.*

The kingfish's bite will usually move back with it, until your hook is as far back as you can get it or else you're pulling your bait through the water sideways. If by then the kingfish are not yet stuffed to the gills with the back ends of your baits, it's time for the stinger rig.

The stinger hook is usually attached with single-strand wire. Cable can also be used. The bait fish in the illustration are a ballyhoo and a small tuna. You can also use mackerel or numerous other fish. If your bait fish is slim like ballyhoo, you can let the trailing hook swing free. Keep in mind that if you troll too slowly, the stinger hook may hang down uselessly, away from the tail.

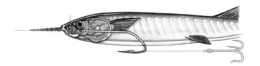

**BALLYHOO STINGER RIG**

If you're using tuna, its belly will keep the hook too far from the tail to do any good. Burying the stinger in your bait's tail will noticeably hinder its action. This will also be true, to a lesser degree, if it's attached with a rubber band. You can minimize this hindrance with a strategically placed swivel, as illustrated.

*Rubber band*

*Swivel*

**TUNA STINGER RIG**

*Never use a stinger rig, even with a regular hook, when trying to set an IGFA record. It and a few other rigs in this book, though commonly used, are against IGFA rules.*

## The snag hook

Another way to use and refer to the treble is as a *snag hook*. I was using a snag hook for years before I ever heard the word "treble." Sometimes we needed bait, and the bait fish just weren't biting. Sometimes the bait fish were so thick, it was foolish catching them any other way.

The novice typically jerks the rod back before reeling in all slack. Most of the force generated by the rod is then dissipated gathering slack line. Also, the commotion caused by slack line can spook the fish. To make sure there is a minimum of slack in the first place, feather your line at the end of the cast (see Chapter 8). And make sure that the cast is far enough away from the fish so as not to spook them.

> **DEFINITION**
>
> A **snag hook** is a treble hook, sometimes weighted, used to snag (impale) fish. You cast it over a school of fish (usually bait fish), then violently jerk back your fishing rod in an attempt to snag (hook) one.

*Never snag by jerking your rod back vertically unless your hook is down and deep.*

Jerking your rod back horizontally applies more hook-setting force and keeps the snag hook in the water where the fish are. If you jerk your rod back vertically, you are likely to jerk the hook out of the water. The closer the treble, the more likely. This can be very dangerous to you or anyone near you.

My favorite use for the treble hook is a method of fishing, not just catching bait. I recommend you try it once or twice even when your real target is bait. Snag a fish, but let it remain with the school. If there is a predator stalking that school, your injured bait is sure to stand out. This method works even if the injury or the treble hook drags your bait to the bottom. Still, I usually prefer to keep it in the school. This means using the smallest size treble hook that will both snag the bait and stand up to the predator.

## The double hook

The most popular use for treble hooks is on lures. However, over the last few years, double hooks have made some headway against them. Double hooks are much easier and, more important, safer to remove. I have a hunch they give the lure a cleaner action, but the difference has to be slight. For all I know, game fish may find a dirtier action more enticing. In any case, the larger the lure, the more I like to see a double hook on it.

# Weedless hooks

*A WEEDLESS HOOK is designed so that weeds do not get caught on it, but its shape and feel may sometimes cost you a fish. Still, if there had been a plastic bag or a hunk of seaweed on your regular hook, that fish wouldn't have hit your bait in the first place. Use weedless hooks when needed.*

Weedless hooks come in a variety of styles and sizes, but only a very small fraction of even the most popular hook styles can be bought weedless. No matter. You can make just about any hook weedless. The lazy way is with a rubber band.

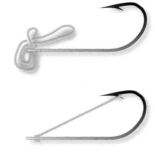

■ **The rubber-band weedless:**
*Thread a rubber band through the eye and back through itself. Pull tight and hang it onto the hook's barb.*

# MAKING A SINGLE-STRAND WEEDLESS

As good as the rubber-band weedless is, fashioning a guard out of single-strand wire is much more effective. Follow this step-by-step to make your own. Note: The thicker the wire, the more likely the fish will feel it. Use the thinnest wire that will get the job done.

1. Cut a length of single-strand wire, double it up, and hang it on the hook shaft.

2. Thread both wire ends up through the hook eye.

3. Using pliers, pull the wire taut.

4. In opposite directions, wrap each wire end around the hook shaft a few times.

5. Wind both wire ends into a haywire twist.

6. Bend the wire toward the hook point, and snip off any excess.

Never buy Brand X hooks by the box. To remind myself of this, I keep a 20-year-old box of treble hooks with my fishing gear. If nitroglycerine was not a part of their smelting process, something just as powerful was. These hooks are guaranteed to explode into at least two pieces if dropped on anything harder than a deep-pile carpet. They sure do have a beautiful shine, though.

# A simple summary

✔ The Seventeenth Golden Rule of Fishing: "If you don't take time to check the sharpness of every hook you use, you're wasting fishing time."

✔ The appropriate hook size depends upon the bait you are using and the fish you're targeting.

✔ The smaller the hook, the less visible it will be to fish and the less likely to affect the appearance or action of your bait.

✔ The smaller the shaft diameter, the easier the hook point will penetrate.

✔ Forged hooks with flattened shafts are the stronger.

✔ The length and width of the hook between point and barb is a trade-off. The shorter and narrower, the easier it will penetrate. The longer and wider, the better it will hold.

✔ When a hook with an offset point can be used, it should be used.

✔ Circle hooks have an excellent hookup ratio and facilitate a quick, safe release.

✔ Barbless hooks make fishing more enjoyable and will cost you fewer fish than you think.

✔ Treble hooks can be an advantage or a liability, depending upon the circumstances.

# Chapter 17

# Sinkers

AS THEIR NAME WOULD INDICATE, sinkers are used to get your bait down in the water column. This does not necessarily mean getting it all the way down to the bottom. There aren't as many different types of sinkers as there are species of fish, but the numbers are closer than you think. Each type has its supposed specific purpose. Fortunately, we can ignore most of these sinkers because no one remembers or can figure out exactly what those purposes were. Unfortunately, that still leaves us with way more types than we need. To keep it simple, we'll limit our discussion to those sinkers you can probably find at your local tackle store.

## In this chapter...
✓ Choosing a sinker
✓ Types of sinkers
✓ Weighty thoughts

SINKERS ADD DISTANCE TO YOUR CASTS AND GET YOUR BAITS DEEPER FASTER

# Choosing a sinker

WHEN CHOOSING A SINKER, *you must consider bottom composition, depth, current, surface conditions, line strength, whether or how far you need to cast, and, of course, target fish. Don't panic. Your average fisherman can usually make this seemingly impossible choice in about 2 seconds flat. To help you learn to do the same, I will temporarily limit your choices to the sinkers illustrated on this page. Many reputable fishermen have survived on less.*

*Never use a heavier sinker than necessary.*

Again, we need to apply the First Golden Rule of Fishing: "Less is better, if it can get the job done." Too much weight can hinder the action of your bait, especially live bait. Some fish don't snap up baits. In an instant, and from inches away, they suck them in, as if their mouths were vacuum cleaners. Your sinker may be too heavy for their vacuum cleaners. If not, its fishy weight can still dissuade a fish from carrying it off. Too large a sinker can even distract a fish from your bait. It can also spook a fish when it moves. During the fight, when a fish is swinging your weight here and there, this may supply the fish enough leverage to throw your hook. On the other hand, it can wear down the fish and prevent it from putting up a sporting fight.

*Your sinker weight is not limited by the manufacturer-recommended lure-weight range printed on your rod.*

SURF WEIGHT

SPLIT SHOT

DIPSEY

EGG

BANK

PYRAMID

# Types of sinkers

THERE ARE MANY TYPES OF SINKERS, *but don't try to memorize what we cover in this chapter. Say you're out in your boat, fishing over a rocky bottom using a pyramid sinker. There's a very good chance that before you lose even half the line on your reel and no more than a dozen pyramid sinkers, it will occur to you that switching to bank sinkers might be worth a try. Even if this does not occur to you, you eventually run out of pyramid sinkers, and probably every other kind you have, until you're forced to switch to bank sinkers by elimination.*

Remember one thing, though: Before you choose your weight, figure out where you want to put your bait and what you want it to do when there. Then, if the weight you choose does not do the trick, figure out which weight will, or figure out something else to do with your bait.

## Split-shot sinkers

Since smaller is better, we'll start out small by first discussing split-shot sinkers. The bait fish attached to one in the illustration is swimming around fine. Though kept near the bottom, it can even drag the weight around. Not on long trips, of course. When your target fish shows up to take this little fellow to dinner, it will not even notice the extra weight added by your split-shot sinker.

You squeeze these tiny weights closed around your fishing line. They come in a number of sizes and are perfect for fine-tuning your rig. To avoid damaging your line, do not close your split shot any tighter than necessary to keep them from sliding along it. Some split shot have protrusions, often referred to as ears, opposite the slit. By squeezing these, you can reopen the weights and remove them. The safest way to open or close split shot is between two fingers, preferably someone else's. If you find using your fingers (or someone else's) too difficult, use pliers, not your teeth. Even if lead were something you should put into your mouth, you still wouldn't want to act like everyone else, would you?

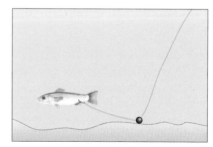

■ **A split-shot sinker** *may be just heavy enough to keep your live bait swimming near the bottom.*

## Egg sinkers

The egg sinker is the most common weight of all. Its smooth, rounded shape helps keep it from getting snagged on a rocky bottom. On a sand bottom in a strong current, it will roll around quite a bit. This seems to bother fishermen a lot more than it should. I don't care how fast the current, any fish worth catching will be able to keep pace with a rolling egg sinker. Unless you've placed your bait exactly where you wanted it, the extra territory covered may expose it to more, larger, hungrier, and stupider fish.

An egg sinker is almost always threaded directly onto the fishing line, just above the swivel. It can be kept in place by adding a split shot directly above it, inserting a toothpick or wooden matchstick into its top hole, or, less desirably, running the fishing line through it twice.

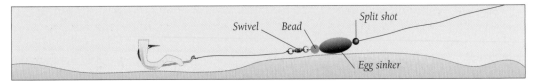

*Swivel*    *Bead*       *Split shot*     *Egg sinker*

USUAL POSITIONING OF AN EGG SINKER

# THE FISH-FINDER RIG

A bead is even more important if you let the line run free within an egg sinker, as in a fish-finder rig. Many fish will not swallow a bait immediately. Instead they will first dash away from other fish or take it back to their "hole." The fish-finder rig allows such a fish to do so without feeling any resistance that might cause it to drop your bait.

"Fish-finder rig" is really a misnomer. Your bait can, but rarely does, move away from your sinker on its own. Even when it does, it does not "find" fish any more than it "searches" for them. A much better name would be "slip-sinker rig" or "free-bait rig." In any case, let's save this weighty problem for those quiet moments when the fish are not biting.

Using the fish-finder method, you should remove all slack from your line. Wait with your bail open and your finger on the line ready to detect any line movement. A steady pull may be no more than the current, while a series of sharp jerks is almost certainly a fish. You cannot be sure if you do not hook up, but an examination of your bait may provide some clues.

The split shot or toothpick should be placed so as to hold the egg sinker snug against the knot. This keeps the sinker from banging on the knot, especially during the cast. A worthwhile option would be a soft bead between swivel knot and sinker.

*When you get a hit without a hookup, never rush to retrieve your line to see if you still have your bait. Be patient. Give that fish a second chance. You may never get your bait back to the right place again.*

## Bank and pyramid sinkers

You can also use bank and pyramid sinkers in place of egg sinkers on the fish-finder rig. However, the bank and pyramid sinkers have other, more important uses. With the three-way swivel rig (*below*), you can use either sinker. The bank sinker is your best choice if you want to avoid getting snagged on a rocky bottom, but it will not hold its ground on a sandy bottom in a strong current. The pyramid sinker is your best choice for these latter conditions, but it is almost a sure snag on a rocky bottom. This three-way swivel rig is most effective when your line is taut enough to keep the bait just off the bottom. It makes sense to have a second three-way swivel a foot or more above the first. It makes even more sense, at least until you catch your first fish, to use two different baits.

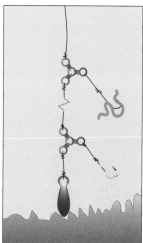

THREE-WAY SWIVEL RIG

*Sacrifice your weight to protect your line. Tie on your weights with line substantially weaker than your main line. In fact, if you're wasting a lot of time fighting hook snags, consider saving this time by sacrificing a few hooks (and fish) instead. Use a leader weaker than your main line.*

## Clinch-on and rubber-core sinkers

Clinch-on and rubber-core sinkers are perfect weights to use with spinning tackle. Their streamlined shapes make for longer casts and less commotion in the water. You should have no trouble finding them in sizes from ⅛ of an ounce to 1 ounce.

These sinkers make adjusting your weights easy because you can put them on and take them off without cutting and retying your line. With the clinch-on, you merely place your line in the groove, then seal the groove by bending down both ears. With the rubber core, you place your line in the groove, then twist the rubber ears a turn in opposite directions.

RUBBER CORE

The advantages to the clinch-on are price and its ability to either slide freely, as in the fish-finder rig, or lock in place. You choose by either pinning or not pinning the line down with one of the sinker ears. The advantages to the rubber core are ease of use and no worries about damaging your line.

## Surf weights

The surf weight, when its wires are bent back, will hold well in a fierce current. A fish or fisherman can still break it free with little trouble. Despite its name, the surf weight can also be used on a rock or refuse-strewn bottom. Just make sure your line is strong enough not to break before this sinker's wires straighten. The breakaway surf weight is a refinement of the surf weight. When retrieved, its wires spring free and trail behind.

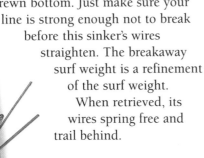

BREAKAWAY
SURF WEIGHT

■ **A heavier sinker** *may be the answer when you want to cast your bait farther, get it deeper faster, or keep it stationary on the bottom.*

## Cigar, keel, and dipsey sinkers

The cigar and keel sinkers are designed for trolling. The swivels built into them are intended to lessen line twist. A keel sinker without a rear swivel may help prevent a rigged bait from spinning. You should have no trouble finding cigar sinkers in sizes from 1 ounce to 1 pound. The largest keel sinkers you will find probably will not weigh more than a few ounces.

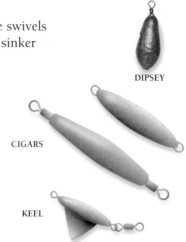

DIPSEY

CIGARS

KEEL

The dipsey sinker is the little freshwater cousin of the bank sinker. It sometimes comes with a built-in swivel for a loop.

## Breakaway sinkers

If you fish long enough, there will come a time when you'll need a weight to get your bait down, but you won't want it on during the battle. A heavy weight can ruin a fight by dampening the sensations of it, or by wearing out the fish. You can attach breakaway weights to your line, usually at the swivel, with thread or wire weak enough to break away as soon as the battle begins. The weights themselves don't have to be lead. Rocks, spark plugs, and countless other things can get the job done.

*Candy Life Savers are great melt-away release devices, especially if you want to lose your weight before the bite. That way there won't be any resistance from a weight to spook a fish. Also, if your bait is live, it will be freer to move around naturally.*

# Weighty thoughts

WHENEVER YOU USE BREAKAWAY WEIGHTS, keep in mind that *few things give a fisherman more pleasure than finding a new fishing spot. Few things disturb him or her more than returning to find a favorite spot changed for the worse. Unfortunately, fishermen sometimes contribute to these changes.*

■ **When you find a fishing spot** *as picturesque as this, make sure you leave it just as picturesque for the next fisherman.*

<u>*The Eighteenth Golden Rule of Fishing:*</u> *"Always leave your fishing spots as close as possible to the pristine conditions you found or had hoped to find."*

I hesitate to turn the subject of weights into something heavy. Still, I must add that lead is a toxic substance. For years there has been a running debate on the dangers lead sinkers pose to the environment. In the UK, lead sinkers have lost this debate. Proven by some studies to be lethal to birds when ingested, accused by other studies of much more, lead sinkers are already banned in the UK. The US Environmental Protection Agency (EPA) has proposed a phase-out of lead, brass, and zinc sinkers less than 1 inch in diameter. Suggested substitutes include bismuth, steel, tungsten, antimony, and turpentine-resin putty. At present there is not much you can do, but do what you can.

# A simple summary

✔ The Eighteenth Golden Rule of Fishing: "Always leave your fishing spots as close as possible to the pristine conditions you found or had hoped to find."

✔ Choosing a sinker, you must consider bottom composition, depth, current, surface conditions, line strength, whether or how far you need to cast, and, of course, target fish.

✔ Never use a heavier sinker than necessary.

✔ Pyramid sinkers are used to hold a bait in place on a sandy bottom with a strong current.

✔ Bank sinkers are used to minimize snags on a rocky bottom.

✔ After a hit without a hookup, never rush to retrieve your line just to check your bait. Give that fish a second chance. You may never get your bait back to the right place again.

# Chapter 18

# Bobbers

THERE IS SOMETHING MAGICAL about seeing a bobber dip ever so slightly into the water and send out a series of perfect, concentric circles. These tiny waves signal that a fish has just nibbled at your bait and that, in an instant, that fish may nibble again or, better yet, yank your bobber completely underwater and take off on a run. I don't care how small your quarry is or how bored you were in the preceding moments, that magic instant, even if you're seeing it for the ten-thousandth time, will fill you with the same anticipation and excitement as the first time, even if you experienced that first time as a small child.

## In this chapter...
✔ Types of bobbers
✔ Using bobbers

BOBBER MOVEMENT IS A CLUE TO THE TYPE AND SIZE OF THE FISH MOVING IT

# Types of bobbers

**THERE IS A HUGE VARIETY** of **bobbers** available today. Here are the ones you are most likely to need.

## Cork bobbers

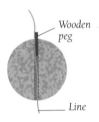

*Wooden peg*

*Line*

**SECURING A CORK BOBBER**

A cork bobber is merely an unpainted cork ball with a hole drilled through the middle and a wooden peg to fit that hole. You thread your line through this hole before tying on your leader or leaderless hook. Then you slide the bobber along the line until the distance separating it from the hook is the distance below the surface you want to position your bait. You lock the bobber in place by pushing the peg into the hole.

## USING PLASTIC BOBBERS

In the days when chemists ruled, it came to pass that bobbers of the cork design were born again in plastic. They were soon further refined with a button that offered a distinct advantage over its cork and plastic predecessors. You could add, remove, and reposition it without cutting and retying your line. Although these popular plastic button bobbers are simple to use, I have witnessed much fumbling with them over the years.

*Button*

**PLASTIC BOBBER**

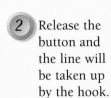

*Button depressed*

*Line*

*Bottom brass hook*

**1** Press the button on top of the bobber; you will see a hook appear at the bottom. Lay the line over the hook.

**2** Release the button and the line will be taken up by the hook.

*Line is caught*

## Slit bobbers

The little brass hooks that catch and hold the line to the plastic bobbers make some fishermen, especially ultralight-tackle enthusiasts, nervous about line damage. This is part of the rationale behind the slit bobber. Usually made of Styrofoam, it uses a peg to position it and has a slit through to its diameter for placement and removal without any cutting and retying.

## Balloon bobbers

The balloon bobber is really no more than a simple balloon tied onto the swivel eye. It has some distinct advantages over all other bobbers, and surely would have been invented eventually in the form of a bobber if it had not been invented as a toy first. One very real advantage of a balloon is that when a fish puts up a good fight, the balloon usually bursts fairly soon, thus freeing both fish and fisherman from a cumbersome source of resistance. Another advantage is that one size fits all. You can blow it up to the appropriate size for any bait.

*Line is laid in hook*

3 Press the outside edge of the button to reveal a brass hook at the top. Lay the line in this hook.

4 Release the button to catch the line. You're ready to go.

*If you're facing into the wind, the smaller the balloon, the longer it will take the wind to blow your bait right back to you. If the wind is at your back, the larger the balloon, the faster the wind will carry it away from you. This means bait placement will not be limited by your casting ability, but rather by the amount of line on your spool.*

You should already be thinking, according to the First Golden Rule of Fishing: "Less is better, if it can get the job done." In general, you're right. However, there are some very curious, if not fearless fish, such as cobia and dorado. The larger your bobber, the more these exceptions to the rule may be attracted to your bait. In fact, when going after species such as these, it would pay to check your local army-surplus store. They may have an old blimp or two in stock.

## Casting bobbers

The casting bobber is more than just a bobber. A port in it allows you to add water for weight to improve your casting distance. Of course the more water you add, the less buoyant the bobber. Therefore, it pays to have this bobber in a few different sizes.

*Some ingenious fisherman figured out that you can use water-filled bobbers to cast flies with spinning tackle. Of course this is not the same thing as fly-fishing. If you ever get the urge to give some purist fly fisherman apoplexy, tell him or her that it is.*

**INTERNET**

**www.marineweather.com**

*At this US site, you can look up your state's fishing regulations. You should. Ignorance is no defense, even against fishing regulations.*

A word of warning about "fly-fishing" with a casting bobber: If a game warden catches you in a fly-fishing-only area, don't even think about trying to convince him or her that you're fly-fishing. Just pay your fine as quickly as possible, and hope the warden doesn't remember your face.

■ **One of the few real drawbacks** *of spinning tackle is fly-fishing-only areas.*

# Sliding bobbers

The sliding bobber does just that – it slides right up and down your line. Chances are, someday you'll need one. Let's say you want to set your bait close to 10 feet below the water's surface, 50 feet from where you're standing. Assuming you're less than 10 feet tall and so is your spinning rod, you're going to have 20 feet of line on the ground before your cast. Unless you can cast better than I can, you'll still have close to 10 feet of line on the ground after your cast.

Fortunately, I can offer you three ways to solve this problem. The first way would be to take the bait in hand, swim out 50 feet, and drop it. Or you could cast your bait from the top of a 20-foot ladder. Still, even from there, the 20 feet of line hanging from your rod tip will make this quite a challenge, probably too much of one. The third solution, and my personal choice, would be to thread a sliding bobber onto your line. Not only are sliding bobbers cheaper than 20-foot ladders, they're substantially easier to fit into your tackle box, not to mention carry around.

## Casting with a sliding bobber

Once you have rigged your sliding bobber, you cast as you normally would, not noticing any difference until 20 feet of line has already left your spool. That's when the stop knot vibrates your line guides on its way out. This should not lower your casting distance too much. If it does, just put on a larger bobber, a larger sinker, or both. When your weight hits the water, it will take your bait down, and your line with it. The bobber and the bead atop it will stay on the surface as the line slips through them. When the stop knot hits the bead, they together keep the bobber from sliding further up the line. This stops your bait's descent at the specified depth.

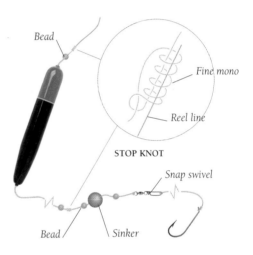

Bead

Fine mono

Reel line

**STOP KNOT**

Snap swivel

Bead

Sinker

■ **A sliding bobber** *should be rigged as shown in this diagram. With the bobber hanging in a comfortable casting position a few inches below your rod tip, you'll have a very manageable few feet of line between it and your hook.*

*Notice that the sliding bobber is cast tapered end first to lessen air resistance and water disturbance. In comparison to round bobbers, cylindrical ones also make for a cleaner fight, causing less water resistance when either fish of fisherman is pulling them one way or the other. Whenever casting distance or minimum water resistance is critical, choose cylindrical over round bobbers.*

# Floats

These sensitive bobbers are freshwater mainstays. Designed for minimum water resistance, even the gentlest nibble will cause substantial up and down movement. This is especially helpful when the water's surface is disturbed enough to obscure the ripples a bobber makes. Less resistance also means less-spooked fish, in that there is less commotion over a fish's head when it bites and less resistance when it runs with the bait. Floats also prove useful in saltwater, but should be placed back into your tackle box long before the white caps arrive. These floats come in enough different styles and sizes to suit just about every type of fishing in every river, lake, pond, pool, and mud puddle in the world.

## Positioning floats

Floats are attached at both top and bottom with the use of rubbers, or at the bottom only by running your line through a ring. For the latter method, you set the depth of your bait by locking the float in place with a split shot to each side of it.

> *Trivia...*
>
> *Warning: Referring to floats as bobbers is guaranteed to offend the purists. However, this guide is not written for purists or people who would think twice about offending them.*

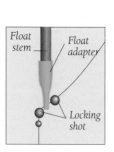

Float stem — Float adapter

Locking shot

**LOCKING SHOT**

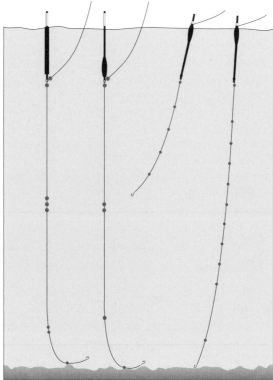

*Use shot about 6 inches from top of float*

**BACKSHOTTING**

■ **You can fine-tune** *both your casts and the speed your bait sinks by the placement of your split shot.*

Add to your casting distance and get your bait down quicker by attaching split shots between float and hook. To get additional distance, switch to a larger, more buoyant float that can support more split shots. For easier casting with less danger of tangles, decrease the size or frequency of these split shots toward the hook. The quicker you want your bait to sink, the more you weight the line toward the hook end. If you expect to get bites on the way down, you do the opposite.

*When the wind is a problem, you can lessen its effects by attaching a split shot a few inches before the float. This sinks the section of line adjacent to it. Also, keep your rod tip low. In fact, you can even place it in the water to try sinking your line completely.*

### Bite indicators

Floats can naturally be used like standard bobbers to suspend a bait in the water column and signal bites. In addition, they can be used to signal bites when bottom fishing. If a fish lifts your bait instead of pulling it down, this bobber will pop up and float on its side instead of disappearing below the water's surface. This technique necessitates your weight barely reaching the bottom and your bobber almost fully submerged. To accomplish this, you have to know the exact water depth, something indeed valuable to know even if you just want to place your bait near the bottom.

### Calculating water depth

One easy way to find your exact water depth is to use our old friend the sliding bobber. Attach a temporary sinker to your hook, one large enough to submerge the bobber. Place a stop knot (or a gently closed split shot) at a distance from your hook equal to your estimate of the water depth. Now cast this rig to the spot you want to fish. If the bobber sinks, raise the knot and cast again. If the bobber floats free, lower the knot and cast again. Keep resetting the knot until the bobber is visible, but not as visible as if it were floating free. That is your water depth.

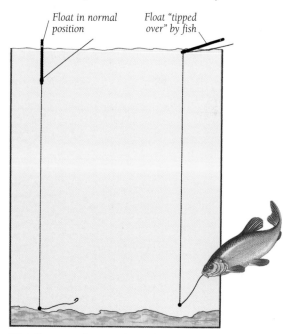

Float in normal position

Float "tipped over" by fish

■ **A float** *can be rigged to indicate when a fish lifts a bait off the bottom, as opposed to when it runs with a bait or pulls it down in the water column.*

# Using bobbers

ONE OF THE MORE SATISFYING ASPECTS *of using a bobber is developing the ability to tell the type and size of a fish just by the way it moves your bobber. A trophy fish may take off on a run that will distinguish it from any nibbler, yet a real monster may just glide away taking its own sweet time. Sometimes you'll guess wrong. Still, if you guess right, you'll have a better idea when or if to try setting the hook.*

### When the current is strong

Most bobbers can be used in strong currents. However, you must remain conscious of how this condition will affect the bait hanging from them. Say the water is 6 feet deep and you want your bait 1 foot off the bottom. If there is little or no current, merely leave 5 feet of line between bobber and hook, as in Figure 1 (*below*). However, strong current can keep your bait well off the bottom (Figure 2) or even right on the surface (Figure 3). You can solve this problem by placing a sinker wherever you care to above the hook, then leaving 5 feet of line between sinker and bobber. Before you do so, it pays to remember our First Golden Rule of Fishing: "Less is better, if it can get the job done." You want to get your bait down with the least amount of weight. This is a far more important consideration than having your line form a pretty right angle at the sinker (Figure 4). So use less weight and a little more line, as rigged in Figure 5.

FIGURE 1

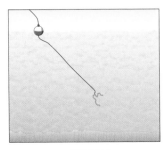

FIGURE 2

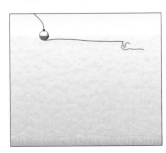

FIGURE 3

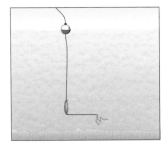

FIGURE 4

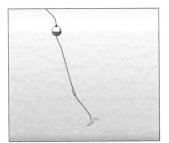

FIGURE 5

## When fishing with live bait

The position of your bait beneath your bobber must also be taken into consideration when hooking live bait. The one in Figure 6 (*below*) is free to swim anywhere between the water's surface and a depth equal to the length of line between bobber and hook. If you want to keep this bait down without the use of a sinker, try hooking it back near the tail as in Figure 7. So you will know this bait is down, use a bobber small and sensitive enough to indicate when your bait is trying to get down farther than the bobber will allow. This should happen quite often. Now, if the current is strong and you are using a sinker, in order to give your live bait a more natural presentation, you can hook it through the lips or nostrils as in Figures 8 and 9.

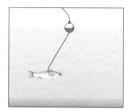

FIGURE 6

FIGURE 7

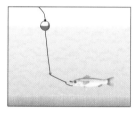

FIGURE 8

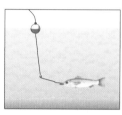

FIGURE 9

*If your bobber remains perfectly still for more than a few minutes, switching to a livelier bait may be a good idea.*

# A simple summary

✓ A bobber allows you to keep your bait anywhere in the water column. It also alerts you when a fish hits your bait.

✓ Cylindrical, as opposed to round, bobbers are better for casting, less likely to spook a fish, and interfere less when you are fighting a fish.

✓ Casting bobbers that can be filled with water will add to your casting distance.

✓ A sliding bobber can tell you the water depth.

✓ In a strong current, an unweighted bait will not hang straight down from a bobber.

# Chapter 19

# Swivels

A TWISTED LINE is far more likely to tangle. Untangling it will cost you time and cause you aggravation. Twisting also weakens line, costing you either fish or the time and money required to replace the line. If you're using spinning tackle and want to keep your line from getting twisted, in most instances you must use a swivel.

## In this chapter...
✓ The job of a swivel
✓ Types of swivels
✓ Types of snaps
✓ Choosing a swivel
✓ Using swivels
✓ When swivels fail

**FIXED-SPOOL REELS ARE MORE LIKELY TO REQUIRE A SWIVEL THAN REVOLVING-SPOOL REELS**

# The job of a swivel

**AS ITS NAME SUGGESTS,** *the job of a swivel is to swivel. No mystery there. They're most often used to connect your terminal tackle to your line. Some baits and lures are designed to spin. Swivels help them spin better. Others spin just to spite the fisherman. Swivels help keep these baits and lures from twisting your line.*

*If you look down at your reel and see line springing off of it in doubled, twisted coils, or you see short lengths of coiled, doubled spikes projecting from your spool like cute little hedgehog quills, then your swivel is not doing its job. Change it, preferably for a better one.*

The spinning reel itself is part of the problem. In order to coil a garden hose or a rope on the ground, you must twist it as you do so. Otherwise the rope or hose will not lie flat. A spinning reel, because the line is retrieved over the end of the spool, must also put a twist in the line to lay it flat.

Not surprisingly, just about any swivel you can buy will swivel. Unfortunately, this is not enough. The true test is when these swivels find themselves between a fisherman pulling one way and a big fish pulling another. A quality swivel must be strong enough not only to bear this load, but also to swivel under it. Corrosion decreases the efficiency of swivels. Wear weakens them.

# Types of swivels

**FORTUNATELY, WE CAN KEEP IT SIMPLE** *and still cover all the different types of swivels you will probably ever run into. That's likely more than you'll ever need.*

## Ball-bearing swivel

The ball-bearing swivel is my swivel of choice. These beauties spin like tops even under load. I like the streamlined shape of them too. No way do I want a swivel dog-paddling in front of, and distracting attention away from, my bait.

**BALL-BEARING SWIVEL**

Are ball-bearing swivels the only swivels you should ever use? No, they're expensive and often unnecessary. When you're trolling high-priced lures or meticulously rigged baits on premium line, or when you're casting spinners or spoons that like to twist your line into pretzel shapes, then ball-bearing swivels will save you more than they cost. For other, less demanding types of fishing, you can often save yourself a few bucks.

You can buy ball-bearing swivels without the pictured rings. I don't recommend this. Your particular snap swivel (see Chapter 6) may prove difficult to attach. Also, a ring is gentler on line and leader material. For this reason, if your swivel has only one ring, don't waste it on a snap if you can attach the snap to the other end of the swivel. Make sure these rings are solid and welded, not split rings. Welded rings are much, much stronger.

## Barrel swivel

For bottom fishing, especially the back-breaking, snag-a-minute variety, the much cheaper barrel swivels are often good enough. Notice that the barrel swivels pictured below have two different types of eyes. One type has both eye ends tapered and anchored within the barrel. The other has an eye formed by twisting one end around the other, and anchoring that other end within the barrel. Now, I have not done any scientific tests, but the first method appears to require more intricate work. It's also more prevalent in higher quality swivels. This would indicate superior quality in itself.

*If you flick the eye of a barrel swivel with your finger, it will spin like a top. Don't be misled. Tie a loop of line to one eye and a 5-pound weight (a sugar bag, for example) to the other. Now see how well this swivel spins, if you can get it to spin at all. Judge how well it spins by how well it keeps the loop of line from twisting.*

**BARREL SWIVELS**

## Three-way swivel

Three-way swivels are used mainly for bottom fishing. They all get the job done. Any substantial difference is probably more a matter of the quality of manufacture than it is of the design. Take special note of my ingenious do-it-yourself contribution, the third of the three illustrated below. A careful study of the picture will enable you to duplicate this feat of engineering.

THREE-WAY SWIVEL

OTHER THREE-WAY SWIVELS

## Conger eel hook and swivel

The strange, primitive-looking conger eel hook and swivel, if made with some real craftsmanship and the right materials, could possibly work on game fish. Unfortunately, I have never seen one that didn't look as if it had been whipped up in a dark tool shed, in less than 2 minutes, by someone with one hand holding a hammer and the other one in a cast. I would not trust these slipshod contraptions either to swivel or stay in one piece.

CONGER EEL HOOK AND SWIVEL

# Types of snaps

THERE ARE EVEN MORE TYPES OF SNAPS *than there are types of swivels. They all have their supposed advantages, with the emphasis on supposed. My suspicions are that many of these advantages in no way apply to fishing. Therefore, we will restrict our discussion to only those snaps I have figured out how to both open and close, and only the most noteworthy of these. The better snaps, though pictured here with one or the other, are sold attached to both barrel and ball-bearing swivels.*

*Lures work better attached to snaps with uniformly rounded ends.*
*Many crankbaits work better tied directly to your line without swivels.*

## Standard (safety-pin) snap

The standards inherent in the standard snap are actually too low to qualify it as standard. I prefer to use its other slightly less common name – the safety-pin snap. This name comes from its appearance, not the unfortunate fact that it is worth about as much as something you would likely find stuck to a discarded diaper. I have seen these snaps fail too many times. Though hard to fathom how, I think the end of the pin usually gets pulled lengthwise from the locking plate. In any case, these snaps are rumored to have popped open when either fish or fisherman have looked at them the wrong way. I advise you not to look at them, not to mention buy them.

SAFETY-PIN SNAP

## Interlock snap

The interlock snap is a vast improvement over the safety-pin snap, which makes it sound much better than it is. I would avoid using it except in its smaller sizes when targeting small fish with very light tackle.

INTERLOCK SNAP

## Crosslock and duolock snaps

The crosslock and duolock are far more dependable. These excellent snaps also come in greater strengths. In addition, they are much smaller than the interlock at comparable strengths. One nice advantage is that they open at both ends. This ability often proves useful, sometimes for odd reasons. You should always keep a few crosslock or duolock snaps handy.

CROSSLOCK SNAP

## Coastlock snap

For the same reason I told you to keep the crosslock and duolock snaps handy – the fact that they open at both ends – I choose to rely largely upon another type of snap, the coastlock. It may be my paranoid side gaining dominance, but the fewer ways a snap can open, the better. If you're buying a safe, you don't go looking for one with two doors unless you have a very good reason for needing that extra door.

COASTLOCK SNAP

# Using swivels

THE QUICKEST AND MOST CONVENIENT WAY *to change your terminal tackle is to use a snap swivel. Do so, and your bait will spend a lot more time where it can accomplish the most good – in the water. However, the less hardware next to your bait the better. This is where the fish is going to stick its nose, the exact place you would put your swivel if you wanted the fish to see it. Also, putting a snap swivel there, where it can get popped open, is asking for trouble.*

*Avoid attaching a snap swivel directly to your hook and, to a lesser degree, to a plug, even if the snap is a distance from the closest hook. If you insist on using a swivel in either situation, try to attach a simple swivel without a snap.*

The optimum place for a swivel is between line and leader. You can't make a safer, stronger connection. There's no reason you have to use a snap swivel. You can attach the wire directly to a snapless swivel using a haywire twist (see Chapter 7).

When casting, using a swivel between line and leader limits the length of your leaders. Even if you could find a swivel small enough to fit through your line guides, you would not want to take a chance on damaging these guides. Any length leader over a few feet diminishes your casting distance. Longer lengths may prevent you from casting at all. If necessary, you may have to forgo the swivel, tying your line to a monofilament leader using a knot that will travel through your guides.

# When swivels fail

I KNOW OF ONLY TWO WAYS TO UNTWIST *a severely twisted line: the first requires deep water and the second a boat. The first works if the water is deeper than the length of twisted line. Tie on a balanced weight that will not spin of itself. Let out all the twisted line. Allow it to hang a few minutes. The line should untwist. A far better method requires a moving boat. Cut off all terminal tackle and let your line unwind into the water. It will retrieve minus the twist, guaranteed.*

## Swivels aren't the only things that spin

Allow me to end this chapter with an interesting fact of very questionable value. An alligator can twist your line like nothing else dead or alive. These stubby-legged, would-be ballerinas can pirouette faster than anything in a tutu. Instinctively, they spin underwater to drown the prey in their mouths. I must mention that, when hunting alligators, rods and reels are not your equipment of choice. Even if you prove skillful enough to reel an alligator up onto dry land, don't make any quick assumptions about who actually has whom. Alligators have not only been known to run faster than humans, they have been known to run faster than humans being chased by alligators.

■ **Don't mess with an alligator:** *Be sure to run if you get anywhere near one!*

## A simple summary

✔ Swivels help prevent your line from twisting. They also help artificial baits that are supposed to spin do just that.

✔ Snaps make convenient, sometimes superior, terminal-tackle connections.

✔ Ball-bearing swivels are far superior to any other type.

✔ Split rings are much weaker than welded rings.

✔ For bottom fishing, the more economical barrel swivel is often good enough.

✔ All swivels swivel. Only a quality swivel will do so under load.

✔ Avoid safety-pin snaps.

✔ Choose the smallest swivel that will get the job done.

✔ Dark swivels are preferable to bright ones and likely of better quality than uncolored brass.

✔ Avoid attaching your snap swivel directly to your hook.

✔ The best way to untwist a line is to cut off all terminal tackle and unreel it behind a moving boat.

# Chapter 20

# Leaders

RARELY IS YOUR CHOICE OF LEADER ARBITRARY. Different leader materials and styles have their advantages and disadvantages. There's usually a specific leader most appropriate for a particular type of fishing at a particular time. This chapter will help you choose that leader.

## In this chapter...

✓ The purposes of a leader

✓ Choosing the right material

✓ Rigging your leaders

THIS FISHERMAN'S SHOCK LEADER MAY BE LONGER THAN HIS RUNNING LINE

# The purposes of a leader

A LEADER CAN SERVE A NUMBER OF PURPOSES, *sometimes one at a time and sometimes in combination. Most often, its purpose is to put some extra muscle where it can do the most good. Fact: If your line breaks, you lose your fish.*

## Added strength

The most vulnerable part of your line is the section closest to the fish. It needs protection from inanimate objects such as rocks, coral, oysters, sunken ships, submerged tree trunks, and submerged electric ranges, for example. Your line also needs protection from animate objects, mainly the fish you're trying to catch. I'm not just talking about their teeth. The mouths of some fish are covered with small protuberances every bit as rough as the surface of a rasp. In addition, the fins, tails, and especially gill plates of some fish can wear mono line or cut it in two. Some species have even developed protuberances as sharp and quick as switchblade knives.

We've already discussed the advantages of using the lightest test line that will get the job done – longer casts, more line on your spool, and such. Let's say you're targeting a fish that supposedly requires 12-pound test. Well, you might just be able to get the same results with a 12-pound leader on 10-pound test. Or you can add a safety factor with a 15- or 20-pound leader. Once you have that safety factor, you might want to lower your line test to 8 pounds.

I'd like to be able to claim that I'm letting you in on some secret technique, but unfortunately this is standard operating procedure for your average fisherman, and it has been for a long time. It's more of a necessity than an option when you're working with extreme line tests. I doubt you will break any 2-pound test records without a leader on the end of it. At the other extreme, many big-game fishermen use 300-pound test for leaders, but none of them fill their reels with it.

■ **It's surprising** *what you can reel in if your leader is considerably stronger than the rest of your line!*

*A leader is almost mandatory in saltwater due to the range of species available. Still, if the fish are not biting in your area, you may want to try without a leader to see if there are, in fact, fish in your area.*

## Casting

If you are using a very heavy weight, say for long-distance surf casting, your line can take more than a beating. It does no good to cast a bait 200 yards off a beach if that bait takes only a few feet of your line with it. Instead of limiting the distance of your casts by using a smaller weight, you can add a **shock leader**. This leader of higher test monofilament, if strong enough and long enough to go around your spool a half dozen times, will take the brunt of your casts without snapping.

> **DEFINITION**
>
> *A **shock leader** is a wind-on leader, attached to your line with a knot instead of a swivel so it will pass through you rod's line guides. However, it is also long enough to go a half dozen times around your reel's spool when you are in casting position. This allows the shock leader, not the relatively weaker line, to take all the force of your cast.*

■ **Using a shock leader** *should prevent your line from snapping when long-distance surf casting.*

## Landing

The strength of your leader gives you an additional advantage during the end game. Your drag is set according to your line strength. Once you've grasped the leader, you can apply as much additional pressure by hand as your leader will allow. If you're using reel-on leaders, attached with a knot instead of a swivel, you don't have to grab it. As soon as you have a few turns on your spool, you can then tighten your drag and reel the fish all the way in.

*There are instances when you may want a leader weaker than your line. Thirty-pound test line with an 8-pound test leader will catch you more bait faster. Fishing an area full of snags, you may want to sacrifice some hooks or lures rather than your line and time.*

## Protection from wear and tear

A leader does more than protect your line from damage that will cost you a fish. It also protects it from attrition. The first few feet or yards of your line will be the first to show wear and damage. Any less-than-perfect line must be removed immediately. Every time you snip off a piece, you're decreasing the level of your line in relation to the front rim of your spool. This increases the friction between line and spool whenever you cast.

■ **When long-distance surf casting,** *a shock leader is usually mandatory.*

More friction means shorter casts. Though each increment of lost line may seem insignificant in itself, these increments add up quickly. Soon you'll be watching your casts fall inches short of their target. It's then that you have no choice but to change or refill your spool. Using a leader to take the brunt of the wear and damage fishing inflicts will lengthen the life of your spools, and lessen time spent refilling them.

*Even if your line looks perfect, it pays to retie your terminal knot whenever a fish or a snag has put it under substantial stress.*

## Camouflage

Leaders serve another purpose that doesn't concern us now but should be mentioned in passing – camouflage. Keeping it simple, we're sticking to spinning tackle, and therefore monofilament, the least visible of lines. However, even fishermen who use other lines, such as Dacron, often like to add a less visible mono leader. Remember that for the future. You will catch more fish.

# Choosing the right material

**ALMOST ALL FISHING LEADERS** *are made from only four simple, common materials – monofilament, single-strand wire, twisted or braided cable, or nylon-coated cable. Each of these materials has advantages and disadvantages that can come directly into play depending upon the species of fish you target or the species that happen to target your bait.*

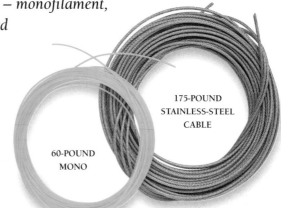

175-POUND STAINLESS-STEEL CABLE

60-POUND MONO

## Monofilament leaders

A fisherman's first choice in leader material should be monofilament. It is less visible to fish. Its suppleness enables your lures and rigged baits to take on a livelier, more natural action. This suppleness also makes monofilament leaders the easiest to cast. Also, during the end game, when your fish is close, grabbing a mono leader is somewhat easier and slightly safer than grabbing wire.

If monofilament were the perfect choice for every type of fishing, it would be the only choice. It's neither. A 1-pound mackerel can slice through a 100-pound test mono leader so fast and so effortlessly, a fisherman may not even realize he's had a hit. So, if you're in a neighborhood frequented by pike, walleyes, muskies, barracuda, mackerel, wahoo, shark, or any other sharp-toothed species, you may have to find yourself a leader material other than monofilament.

Even a fish without teeth, if big enough and strong enough to put up a long fight, can eventually wear through the thickest mono leader. This is why some marlin fishermen prefer cable leaders.

## Trivia...

*There's one rare breed of fishermen that prefers mono only when toothy critters are around. Some marlin fishermen can't be bothered reeling in a line with a barracuda or wahoo on the other end. Too much trouble. Too much time wasted. They would rather these fish slice right through their leaders, taking $50 to $100 marlin lures with them. This can be interpreted as proof of the high intelligence and ingenuity of the human mind. On the other hand, it can also be taken as proof that some people just have too much money to throw around.*

259

## Single-strand wire leaders

Single-strand wire is the fisherman's second choice simply because it gets more hits than any other leader material except mono. The main reason for this is relative visibility. Single-strand, in comparable strengths, is much thinner than either mono or cable. Attaching it with a haywire twist (see Chapter 7) does not require any tools except a wire cutter and is not much more time-consuming than tying your average knot. When trolling, where fish usually come up from behind a bait, single-strand is only slightly more visible than mono. There is no easier material to use when rigging ballyhoo, squid, and many other baits. It is also less expensive than cable.

40-POUND
SINGLE-STRAND
WIRE

In this book single-strand wire means stainless steel and nothing else. In freshwater you can get away with wire that will rust, but price is the only advantage and it's not enough of one. Monel, also a single-strand wire, is for wire lines, not leaders. Stainless steel is the only wire to use. In fact, single-strand wire is often referred to simply as "stainless," and vice versa.

*The flash of the wire can sometimes draw attention — and even strikes — away from your bait. For this reason, stick to the coffee-colored variety. However, be aware that this color can wear off, especially from trolling.*

Single-strand wire does have its drawbacks. It's stiffer than both mono and cable. This is detrimental to the action of your baits. You can minimize this effect when attaching a lure by doing so with a nice wide loop instead of a short, narrow slit. Single-strand also kinks quite easily. Large, powerful fish often help it kink by wrapping themselves up in it. Fishermen, both powerful and weak, sometimes do the same. The results can be far more serious than a lost fish. You can severely cut yourself.

*Never straighten a kink in single-strand wire. You will weaken it. You must cut out any kinked sections or discard the entire leader. Also, the straighter the single-strand, the less visible it is.*

**INTERNET**

www.geocities.com/
Yosemite/3133/
ma_ar014.html

*This article on wire leaders, discusses the pros and cons of several different types. Take a look.*

## Cable leaders

Cable, which is braided or twisted wire, is more flexible and kink-resistant than single-strand, especially when nylon-coated. This coating also protects against fraying. For these reasons, cable will last longer than single-strand and is better suited for battles with larger fish that jump and spin. Its suppleness – again, especially the nylon-coated variety – gives your baits better action than single-strand.

50-POUND
TWISTED
WIRE

Cable does have its drawbacks. The most serious is that it will get fewer hits than monofilament or single-strand. This is most likely due to the fact that it's thicker than single-strand and opaque, making it more visible to fish.

*In rough, murky water during low-light conditions, you may be able to get away with more visible leaders for the safety factor they supply. Just remember, the better the visibility, the less visible your leader better be.*

Plastic-coated cable is easier to handle than uncoated. The plastic also adds abrasion and corrosion resistance. However, it adds thickness that, pound for pound, makes coated cable much more visible. Watch out for signs of corrosion, thus weakness, beneath the plastic coating.

■ **There's not a sailfish in the ocean** *that can't be caught with a monofilament leader.*

# PART
# FOUR

RIGGING BAIT CORRECTLY TAKES TIME, BUT IT PAYS OFF

# Chapter 21

# Natural Bait

NATURAL BAITS are made from natural materials – vegetable as well as animal. Bread and oats are just as natural as salmon eggs. Natural baits naturally include minnows, mullet, menhaden, shrimp, squid, and many, many other baits that once were, but – unfortunately for them – are no longer, among the living. Depending upon conditions and target species, they are often the bait of choice. You can use natural baits to catch fish, to catch bait fish, or as chum.

In this chapter...

✔ Buying it
✔ Catching it
✔ Preserving it
✔ Rigging it
✔ Using it

# Buying it

NATURAL BAIT SHOULD BE FRESH and well preserved. It should not have a strong odor. Shrimp should retain a firm and elastic feel. Fish should have bright red gills, clear eyes, and shiny skin. If such bait was never frozen, and you keep it cold while fishing, afterward you can possibly freeze it yourself for the next trip. If it's been frozen, you can freeze it again for use as chum.

If possible, buy only vacuum-packed frozen bait. When not possible, make sure your bait is tightly packed with little air inside. It will be practically impossible to check the gills and difficult to see the skin but, again, the eyes should be clear and the skin should not have the dull, dried-out indications of freezer burn.

## Trivia...

Catfish bait is one exception to the freshness rule. In fact, I've always had a hunch that run-over skunk would probably be a dynamite bait for catfish, and it would not have to be freshly run-over skunk either. Still, I am proud to say there are some things I wouldn't do to catch a fish – at least one thing, anyway. If you can't say the same, be prepared to eat your catfish alone. You might try smothering it in ketchup. Applying some to yourself would not hurt either.

# Catching it

THE BEST WAY TO GET NATURAL BAIT is to catch it yourself. You can then use it fresh or carefully freeze it. Some bait fish are better caught with nets, some with baited hooks, others with artificial baits. It often helps to first attract bait fish in large numbers with chum.

Your tackle store stocks various equipment for catching bait. If they can't explain to you exactly how and exactly where to use it, find yourself a tackle store that can.

■ **Why buy bait** when you can catch it? Because some days you just can't catch it!

# Preserving it

*AS SOON AS YOU CATCH YOUR BAIT, take steps to preserve it. This usually means keeping it alive or keeping it cold. Some whole baits or large strip baits, especially those to be used for trolling, should be toughened up by soaking them in an ice-cold water/kosher salt solution. Not only will you be able to cast harder and troll faster, you will waste less time changing baits and fishing deteriorated ones without even knowing it.*

Freeze your bait in either vacuum-pack bags or soft plastic ones that will allow you to squeeze out nearly all the air. This will prevent freezer burn. If you feel the thin plastic bags are not sturdy enough, then double wrap your bait by placing the more pliable bags inside thicker ones.

*Never allow saltwater bait to come into contact with freshwater, unless, for some weird reason, you want it to fall apart.*

Frozen bait should be defrosted gradually in a cool place. When you can't wait, place it in a watertight plastic bag, then submerge it in water. If you're fishing in saltwater, use saltwater.

## NATURE'S OWN REFRIGERATOR?

I was once camping on a secluded beach where the only problem in catching a nice fish was first catching the bait. I had no cooler, and every morning I had to make dough balls out of increasingly stale bread in order to catch a small bait fish.

One day I tried to store what remained of that small fish for some afternoon fishing. Skeptically, I buried it in the sand. When I dug up that fish, it looked as if it had come right out of a refrigerator. For the hell of it, I buried it again that evening. To my amazement, I used that bait for 2 more days. Any deterioration was negligible. I'm sure it would have been good for another day, but an animal dug it up that night.

I have no idea why the sand preserved this fish. I don't know if would have happened in another place or another time. I haven't needed to try it again. I'm not saying it'll work for you, but it worked for me. If you ever have the need, why not try it?

# Rigging it

IN ORDER TO RIG YOUR BAITS *you need at least two tools – a knife and fishing pliers. I recommend a reasonably priced, stainless-steel, fillet-style knife. If it doesn't have a scaler on the back, get a separate scaler. A quality apple corer works fine. Never dull your knife blade by using it to scale fish. A sharpener is another thing you'll need, otherwise the most expensive knife will soon be worthless.*

> *The Nineteenth Golden Rule of Fishing: "A good fisherman always brings a spare knife."*

It does not pay to buy cheap pliers either. Even if they work the first time you use them, they won't last long. On the other hand, you don't need a status-symbol, luxury model. Use that money for a down payment on a boat. Then you can invite along the owner of a serviceable pair of pliers.

## Shrimp

Deceased shrimp are a very popular bait, and deservedly so. You can buy them already deceased, or use the frozen leftover live shrimp from your last trip. There are various ways of hooking them. When using pieces, remove the shell. When using whole shrimp, leave on the shell to help keep them on your hook.

BETTER HOOK CAMOUFLAGE          BETTER HOOK HOLD          BETTER CASTS WITH A JIG HEAD

## Mullet

Mullet is one of the most versatile baits. It can be used whole and cut, for bottom fishing, drifting, *cast and retrieve*, and trolling. I illustrate how to prepare and rig mullet chunks for bottom fishing on the following page. This method can be applied to countless other bait fish.

> **DEFINITION**
>
> **Cast and retrieve** *involves casting a bait (artificial, natural, or live) and retrieving it at a speed and with a motion intended to entice strikes.*

When preparing mullet for cast and retrieve or slow trolling, there is a real advantage in leaving on a piece of the tail to give your bait a "live" action. I call this a strip-and-tail rig. It may take you a few tries to get the knack of splitting the tail down the middle. A sharp knife is a must, and a flexible blade is an advantage. If you don't get four baits out of a tail, you've definitely done something wrong, most likely the count. I prefer to use the strip and tail with a single-hook pin rig. The pin rig is made the exact same way as the single-strand weedless hook illustrated in Chapter 16, except you finish it by bending the wire to hold the bait, not to guard the hook point.

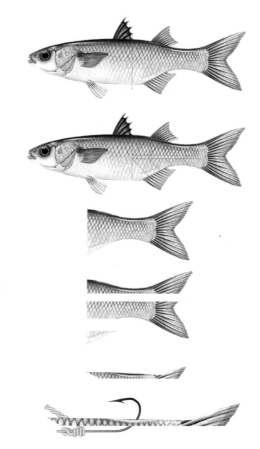

■ **Mullet chunks** *can be used for bottom or drift fishing.*

■ **The strip-and-tail rig** *can be used for trolling, cast and retrieve, and drift fishing. Trim it to approximately ³⁄₁₆ of an inch in thickness, and bevel the front edge.*

Usually, cut mullet is not as desirable a bait as shrimp or squid. However, when shrimp or squid are not getting bites, don't hesitate to try mullet. Sometimes your bait of choice will get outperformed by your second or last choice. Also, when a bait suddenly stops working, the fish may be onto you. Changing baits just might fool them. It pays to bring along mullet or another bait as a backup.

# Ballyhoo

Ballyhoo (balao) is a good cut bait, but it's an excellent trolling bait. The rig illustrated below is perhaps the most popular whole-fish trolling bait in the world. It is often used for drift and other types of fishing too. Trolled ballyhoo should swim and skip along the surface of the water. If you want it to stay under, insert the hook as illustrated below, then thread an egg sinker onto the wire. Insert it gently and snugly between the gill plates. Only then take the wraps with the copper wire to secure it in place. Before you add a ballyhoo to your spread, hold it in the water close enough to the boat to make sure it isn't spinning and looks natural. Ballyhoo should be pulled by the pin, not the hook. If the hook bend is distorting the ballyhoo by pushing forward or backward against the hook hole, you must enlarge this hole with a knife.

1. Attach the hook to single-strand wire with a haywire twist. Leave a ½-inch "pin" pointing in the opposite direction to the hook bend. Attach copper rigging wire with a few turns around the pin.

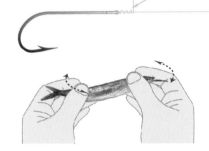

2. Bend the ballyhoo (as gently as possible) from side to side to break the backbone in a few places.

3. Empty what you can from the fish's stomach by squeezing gently with two fingers, moving from the front of the stomach to the vent.

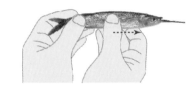

4. Lay the rig over the ballyhoo with the pin halfway between its eye and upper bill tip. Use the hook point to mark the belly where the hook should emerge.

5. Bend the ballyhoo. Open the gill plate and slip the hook into it. Guide the point through the mark on the belly. Push the pin up through the center of the head. Break off half of the bill by pulling down. Skin should come with it, leaving a groove for the wire.

6. Lay the leader in the groove under the beak. Wrap copper wire around the pin then down to the end of the beak. Slide the end under the last wrap. Pull tight. Wrap in the other direction until you have only enough copper wire to secure under the last wrap.

# Squid

Squid is an excellent bait. It can be cut and rigged like mullet chunks or strips. The tentacles can be used to cover the hook or to trail behind like plastic worms. It can also be rigged whole for drift, pier, or bridge fishing. The easy way to do this is with tandem hooks (explained in Chapter 16). Make sure the trailing hook pierces the squid's head, preferably with its bend centered between the eyes. This can be accomplished by using a combination of various-sized hooks or combinations of the same-sized long- and short-shanked hooks. These rigs can be made on the spot, but it pays to have various tandem hook sets available ahead of time.

The only problem with the tandem-hook rig is that, if your target fish is a picky eater, the sight or taste of all that metal may take away its appetite. If you have the time and are willing to take the trouble, use the more natural and durable trolling rig shown below, even when you're not trolling.

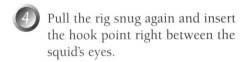

*For sewing baits, a set of bait-rigging needles is nice, but a cheap set of carpet needles gets the job done.*

1. Attach a hook to your single-strand wire leader with a haywire twist, and thread on a bead, a sturdy plastic drinking straw, and an egg sinker.

2. Run the single-strand wire under the squid's mantle and out through its point. Pull the sinker snug. Measure the distance between the squid's eye and the hook bend.

3. Slide the rig back out and cut from the straw the length measured in the previous step.

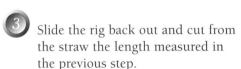

4. Pull the rig snug again and insert the hook point right between the squid's eyes.

5. Stitch the hook in place with a piece of dental floss or Dacron line.

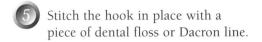

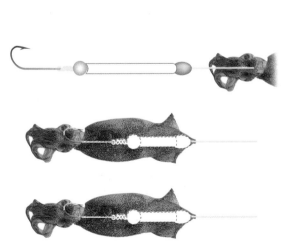

# *Using it*

REMEMBER THAT BOTH THE SIZE of your bait and the size of your hook must suit both your quarry and each other. One of the commonest novice mistakes is to put too much bait on the hook.

The Twentieth Golden Rule of Fishing: *"Too large a bait on a hook does little more than increase the chances a fish will strip it."*

There are many great natural baits we haven't mentioned. Sardines, for example, are dynamite. How you rig them depends upon the hook you use. Whatever hook you use, it should be the smallest that will do the job. In a soft bait such as sardines, you can bury it completely, including the point. I prefer to always leave at least part of the point clear. This insures the point will not skewer a fish scale that will prevent it from penetrating.

## No bites?

When the fish are not biting, don't hesitate to change baits, switch baits, and try new baits. There are no bait stores on offshore oil platforms, yet

■ **Sardines are oily enough** *to send out their own chum slick.*

some of my most enjoyable fishing took place during my roughneck days. We caught beautiful fish with just about anything we could pilfer from the kitchen – raw beef, chicken, and my favorite, turkey. More surprising was what we found inside those fish – chicken bones, steak bones, whole raw unpeeled potatoes. Someone even caught a grouper with a toy rubber gorilla inside.

One morning, out of the corner of my eye, I saw a kitchen worker dump a can of biodegradable garbage over the side. While the rest was sinking, about a dozen squeezed-out orange halves remained floating on the surface. I thought I was seeing things when it looked as if a fish scarfed down one of them. I knew different when a big tuna came halfway out of the water to get another orange half. I stood there watching with my mouth open as that big boy returned for pass after pass until all those orange halves were gone. I have seen more than enough tuna up close to know that it's impossible for them to smile. I also know that orange-eating tuna had a grin on its face as wide as Cool Hand Luke's.

_The Twenty-first Golden Rule of Fishing_: "Bring a variety of baits.
Even if you plan on using only artificial bait, always bring along at
least a small amount of natural bait – to use as bait, as bait to
catch bait, or as chum."

# A simple summary

✔ The Nineteenth Golden Rule of Fishing: "A good fisherman always brings a spare knife."

✔ The Twentieth Golden Rule of Fishing: "Too large a bait on a hook does little more than increase the chances a fish will strip it."

✔ The Twenty-first Golden Rule of Fishing: "Bring a variety of baits. Even if you plan on using only artificial bait, always bring along at least a small amount of natural bait – to use as bait, as bait to catch bait, or as chum."

✔ Well-preserved bait fish have bright red gills, clear eyes, and shiny skin.

✔ The best way to get natural bait is to catch it yourself.

✔ Never allow saltwater bait to come into contact with freshwater.

✔ Frozen bait should be defrosted gradually.

✔ In order to rig your baits you need at least two tools – a knife and fishing pliers.

✔ Mullet is one of the most versatile baits. It can be used whole and cut, for bottom fishing, drifting, cast and retrieve, and trolling.

✔ Ballyhoo and squid are both excellent baits.

✔ Remember that both the size of your bait and the size of your hook must suit both your quarry and each other.

# Chapter 22

# Live Bait

EVEN IF YOU PREFER ARTIFICIAL BAIT, it's always a good idea to take some live bait along. Fish are finicky. Sometimes they want only artificials and sometimes only live bait. Sometimes they even prefer dead bait to anything else. In any case, live bait makes for a nice change of pace. It may get you a larger fish of the same species, or one of a different species.

In this chapter...

✓ Buying it

✓ Catching it

✓ Keeping it live

✓ Rigging it

✓ Using it

HOW YOU CATCH LIVE BAIT AFFECTS HOW LONG IT STAYS ALIVE

## Fiddler crabs

Catching fiddler crabs necessitates making a fool out of yourself. These crunchy morsels are a matter of taste that many fish have yet to acquire. However, to some scaled gourmands, such as sheepshead, they are irresistible. If you find the lure or taste of sheepshead irresistible, get ready to make a fool out of yourself.

You want to show up when the fiddler crabs are strolling the beach en masse, at low tide more often than not. Bring a friend or two, types who are not easily embarrassed. One of you has to carry a bucket. Charge onto the beach, making all kinds of noises, and also making a circle perhaps 20 yards across. Toss the bucket into the center. Continuing to run, space yourselves as evenly as possible around this circle, trapping as many fiddler crabs as possible.

■ **Fiddler crabs** *are easy to catch, and they make catching sheepshead easier.*

Once the crabs are surrounded, they will take off scuttling, as fast as they can, away from the stomping and yelling idiots. This enables you to gradually collapse your circle until the fiddler crabs are doing their scuttling over and under each other, three or four layers deep. By then you should be close enough to the bucket to start tossing the crabs into it. You do so with your hands, as fast as possible. No matter how fast you toss them, once in a while a faster crab will get its claw on you. I make no guarantees, but I have never seen anyone even slightly injured by a fiddler crab. Most pinches won't even hurt. However, when they get you on the webs of your fingers, you'll definitely feel it. You may even yell, at the same time shaking your hand to loosen the crab's grip. By then you'll probably have more than enough fiddler crabs for a day's fishing.

*If you're the type of fisherman who avoids scenes, look for your fiddler crabs on secluded beaches. If you find this impossible, I suggest a simple disguise, one that will not fall off when you are running in circles. Groucho Marx glasses — bushy eyebrows, nose, and mustache attached — will do fine.*

# Keeping it live

### FIDDLER CRABS WILL LAST FOR DAYS

*if you just keep them damp. Filling the bottom of your bucket with damp sand should be enough to do the trick. Blue crabs, a much larger variety, can be kept damp or in water. Earthworms must be kept in a cool, dark place. If you have to store them for more than a couple of days, throw in some chopped hard-boiled egg.*

Bait fish and shrimp can be kept in a floating bait bucket, or a refreshed or aerated bait well. Even an aerated well should be refreshed regularly with "new" water, if possible. This dilutes toxins given off by the fish and retards changes in water temperature toward air temperature. If you can't refresh the water and its temperature is rising, you can try tossing in a sealed container (a plastic water bottle, for instance) of ice. It's extremely important that you remove all dead or injured toxin-spreading baits immediately.

■ **Whichever live bait** *you use, remember to keep it in the right conditions. Otherwise, when you come to use it, you may find it's live no more.*

How a bait fish is handled when caught can have an extraordinary effect on how long it will live. The longer you intend to keep a bait alive, the more important this fact.

### Fish sensitivity

¼ inch

6 inches

Fish have a coating of slime that protects them from disease, among other things. Even when they're caught by net, some of this slime is removed. There are species of bait fish so sensitive that, when caught by net, they're unlikely to last overnight. These fish must be caught by hook and never touched by hand. This can be accomplished with a homemade de-hooking device. You can make one out of a coat hanger. If available, use a nonrusting metal. Only one hook is necessary, but with two you can't pick it up by the wrong end. Also, if the hooks are at any angle except opposite, the de-hooker will be easier to grab because it will not lie flat. Just catch the line with the de-hooker, hang the fish over the well, and pull down on the line until fish hook meets de-hooker hook. If the fish isn't already in the well, just jiggle the de-hooker and it will be – untouched. If the bait fish is a sensitive species, and it hits the ground or deck, you may as well return it to the water then and there.

*If you have to handle a bait fish (or a fish you intend to release), wear wet gloves. If you don't have gloves, wet your hands.*

■ **This homemade** *bait de-hooker is at least as fast and simple to use as any store-bought one.*

# Rigging it

HOW YOU RIG A LIVE BAIT *will help determine how long it stays live, how live it appears, and where it appears.*

## Rigging a fish

No matter where you're fishing, it's always worthwhile to put out a live fish below a bobber. This rig works with 1-inch minnows or 5-pound snappers. The bobber should be just large enough to prevent the bait fish from pulling it completely under.

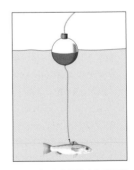

**LIVE FISH BELOW A BOBBER**

Because the bait fish may end up hanging from this bobber, make sure you place the hook so the bait will hang naturally. I choose to believe a bait fish looks most natural, dorsal fin up, belly down.

*The hook you use with a live bait must allow it a maximum of freedom and do it a minimum of damage. This relates to the First Golden Rule of Fishing: "Less is better, if it can get the job done."*

## Hook size

The hook should be as small and as thin as possible. Whatever the size, a less visible short-shank is preferable. The only exception is if you're not using a leader and need some extra shank to keep the fish's mouth away from your mono. You can insert the hook in a number of places. The brain and spinal cord are not two of them, unless for some reason you want your live bait dead or appearing so. If you're using a slender fish such as a minnow, you must be especially careful not to injure the spinal cord. The hook should be placed between it and the dorsal fin, closer to the dorsal.

## Going deeper

If you want to get your live bait fish down deep without a weight, hook it in the hindquarters. Sometimes hooking it above the center line works better, sometimes hooking it below. This depends upon species of bait fish, species of fisherman, phases of the moon, and who knows what else? In any case, fishing is not rocket science. Try both ways. It won't cost you any more than a few minutes and a bait fish. Once you do figure it out, this rig allows you to take it easy and let the bait do the work.

**HOOKING THE HINDQUARTERS BELOW THE CENTER LINE**

**HOOKING THE HINDQUARTERS ABOVE THE CENTER LINE**

## Rough waters

If there's a strong current, or you're the energetic type of fisherman who likes to work a bait by retrieving it or making it dart here and there, then place your hook as far forward as you can get it. Again, you have a choice, something most less-than-energetic fishermen would just as soon do without. You can place your hook vertically through the lips or horizontally in one nostril and out the other. Your choice should depend upon how well the hook will hold, how lively the bait remains, and how long it stays alive.

**HOOKING THROUGH THE LIPS**

**HOOKING THROUGH THE NOSTRILS**

## Rigging a worm

Earthworms, or night crawlers, are an ideal bait. Pass your hook once through the smooth collar of the worm, then, working with the longer end, once or twice again if you like. Always leave the ends swinging free for more action. This rig works nicely from a bobber. If you're after catfish or some other bottom feeder, you can forget the bobber and cover the entire hook with worms.

The worm rigs illustrated here (*right*) are ideal if you don't want to be bothered hooking small fish and don't mind losing a few bites off your worm. These rigs also enable you to retrieve the worm as if it's swimming, or bounce it along the bottom as if it's doing who knows what. The straighter the worm is rigged, the less likely it is to spin.

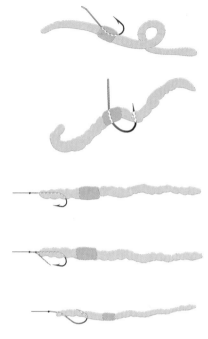

A SELECTION OF WORM RIGS

### Choosing your hook

Note that the hooks used in the top two images above are short-shanked, which means more worm and less metal. This is the recipe fish prefer, thus lessening the likelihood of them spitting your hook. Also, keep in mind that an exposed hook point is slightly more likely to get you a *hookup* than a buried point or a weedless.

Most of the rigging methods for earth worms can also be applied to caterpillars, grubs, sandworms, or bloodworms. Use your imagination. Slow fishing days are the ideal time to do so.

> **DEFINITION**
>
> *A hit or strike qualifies as a **hookup** if the hook point penetrates and holds for at least a few seconds.*

### Trivia...

*I will freely admit that I've never been able to figure out the logic behind hooking a worm through the collar. Perhaps it's aesthetics. Whatever the logic, there is an excellent reason. If you don't hook the worm through its collar, some clown will point out your "mistake." When this happens (notice I didn't say "if"), your best defense is to ask, "Why?" There's no chance this will get you an answer, but it will get you some silence.*

EARTHWORM

## Rigging a leech

Leeches are probably the most convenient bait around. If you can't find them at the bait store, just go somewhere they can find you. This method allows you to carry them around with both your hands free. However, I should mention that your skin turning purple is a sure sign that you're carrying around too many. In this case, or when you need one for bait, just touch it with the hotter end of a lit cigarette (usually the end opposite the filter).

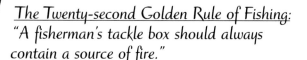

**LEECH RIG**

_The Twenty-second Golden Rule of Fishing:_
_"A fisherman's tackle box should always_
_contain a source of fire."_

I guarantee there will come a day you'll be glad you have a source of fire in your tackle box, and I am not just talking about the time an attractive member of the opposite sex will ask you for a light. A cheap, throwaway butane lighter is perfect for the job. Just keep it in a watertight container or you may need to bum a light to light it. By the way, you hook a leech just behind its sucker.

## Rigging a live shrimp

Shrimp is the queen of live baits. It will catch just about any fish that considers shrimp bite size, and that includes some surprisingly large fish. Most people who enjoy catching fish would also enjoy catching shrimp. We won't get into the how of this because there are too many places where shrimp can't be caught and too many different ways of doing it where they can. If you're in an area where they can be caught, find a tackle store that wants to sell you the needed equipment enough to explain how to use it.

■ **If the fish** _won't take your live shrimp, chances are there are no fish anywhere near your shrimp._

_If you're going to the expense and trouble of using live shrimp, make sure they look the part. This entails using the smallest, thinnest hook possible, so as to do the shrimp the least damage and allow them the most movement. What appears like a little hook to you may feel like a 2-ton anchor to a shrimp._

# Using it

**KEEP YOUR LIVE BAIT ALIVE.** *This sometimes necessitates cutting down on the power you put behind your casts.*

"The farther you cast, the more fish you will catch," is not one of the Golden Rules of Fishing. Once you get a bait where you want it, let it do the work. The less you bother it, the less pressure you put on it, the longer it will last. Eventually, if you don't get a hit, check your bait. If it's dead, check sooner the next time. If it's lively, then you can wait longer.

**INTERNET**

**www.fishingminnesota. com/fishinfo31.html**

*This page of the Fishing Minnesota web site contains an article called "Secrets to Super Bait," and it goes on to offer you just that.*

<u>The Twenty-fourth Golden Rule of Fishing</u>: *"You can't use live bait if ya done kilt it."*

## Trying other baits

If you have a lot of live bait, switch often. If you don't have a lot, and the fish are really biting, try naturals or artificials. They may work just as well. You can save

■ **This tackle-store** *owner may be able to pass on a trick or two about catching lunkers, or at least mounting them.*

the live bait for when the fish get picky. If you have no live bait and are using naturals or artificials, take a break to catch a live bait. Attach it to that spare rod of yours, perhaps hanging from a bobber as shown on page 282. Cast it out, then go back to your artificials and naturals.

*Even if you have no intention of using live bait, always bring along hooks small enough to catch some. One live bait just may save your day.*

# A simple summary

✔ The Twenty-second Golden Rule of Fishing: "A fisherman's tackle box should always contain a source of fire."

✔ The Twenty-third Golden Rule of Fishing: "If you don't know if there are fish, or exactly where they are, for your first attempt choose the bait and rig most likely to get you a strike, not the bait and rig most likely to get you a fish." Once you know there are fish, then focus upon catching them.

✔ The Twenty-fourth Golden Rule of Fishing: "You can't use live bait if ya done kilt it."

✔ Immediately remove any dead or dying bait from your bait bucket or well.

✔ Chum is just as helpful when catching bait as it is when catching game fish.

✔ How a bait fish is handled when caught can have an extraordinary effect on how long it will live.

✔ If you have to handle a bait fish (or a fish you intend to release), wear wet gloves. If you don't have gloves, wet your hands.

✔ The hook you use with live bait must allow it a maximum of freedom and do it a minimum of damage.

✔ Even if you have no intention of using live bait, always bring along hooks small enough to catch some. One live bait just may save your day.

## Chapter 23

# Artificial Bait

THERE'S SOMETHING VERY SPECIAL about catching a fish on an artificial bait, or lure. Some would claim, as the first three letters of "artificial" would indicate, that there is an art to it. Though I had seen other fishermen succeed numerous times, I think, irrationally, that I doubted I ever would. There seemed to be a magic to it, catching a live fish on a strange piece of wood or plastic. Looking back, this belief in itself was probably the reason success eluded me for so long. To catch a fish with artificial baits, you have to use them carefully, persistently, and, most important, with confidence.

In this chapter...
- ✔ Lure size
- ✔ Lure color
- ✔ Types of lures
- ✔ Using lures

THE RIGHT LURE ALSO REQUIRES THE RIGHT TECHNIQUE

# Lure size

*SIZE IS IMPORTANT. Admittedly, I have caught 9-foot marlin on 2-inch bonito lures, and foot-long bonito on 2-foot marlin lures. That is, actually caught. Who knows how many mismatched fish I must have almost caught? Many times I've stood wondering what the hell these fish could have been thinking, knowing for sure that thinking had nothing to do with this riddle. Still, despite all the exceptions, size is important.*

*Whenever I troll five or more lures, I try to start out by including one oversized lure and one undersized lure in the spread.*

An oversized lure in a spread not only gives me a better chance at a trophy fish, the commotion it causes may act as a teaser. Even if a fish eventually goes on to hit one of the middle-sized lures, it may have been attracted to the spread by the oversized one. The undersized lure gives me a chance at a fish too small for the other lures. You may be asking yourself why I need a small fish. The answer is that, for my first fish, I will take any fish. Once the first fish is caught, my fishing becomes more relaxed and enjoyable. Often, the small lure starts the action.

## The hookup ratio

To a point, the smaller the lure in relation to the fish, the better the *hookup ratio*. You have a better chance of hooking a large fish on a small bait, as opposed to a small fish on a large bait. Also, generally, the smaller the species of fish, the more there are of them. This means – again, generally – the smaller the lure, the more fish you have a chance of catching. If you're after a particular fish and know what it's feeding on, use the artificial that most closely matches this food, size included. If you're not sure what size, make an educated guess, then, instead, choose a slightly smaller lure.

> **DEFINITION**
>
> A **hookup ratio** *is the number of hooked fish compared to the number of strikes. A successful fisherman strives constantly to improve his or her hookup ratio. This entails searching for and eliminating the reason behind every missed strike.*

PLASTIC SQUID

LARGE PLASTIC SQUID

■ **By choosing** *a smaller bait over a larger one, you can increase your number of potential strikes.*

# Lure color

COLOR IS ALSO IMPORTANT. *I probably have a favorite color combination for just about every species of fish I go after. Still, I never stick exclusively to one color combination for any particular species. If a lure is not producing that day, before I give up on it, I'll often switch to the same model in a different color.*

## Dark vs bright

According to more than one supposedly scientific study, fishermen should use predominantly dark lures on overcast days and during the low-light hours after dawn and before dusk. Conversely, they should use bright lures on bright days. Dark and bright lures are supposedly more visible to the fish at these times. I realize this may seem counterintuitive to you but, actually, the thinking, if not the science, is sound. The less light, the fewer colors of any shade the fish can see. What they can see are silhouettes, and darker lures make more distinct outlines. When the light is bright, colors become more distinct and outlines less so. Therefore, lighter, brighter lures are called for.

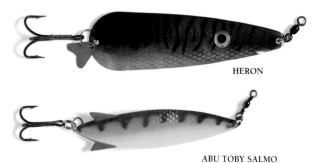

HERON

ABU TOBY SALMO

■ **A dark-colored lure,** *like the heron, is best used on overcast days, while a bright abu toby salmo is good for well-lit days.*

Of course, the real world brings us complications. Even when the sun is bright enough to give the rocks melanoma, if the water is murky, you may be better off with a dark lure. The same is true if you're casting into a heavily shaded area. Also, keep in mind when running lures deep that colors fade with depth. Shorter wavelengths, such as orange and red, disappear faster than blues and greens. For all you know, that red lure of yours may be deep enough to turn blue. One last complication is that the actual color of a lure may sometimes be less important than its relative color. Many trollers like to have all the lures in their spread a single color, except for one. They do so in the belief that the odd color lure will get the most hits. You see, fish are similar to people. They pick on the oddball.

I never strictly follow the color rules, but I do lean toward them. Say I am using a favorite lure with a color that runs counter to these rules, and that lure is not producing. When I change lures, chances are I'll change to one that obeys these rules.

# Dark on top, white on bottom

An interesting aspect of color is that nearly all fishing plugs resembling fish are dark on top and white on the bottom. If you've wondered why, I hope you haven't been searching for any deep philosophical reason. They're colored that way to resemble fish, almost all of which are colored the same way. Fish are colored that way because it makes them less visible from above and below. A predator looking up from and through the depths toward a bright sky is far less likely to spot your typical white-bellied fish than his nonconformist schoolmate doing the backstroke. Conversely, a predator looking down into the dark depths is far less likely to see the dark back of a fish than the belly of another backstroker.

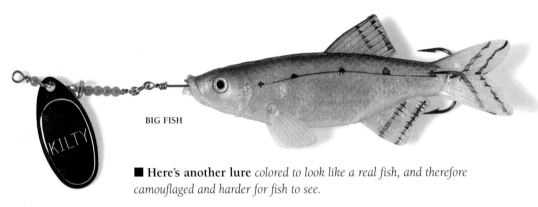

BIG FISH

■ **Here's another lure** *colored to look like a real fish, and therefore camouflaged and harder for fish to see.*

Interestingly, at least to me, is the fact that every other aspect of your average lure was probably designed to make it more visible. Why shouldn't the manufacturer also color the belly dark and the back light, the hell with how fish actually look? Though I have not found the answer to this question, I have not lost enough sleep over it to make me repaint some lures to see how they will work. This brings us to another interesting theory about color.

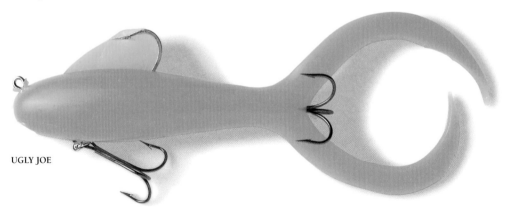

UGLY JOE

■ **Bright lures** *attract attention and strikes on bright days.*

# Confidence counts

Many successful fishermen consider lure color irrelevant or close to it. They don't care what color a lure is, as long as it has the right shape and action. I am not one of these fishermen, but I can see that they may have a point.

<u>The Twenty-fifth Golden Rule of Fishing:</u> "The most necessary, most important requirement for an artificial bait is your confidence in it."

Let's say that you see on TV that the best color lure is chartreuse with rhinestones. So you take out a second mortgage on your house and purchase one of these miracle rhinestone beauties. You're so anxious to try it that you actually stop on the way home. That scenic spot on the river where it runs between the sewage treatment and a nuclear power plant had proved too picturesque to pass by. Fifty casts later you have nothing to show for your purchase except a mortgage-payment schedule. Your arm may be killing you, but there's no way you're going to give up, not after the cash you've laid out. No, you make up your mind to try 50 more casts. After those, you decide on 50 more. Well, you have about 5 minutes of light left and a few remaining threads of shoulder tendon, when you get a hit strong enough to knock the smell of sewage out of your nostrils. Sure enough, you haul in the biggest fish you ever caught on an artificial. The idea does not occur to you that this was the first time you ever stuck with a lure for more than a dozen fruitless casts. No, the idea that does occur to you is that of taking out a third mortgage.

## Is it really any better?

Well, this lure becomes your pride and joy. You use it almost exclusively, and you catch many more fish with it. Again, it never occurs to you that maybe its color is not so important, not even after most of that color is scraped off. It never occurs to you that if you had given the same chance to any of a dozen lures lying forgotten in your tackle box, they might have proved equally effective. No, you're sure that chartreuse with rhinestones is the only lure-color combination that really works. Well, I would not waste my time telling you that you may be wrong, or that those people who think color is irrelevant may be at least half right. However, I will waste my time to repeat once again the Twenty-fifth Golden Rule of Fishing: "The most necessary, most important requirement for an artificial bait is your confidence in it."

**INTERNET**

www.inthebite.com/misc/
previouspoles5.shtml

*This page of InTheBite.com gives details of some of their previous readers' polls, including which lure color combinations work best.*

# Types of lures

*I HAVE ALWAYS FELT that a lure's shape was far more important than its color, and that its action was more important than its shape. At the risk of shocking you, let me state that different types of lures have different actions. Even different lures of the supposedly exact same type can have different actions. Some lures sink and stay underwater. Others stay on the surface. Still others stay on the surface unless jerked or retrieved fast enough to make them dive. These lures can be made to surface and sound like a playful dolphin. The action of some lures is almost completely inherent in their construction. Other lures rely almost entirely upon the fisherman's retrieving technique. The actions of most lures depend upon a combination of construction and technique.*

*A few of the lure types we will mention have subspecies that give off scents, blink on and off, and do other things I've succeeded in wiping from my memory. Soon, no doubt, they'll be joined by lures that whistle, sing, rap, beg for mercy, talk dirty, bleed, and belch. I recommend that you show all of them the same disdain that fish are surely to exhibit.*

It would be helpful to divide our discussion of lure action by the different types of lures that concern us. Unfortunately there is some overlap in types. Terms such as plug, popper, and stick bait mean different things to different people. So, I'll keep it simple by dividing lures into temporary, imaginary, made-to-be-forgotten, disposable, and, above all, biodegradable categories – lipless plugs, lipped plugs, poppers, worms, jigs, spinners and spoons, and their offspring.

ABU GLIMMY

ABU ATOM

■ **Even when worked** *at the same speed in the same conditions, the actions of two seemingly identical lures can be completely different.*

# Lipless plugs

The lures on this page are all lipless, which has nothing to do with the lips some of them do have painted on. The lips we are talking about, the ones these lures don't have, are the plastic or metal spoonlike projections on the lower jaws of some lures.

The first lure is a lipless floater with a relaxed swimming action. It can be retrieved at a steady, leisurely pace. You can also add some short jerks, supplied by your wrist. However, most often it is cast near where you think the fish are, say some lily pads. Instead of retrieving it, you alternately twitch and allow it to rest. This technique keeps the lure within the fish's strike zone for a longer time.

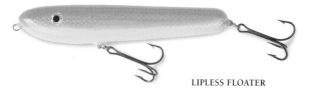

LIPLESS FLOATER

The second lure is sometimes called a countdown bait, which means it's suited for the countdown method. Using this method, you cast at a likely spot, counting as you let your lure sink. If it snags on the bottom or fouls with weeds, you waited too long. On your next cast, snap the bail shut and start retrieving one or two counts earlier. You can retrieve this lure at a steady rate, or add some wrist jerks. You can also alternately bring your rod back, then forward again while reeling in the slack. Short, quick arcs give the lure a herky-jerky motion. Longer, slower arcs let the lure hop on the bottom, just off it, or well off it.

COUNTDOWN BAIT

The last lure on this page is an Australian-style plug developed for trolling. The other lures can be trolled, but only at relatively slow speeds. The Australian-style plug can be trolled faster and deeper than any fish-shaped plug I've come across. It has an excellent vibrating action. More to the point, it produces fish, a lot of them. The smaller models are productive, worthwhile casting lures. Some of them do have a bothersome drawback. They're not balanced for casting and require a gentler, and therefore less effective, casting motion.

AUSTRALIAN-STYLE PLUG

# Lipped plugs

The lures shown below are very similar to those on the previous page except, of course, for the addition of lips underneath their jaws. Some of these plugs float, while others sink. Some of the floaters dive when jerked, retrieved, or trolled fast enough. Then they pop back up to the surface as soon as the pressure is off. These plugs can be worked in many of the same ways as the lipless ones. Their lips will accentuate their actions. Generally, the larger the lip, the greater the action and deeper the dive. The faster the trolling speed, the deeper they will run, to a point. Each lure, at a specific distance from the boat's transom, has a limited trolling speed. If this is surpassed, these lures skip uselessly over the water. For example, the crankbait, that fat-bodied, largest-lipped lure below, will go very deep when retrieved, but it has to be trolled slowly. The metal-lipped lure was designed for trolling and can be pulled considerably faster. This doesn't mean it can't be extremely effective when cast. Then again, some seemingly similar lures are not balanced well enough for casting.

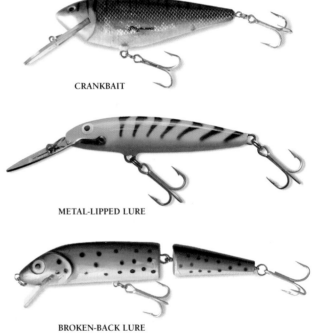

**CRANKBAIT**

**METAL-LIPPED LURE**

**BROKEN-BACK LURE**

## Pros and cons

Both metal lips and plastic lips have their advantages. The metal-lipped lures can be tuned. When one starts doing the sidestroke, this is not because it's tired. The lip is bent to one side. All it takes is two fingers to bend it back again. By lowering the lip, you can make the lure swim deeper. This will also make it vibrate faster and decrease its side-to-side swimming action. Raising the lip will do the opposite. The drawback to this versatility is that a powerful fish can untune these lures. Plastic-lipped lures can't be tuned, but they can't be knocked out of tune unless their lips are broken or chipped. In this case the lure is often ruined.

*The plastic-lipped lure can, in fact, be repaired or tuned, but not back to manufacturer specifications. The lip can be filed down to a shorter length or filed off completely.*

*If you see that your metal-lipped lure is swimming slightly on its side or acting funny, don't be so quick to retune it. Try a few casts. The lure may attract more strikes if it appears injured. In fact, you may end up untuning some of your perfectly tuned lures.*

The broken-back lure has a more realistic, enticing, you could even say sexier, swimming action. For a long while, after my first nice fish caught on a broken-back, this was the only type of plug I would buy. Though I continued to catch nice fish with them, I eventually noticed that friends using "unbroken" lures were doing at least as well, if not slightly better. I have not bought a broken-back since.

## Poppers

The scooped-faced lures on this page are usually called poppers. All of these lures can be cast to a small, likely strike zone, to be kept there for a long time by alternately twitching them and letting them sit, usually until the rings dissipate and the water's surface is flat again. They can also be retrieved with sharp jerks of your rod. The concave face of the lure will dig in, spraying water and making a sound that could be described as a "pop." Again, you'll usually hold off

POPPERS

on the next jerk until the water calms. Of course you don't have to, and you can wait even longer if you like. No fisherman ever got a ticket for overparking a popper.

### Chuggers

The lure at the bottom is really more of a chugger than a popper. It's not meant to be tuned, or, as a matter of fact, untuned. It can be twitched or popped, but it probably works best with a slow yet variable-speed retrieve. If you're getting hits but not hooking any fish, especially at night, try a steady, one-speed, "chugging" retrieve. Remember, at night, the darker the lure color, the better.

A CHUGGER

# Plastic worms

I can't believe that the inventor of the plastic worm, even in his, her, or its wildest dreams, imagined the earth-shaking magnitude of this technological leap for mankind. I can't believe the entire civilized world, if there is such a thing, does not even know this genius's name. It should be right up there with Isaac Newton, or is it Isaac Walton? Hell, it should be right up there with both of them, whoever is which. How could anyone have guessed that with this cross between Jell-O and a bungee cord, mankind would be able to catch both freshwater bass and saltwater sharks, and countless species in between?

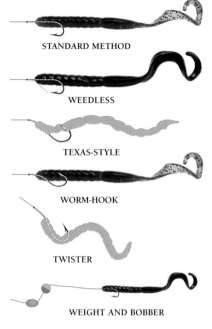

STANDARD METHOD

WEEDLESS

TEXAS-STYLE

WORM-HOOK

TWISTER

WEIGHT AND BOBBER

## Rigging plastic worms

Above right, you can see numerous ways to rig a plastic worm. You can almost double these ways by adding a small cone- or bullet-shaped weight right before the worm on most of these rigs. Scraping your worm along the bottom makes one of the weedless rigs more desirable. Rigging your worm Texas-style gives it the spinning action a lot of fishermen prefer. It also hides the hook point, lessening the chance of a fish spitting your bait. The worm-hook rig hides the hook just as well, and keeps the worm from spinning, if that's what you prefer. Weedless rigs should be avoided unless necessary. They make setting the hook slightly more difficult. You can get some Texas-style action and an exposed hook point with the twister rig. The weight-and-bobber rig keeps your worm just off the bottom. Use the smallest bobber you can find. If it's cork or foam, it can be the smallest one you can find cut in half.

## Retrieving plastic worms

The plastic worm can be retrieved at a slow, steady pace or at a rhythmic pace such as a slow half turn of the handle alternated with a faster turn. It can also be bounced off the bottom. Generally, you shouldn't try to set the hook at the first sensation of a hit. Since the hook is rigged so far forward, give the fish enough time for a good gulp. You can also feed it a little line, or point the rod tip toward it. As soon as you feel a steady pull, set the hook. You will just have to develop a feel for when by trial and error. Fortunately, a fish will often get you off the hook by hooking itself.

**INTERNET**

**www.cremelure.com/ home.htm**

*This is the web site of Creme Lure, manufacturers of plastic worms. Check it out. You may even discover who invented them!*

# Jigs

A plain jig is usually a single hook with a
weight molded around the eye end of the shaft.
It's weighted so the hook point rides up and
away from the bottom, lessening the chance of
snags. This hook can be and has been dressed
with just about anything, but most often with
bucktail, nylon, feathers, or Mylar.

*In a pinch, if you have a hook, a plastic
bag, and a sinker (or something else you
can use as a weight), you can make your
own jig. Cut a half dozen strips (about 8
inches by ½ inch) out of the plastic bags.
Use whatever colors you have and care to
use. Pierce the center of each strip and
thread them onto your line, followed by the
hook, and trim the strips just long enough to hide it. This lure
will be even better for trolling than jigging.*

JIGS

Jigs are probably the most popular lures. A reason for this, aside from their proven ability
to catch fish, is that nearly all jigs are a pleasure to cast. A jig is no cute, dainty little plug.
You don't have to worry about treble hooks catching each other or your line. You don't
have to worry about your jig landing wrong. All you have to worry about is not killing
anybody while casting it. Rear back, let it go, and any decent jig will take off like a rocket.

## Working a jig

There are so many different methods to fish a jig, and so many variations of methods
for different species that, to keep it simple, I'll stick to a few tips and prime examples.
As far as speed is concerned, you can catch fish by working a jig as fast as you can, as
slow as you can, and all the speeds in between. If the fish you're after are on the surface,
then that's where your jig should be. You won't be able to keep it on the surface unless
you use a fast retrieve. This works fine with mackerel. I've never seen anyone work a
jig too fast for them, and I doubt it's possible.

Some jigs produce when they're not even being worked, on the original drop as they
sink. They can also be deadly on the down leg of an up-and-down jigging action. The
biggest factor in this phenomenon is probably the shape of the jig's lead head, though
the hook dressing must play a part. Different shaped jig heads cause different actions –
fast sinking, slower sinking, fluttering, wobbling, and so on.

The basic way to work a jig is first to cast it where you want it. Wait with the bail open and the jig dropping straight down until it reaches your target depth or reaches bottom. Be aware that you must watch the spool carefully. There might be only a moment's pause when the jig hits bottom. Afterward, current or wind may start peeling off more line, but at a different speed. This difference may be slight and very hard to catch. Pay attention. As soon as you spot that pause or speed change, start reeling.

I will describe the most common, basic way to work a jig. Once you get that down, you can add any tricks or embellishments you come across or develop. First reel in any slack line, then jerk your rod back as far and as fast as you care to. Point your rod in the general direction of the jig, again reeling in the slack line. When the line comes taut, jerk your rod back again, then quickly reel in the slack as you again point your rod in the direction of the jig. That's it, over and over again. Simple? Well, not quite so simple.

## Underhand, overhead, and sidearm

There are three basic ways you can jerk back your rod. Let's say you're jigging for mackerel from a high pier. If you follow my recommendations, you'll keep that jig close to the surface, retrieving it as quickly as you can. Perhaps you'll be able to jerk your rod back straight over your head or over your shoulder a few times, but as soon as your jig

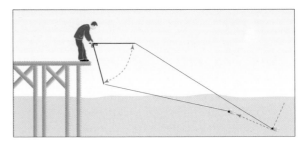

JIGGING UNDERHAND FROM A PIER

gets anywhere near the pier it will start bouncing off the water's surface like a golf ball on a frozen lake. To keep that jig wet, where the fish can get at it, you better start jigging underhand. Fishing from a high seawall or a jetty, you must make use of the same technique, at least when the jig is close in. Otherwise, you may conk yourself or someone standing nearby. Off a boat, you have to be just as careful. Remember, the closer the jig, the lower you must keep your rod.

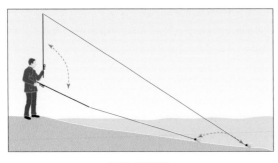

SURF JIGGING

Let's say you're in the surf, and you want to bounce your jig off the bottom on the retrieve. Now the best way to lift your jig is to jerk your rod back over your head or shoulder. This presents some problems. When the jig is far out and the fisherman jerks the rod back, the jig hardly bounces at all. In fact, if the fisherman is a good long-distance caster, he or she is probably digging a trench with the jig. Of course, the closer the jig comes, the higher it bounces. In fact, to keep it from bouncing out of the water, after a certain point the jigging must gradually take on a sidearm instead of overhead motion.

You don't have to keep it on the bottom to give your jig a hopping motion. This action produces fish anywhere in the water column. When you're jigging with a slow retrieve without success, you can do more than change your speed. You can vary it, giving the retrieve a rhythmic pattern.

## Deep jigs

Believe it or not, the lure shown here is also a jig. These types of lures are classified as jigs mainly because they're worked almost exclusively like jigs. I never propagate rumors, but scholarly reasons force me to mention the oft-whispered belief that while both the mother and father of these lures are pure-blooded jigs, the guy that used to deliver the groceries was a spoon (which we'll get to soon).

Now, these jigs are far more streamlined and heavier for their size than any other type. This means you can cast them farther. In fact, fishermen often call on the smaller models when facing winds strong enough to blow any other lure back in their faces. These lures also sink faster, an important factor when fishing deep water. In fact, the heavier of these (from 4 ounces to a pound) are often referred to as deep jigs. While they can be used anywhere, even bounced off the bottom in the surf, large jigs are predominantly worked straight up and down in deep water, which usually requires a boat.

DEEP JIG

### Working deep jigs

All you do is open your bail and let the deep jig drop. If you're worried about snagging bottom, use the countdown method explained earlier in this chapter. Again, watch the spool carefully for changes in rate of drop. If you get a hit on the drop, you want to know it before the fish has all of your line. For the same reason, it pays to know the water depth and your reel's capacity. Once you hit bottom, reel in any slack and start jigging. You can keep bouncing your jig off the bottom by raising and lowering your rod. Alternately, you can also jig it right back to the surface with a pump-and-reel action. Another worthwhile strategy is jigging your lure up about three or four pumps and reels, then letting it fall to the bottom again, and again, and again, and again . . . .

*Keep in mind, the deeper the water and the more mono you have out, the greater the stretch or give in your line. This means that, when deep jigging, you need a rod with real backbone to set your hooks.*

# Jig combos

Choose a jig of the right shape and weight and you can catch anything from bonefish to marlin. In fact, one of the most famous old-time marlin rigs was simply a big jig with a bigger slice of pork rind dressing the hook. For smaller species, tipping the jig hook with a piece of shrimp can prove irresistible. However, the Nobel Prize for Imagination (or perhaps Desperation) should have gone to the strange mind that first married the jig to the plastic worm. I assure you that both families were against this union, and no one with any aesthetic taste gave it a chance. Still, this marriage has done more than last.

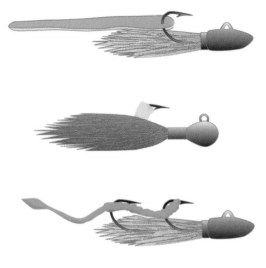

TIPPED JIGS

## Soft-tail jigs

The soft-tailed offspring of the made-in-heaven marriage between jig and worm have multiplied in both numbers and diversity. Soft-tail jigs are extremely quick and easy to rig. The tails, made of the same material as plastic worms, come in various shapes, custom-made for a wide variety of jig heads. Just slip one soft tail off the hook, then replace it with another of a different shape or color. Many, many fish find your standard jig dressed in bucktail or nylon very attractive. Some fish that don't, find a soft-tail jig irresistible.

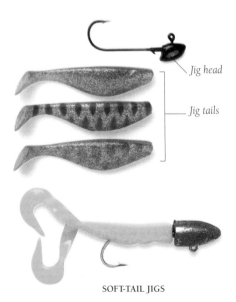

*Jig head*

*Jig tails*

SOFT-TAIL JIGS

I'm always amazed at how slowly you can bounce a metal jig off the bottom and still catch fish. When you're doing this, a soft-tail jig is a marked advantage. During a slow retrieve, you're less likely to set the hook in the course of that retrieve. When you do set it, you're not likely to set it as deep. A fish that takes a bite out of a soft-tail jig is not only less likely to spit it out, that fish is more likely to hook itself. Also, at slower speeds, the tails of many soft-tail jigs give them a more enticing action than that of a standard jig. All things being equal, the slower your retrieval rate, the bigger the advantage of a soft-tail.

# Spoons

The first spoons were almost certainly just that – spoons. Their use probably derives from two indisputable facts. Firstly, fishermen will use anything to catch a fish. Secondly, when eating a fish, a fork is more helpful than a spoon. In any case, spoons do catch fish, and plenty of them. From these facts, we can conclude that either fishermen lucked out, or forks would have worked equally well if anyone had ever tried them. However, knowing that fishermen have tried just about everything, probably including forks, I think we can chalk up spoons to luck.

The spoon is surely a lure that received a lot of laughs until it produced its first fish. Why a fish would go for one is certainly a mystery. Again, vibrations and flash are probably the keys to this mystery. I have heard it said that a spoon imitates a minnow. Not being blessed with the imagination of your average redfish, I can't see it. No matter. Spoons do something to fish, both the freshwater and saltwater varieties.

## Spoon varieties

There are two basic kinds of spoons – single hooked and treble hooked. The single hooked is often weedless. It's also often rigged with pork rind or a plastic worm. Spoons come in chrome, gold, pearl, and a wide variety of

**SINGLE-HOOKED SPOON**

patterns and colors. At one time saltwater fishermen pretty much stuck to silver (chrome) and gold. Today, colors like green mackerel go in and out of fashion. The more concave a spoon, the more wobble it will give you. Perhaps of greater import, a difference in motion indicates a difference in vibrations. An often-overlooked difference is thickness. Thicker spoons are heavier. They sink faster and run deeper. So what does your average fisherman do when a trophy fish steals his spoon? He reaches for one of the same color. Well, that lunker with the shiny new spoon hanging from its jaw might not have even noticed the color. It may have struck because that spoon was the first one in years heavy enough to get down to it.

**TREBLE-HOOKED SPOON**

## Working a spoon

Spoons can be worked like jigs, and often are. Bouncing them along the bottom is very popular. More popular is a steady, slow-to-medium retrieve. With either retrieve, the countdown method can add to your success. Never tie your line or leader directly to the spoon. A split ring and a swivel should come in between. Two split rings and a ball-bearing swivel are even better.

## Spinners

Spinners probably descend from spoons, though any direct links were lost somewhere in fishing antiquity. Spinners are almost exclusively used as freshwater lures. This is mainly because they're not as successful at catching saltwater fishermen as they are at catching saltwater fish. These lures produce fish, tons of them. Admittedly, these are not the largest of fish, and each ton is divided up among many, many fishermen. If you don't mind sharing, get yourself some spinners.

The distinguishing characteristic of spinners is that one part spins around the other. There are exceptions that are not worth getting into. Neither are the distinctions between spinners and their close relatives, such as buzzbaits. In fact, depending on where you are and who you're talking to, the names may be different or interchangeable.

*I doubt any fish will ever ask you the name of the lure you used to catch it. If a fish ever does, just pretend you didn't hear the question, especially if anyone else is within earshot.*

**A SELECTION OF SPINNERS**

## Spinnerbaits

The weird-looking objects below are usually referred to as spinnerbaits. If you're curious as to why, you're reading the wrong book. I debated leaving them out completely, on the good chance that they would lessen your respect for both the intelligence and taste of fish. Ultimately, I decided to leave them in for the odd reason that they are damn good at catching fish. The heavier arm possessing the hook stays on the bottom. This fact, and the protection provided by the upper arm, makes spinnerbaits practically weedless. You can bounce them enticingly off the bottom, or work them anywhere else in the water column. In fact, many fishermen like retrieving them on the surface. The commotion thus caused excites fish as much as fishermen. One retrieve you should definitely try is with the upper arm breaking the surface just enough to cause a wake.

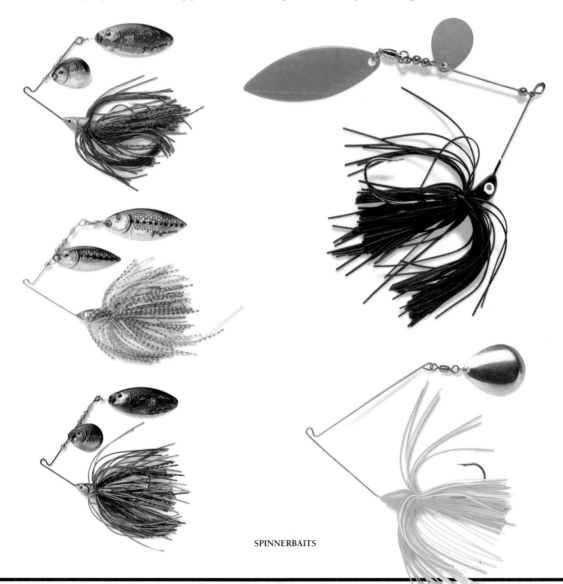

**SPINNERBAITS**

# Using lures

**NO ONE CAN TELL YOU EXACTLY HOW** *fast to retrieve a lure. Different species of fish are susceptible to different retrieval speeds and actions. If you see a fish following your lure without striking, you're probably giving that fish too good a look. Speed up your retrieve. Believe me, that fish could have caught your lure if it wanted to. Even when you're sure you're retrieving at the appropriate speed with the appropriate action, if the fish don't seem to agree, take their opinion seriously. Change something – speed, action, lure, or fishing spot. The first thing I usually change is speed. In freshwater, I tend to slow it down a notch. In saltwater, I tend to go the other way. Try this, or try the opposite. Just try something, until something works.*

**INTERNET**

**www.etackle.com.au/ pages/lureover.htm**

*This "Overview on Using Lures" comes to you courtesy of the Australian web site eTackle.com.*

One thing I can tell you is my strong belief that the more frightened your artificial bait looks, the more likely it is to draw strikes. Sure, the predator is enticed by the unwary. It also strikes to protect its territory. Still, I doubt anything triggers the strike reflex quicker than the sight of fear. Give your artificials a skittish action. Yet, don't overdo it. You do not want them to look unnatural. Nor do you want them darting around so erratically that predators cannot catch them.

*The choice of a lure is not one that you have to live with, not for more than a cast or two anyway.*

■ **Giving your lure** *a skittish action at just the right moment may be just enough to trigger some lunker's strike reflex.*

Experience and only experience will eventually make these choices easy ones. I've had just as much success with sinking lures as with floaters. Still, unless I have a very good reason to do otherwise, for my first lure I usually choose a floater.

It's a pleasure to follow a lure's action in the water. More important, if something happens short of a strike, I'm more likely to see it. Most important, and least important at the same time, a fish striking a surface bait is one of the most exciting, rewarding sights fishing has to offer – one well worth a few possibly wasted casts with a surface lure.

## A simple summary

✔ The Twenty-fifth Golden Rule of Fishing: "The most necessary, most important requirement for an artificial bait is your confidence in it."

✔ Just because some lures are commonly called poppers, don't forget that they sometimes work best when reeled in with a slow, steady retrieve.

✔ Plastic worms will catch freshwater bass, saltwater sharks, and countless other fish.

✔ For deep jigging, because of the stretch in monofilament line, you need a rod with real backbone to set your hooks.

✔ A fish is less likely to spit a jig with a soft tail.

✔ The slower your retrieval rate, the bigger the advantage of a soft-tail.

✔ There's more to a spoon than its color. The more concave, the more wobble and vibrations. The thicker, the heavier. The heavier, the faster it will sink and the deeper it will run.

✔ Different species of fish are susceptible to different retrieval speeds and actions.

✔ If the fish are not striking, change speed, action, lure, or fishing spot.

✔ I strongly believe that the more frightened your artificial bait looks, the more likely it is to draw strikes.

# The Golden Rules of Fishing

1. "Less is better, if it can get the job done." The lighter your line and the terminal tackle attached to it, the more fish you will fool.

2. "Never contaminate your line or terminal tackle with lubricants, insect repellent, sunblock, suntan lotion, or any other substance that will repel fish." These substances are known, for a fact, to take away a fish's appetite.

3. "Keep your line tight." Give a fish slack, and you give it a chance to throw the hook. Also, in order to tire a fish as quickly as possible, it's important that you always maintain maximum pressure.

4. "No matter how far you can cast, the best-looking spot is almost sure to be just out of range." Concentrate on casting accuracy, not on distance.

5. "Gaffs can be just as deadly to fishermen as to fish. Keep gaff tips covered until just before use."

6. "All unneeded fish should be returned to the water unharmed."

7. "Whenever you cover a lot of ground searching for fish – be it by trolling, circling a lake, walking a river bank, or driving from pond to pond – return to the most productive or promising spot for dusk."

8. "To read water you must understand the ambush. To find your target fish, find its ambush site."

9. "When you cast your bait to a spot where you think there may be a fish, cast it as if you're 100 percent positive there is a fish." The more you put into a cast, the more you're likely to get out of it.

10. "When searching for fish, try a few casts at anything that catches your eye." It may have caught some fish's eye also, and it only costs a few casts to find out.

11. "If you can't get the fish to bite on what you brought, try using what's there to catch what's there – a frog off a lily pad, a grasshopper from the bank, a piece of barnacle off a boulder, a piece of shellfish on a grass patch, a crab on a flat, or any bait fish you can catch."

12. "Trophy fish of almost any species are likely to be in the best place to get food without becoming food."

13. "When trolling, unless your lines are tangle-proof, always turn to the side of your longest line."

14. "If the fish are not biting, whatever you do, do not not do anything."

15. "The best place to find fish is where you just found a fish." When you get a strike, keep going back to the same spot until you stop getting strikes.

16. "The most important technique in trolling is to keep your lines in the water." When they aren't, all the other techniques are worthless.

17. "If you don't take time to check the sharpness of every hook you use, you're wasting fishing time."

18. "Always leave your fishing spots as close as possible to the pristine conditions you found or had hoped to find."

19. "A good fisherman always brings a spare knife."

20. "Too large a bait on a hook does little more than increase the chances a fish will strip it."

21. "Bring a variety of baits. Even if you plan on using only artificial bait, always bring along at least a small amount of natural bait – to use as bait, as bait to catch bait, or as chum."

22. "A fisherman's tackle box should always contain a source of fire."

23. "If you don't know if there are fish, or exactly where they are, for your first attempt choose the bait and rig most likely to get you a strike, not the bait and rig most likely to get you a fish." Once you know there are fish, then focus upon catching them.

24. "You can't use live bait if ya done kilt it."

25. "The most necessary, most important requirement for an artificial bait is your confidence in it."

# More resources

## Books

Big Fish and Blue Water: Gamefishing in the Pacific
Peter Goadby, Currently out of print

Fishing for Dummies
Peter Kaminsky, IDG Books, 1997

McClane's New Standard Fishing Encyclopedia
A.J. McClane, Holt, Rinehart and Winston, 1965

Fishing the Flats.
Mark Sosin and Lefty Kreh, Winchester Press, 1983

The Complete Idiot's Guide to Fishing Basics
Mike Toth, Alpha Books, 2000

## Organizations

International Game Fish Association
300 Gulf Stream Way
Dania Beach, FL 33004-9968
(954) 927-2628

The Billfish Foundation
2161 East Commercial Blvd, 2nd Floor
Fort Lauderdale, FL 33308
(954) 938-0150 or (800) 438-8247

# Fishing on the Web

THERE IS A HUGE AMOUNT of information about fishing on the Internet. The following list contains some of the sites that I think are useful. Please note that due to the fast-changing nature of the Net, some of the below may be off-line before you get online.

www.asafishing.org
The American Sportfishing Association is, among other things, a conservation organization. Amazingly, it loans fishing equipment to novices in the same manner as libraries loan books. Log on to find out if there's a branch in your area.

www.cmc-ocean.org
If you want to get involved in marine conservation, the Center for Marine Conservation will tell you exactly how to go about it. This is a US site.

www.cremelure.com/home.htm
Check out this plastic-worm manufacturer's web site. You may even discover who invented them!

www.cyberangler.com
At this US-based site, among other interesting things, you can find your local tides and weather forecasts.

www.dfo-mpo.gc.ca
The site for the Department of Fisheries & Oceans details conservation efforts, reviews marine safety, and provides links to provincial government web sites.

www.etackle.com.au/pages/lureover.htm
This "Overview on Using Lures" comes to you courtesy of the Australian web site eTackle.com.

www.fishingcairns.com
This Australian web site offers instruction on knot tying and much information about fishing in Australia.

## www.fishingminnesota.com/fishinfo31.html

This page of the Fishing Minnesota web site contains an article called "Secrets to Super Bait," and it goes on to offer you just that.

## www.fishingworks.com

Claiming to "help fishermen navigate the Web," this site contains information on pretty much every aspect of the sport, including buying fishing rods.

## www.fishontario.com

This web site provides up-to-date information on Ontario species and the best fishing spots in the province.

## www.fishsa.com/sinkswiv.htm

This page of the Tackle Talk section of FishSA.com gives some information about swivels, but you'll have to scroll past (or read) the stuff on sinkers first.

## www.geocities.com/Yosemite/3133/ma_ar014.html

In this article on wire leaders, the author discusses the pros and cons of several different types.

## home.icdc.com/~vernonsk/

Maybe it's premature since we're talking about your first reel, but this quirky site is about collecting antique reels!

## www.igfa.org

The International Game Fish Association (IGFA) web site lists the rules that must be followed to qualify a catch for an IGFA record. Among other things, it also contains valuable information about the IGFA Junior Angler Program. This web site is a must stop.

## www.insidesportfishing.com/Encyclopedia/Articles/1041.asp

This page of the Inside Sportfishing web site gives in-depth directions on how to set the hook.

## www.inthebite.com/misc/previouspoles5.shtml

This page of InTheBite.com gives details of some of their previous readers' polls, including which lure color combinations work best.

## www.kenschultz.com/articles.asp?article=41

This article, "How to Spool Line," is found at KenSchultz.com, "the angling authority™." It covers spinning gear, as well as spincasting, baitcasting, and fly casting, and should be worth a look.

## www.marineweather.com

At this site, you can look up your state's fishing regulations, and so you should. Ignorance is no defense.

## www.maxima-lines.com

This line manufacturer's web site contains helpful instructions for tying a number of knots, including the Bimini twist.

## www.mustad.no

This hook manufacturer's web site has an interesting article on the history of the fish hook. The fact that it's one history lesson you will never be tested on makes it even more interesting. The site also contains some fish-hook illustrations suitable for framing.

## www.novascotiasalmon.ns.ca

The Nova Scotia Salmon Association's web site provides information on events, projects, programs, and fishing in Nova Scotia. There are also great links to other fishing and conservation organizations in the both Canada and the US.

## www.orvis.com

This fishing equipment manufacturer's site should prove extremely interesting to prospective fly fishermen. It even has an interactive fly-casting lesson.

## www.shakespeare-fishing.com

This manufacturer's web site contains casting tips for spinning, baitcasting, and fly-fishing. It also has, among many other things, maintenance tips for both rods and reels.

## www.sosin.com

Mark Sosin's outstanding web site lists fishing guides, fishing tips, fishing articles, and much more. Be sure to check it out.

## www.sportfishingbc.com

This is a great site for information about saltwater and freshwater fishing in British Columbia. The site includes online articles and maps, and lists the BC fishing hotspots, lodges, and guide packages.

## www.ufish.com/latlontds/loran.htm

This US web page offers links to sites containing some Loran and GPS numbers (coordinates).

## www.weather.ec.gc.ca

This weather site run by Environment Canada covers weather conditions across the country.

# A simple glossary

**Action** When applied to fishing rods, it refers to flexibility. Only experience, and a lot of it, will teach you how to judge a rod's action.

**Artificial baits** Sometimes called lures, plugs, and jigs, among other things, these are inedible baits made out of metal, plastic, wood, Mylar, nylon, feathers, and many other materials.

**Barrel wraps** Neat, uniform coils that resemble a contracted spring. They are a component of many fishing knots.

**Bird nest** A tangled mass of fishing line constructed by a fisherman atop a conventional reel, usually at the end of a cast or attempted cast. Both the bird nest and its method of construction are commonly referred to as backlashes.

**Blank** The unadorned rod shaft made of fiberglass, graphite, and so on.

**Bobber** Sometimes called a float, a bobber is a device made from wood, cork, plastic, or any other suitable floating material. It is attached to your line to keep your bait at a particular place in the water column and, by its movement, alerts you when a fish hits your bait.

**Cast** To send your bait, with the help of your fishing rod, through the air to the place you want it to enter the water.

**Cast and retrieve** Casting a bait and retrieving it at a speed and with a motion intended to entice strikes.

**Chemically sharpened hook** A hook that has been dipped in acid to remove metal burrs that hinder penetration.

**Chum slick** An area of water encompassing a source of chum and the entire continuous spread of that chum.

**Clark's Law** The rule that states: The junk you have will expand to fill all available space.

**Conduit** A huge pipe laid under a road or dike, connecting a canal to a wetland or to a wet something else.

**Conventional tackle** Also called level-wind tackle, refers to just about all fishing tackle with both the reel positioned on top of the rod and a spool that rotates during the cast and the retrieve.

**Deep jigging** Working a lure with sharp jerks of the rod in deep water.

**Downrigger** A device that lowers your trolling lures or baits to a specific depth and keeps them there.

**Drag** On a spinning reel, a set of washers and a spring, plus a knob to adjust the pressure on them. How the drag is set determines the force a fish needs to apply in order to take out line.

**Drop-back** The slack provided on a strike, when a release device frees extra line. This enables the fish to swallow the bait before the line becomes taut, increasing the likelihood of a hookup.

**Edge** A dividing line between two currents, water temperatures, bottom contours, or any of the many other changes that attract fish.

**Faure's Law** The rule that states: If it happens, it must be possible.

**Feathering** Slowing the line's escape from the spool by gently trapping it between finger and spool rim.

**Ferrule** A male–female connection on the fishing rod that allows it to be broken down into two or more pieces. It can be two pieces of metal glued onto the two halves of a rod shaft, or it can be molded into the rod shaft itself.

**Finagle's Law** The rule that states: Once a job is fouled up, anything done to improve it just fouls it up worse.

**Fishfinders** Devices that, with the use of sonar, give you a picture of the bottom, plus any fish between it and you.

**Flotsam** Floating refuse or debris.

**Foul hook** To hook a fish anywhere outside its mouth. This may not bother you, but it bothers the IGFA (International Game Fish Association). A foul-hooked fish cannot be submitted for a record. Ironically, foul hooking usually enables a fish to put up a better fight, especially if that hook is embedded near its tail.

**Freelining** Leaving your reel's bail open to give your bait freedom to swim or to be taken by the current or by a fish.

**Gap** The distance between the shaft and the point of a hook.

**GPS** Global Positioning System. Uses satellite signals to give your position in longitude and latitude.

**Green fish** A fish that is not yet played out (worn out) enough to be safely unhooked or taken from the water. It's still too active to land.

**Hookup** A hit or strike in which the hook point penetrates and holds for at least a few seconds.

**Hookup ratio** The number of hooked fish compared to the number of strikes. A successful fisherman strives constantly to improve his or her hookup ratio.

**IGFA** The International Game Fish Association, the arbiter and keeper of all international fishing records. Among other things, it works to protect the oceans and the fish in them. A year's membership costs less than a cheap rod and reel. Every sportfisherman should join.

**Jigging** This term means to work a lure with sharp jerks of the rod.

**Leader** A length (from a few inches to a few yards) of line or wire attached to the business end of your fishing line. A leader is almost always stronger than the line to which it's attached.

**Leeward side** The side farthest from the source of the wind.

**Live baits** Baits that are alive.

**Longliners** Commercial fishermen who set out lines, often miles long, with thousands of hooks dangling from them. By the time they retrieve these lines, the by catch (nonmarketable species) and fish they are forbidden to harvest, such as marlin, are already dead. Longliners are no friends to sportfish or sportfishermen.

**Loran** A navigation service that uses radio waves to give your position in longitude and latitude.

**Memory** The characteristics of monofilament to retain its shape as, when unwound from a spool and allowed to hang without tension or weight. It will retain the memory of the spool by hanging in a corkscrew pattern.

**Natural baits** Baits derived from natural materials, vegetable as well as animal. Bread is as natural a bait as squid, earthworms, blood worms, crickets, mullet, menhaden, eels, shrimp, minnows, shiners, and many, many other things. The term natural baits is not usually meant to include live baits, which, it could be argued, are more natural than the no-longer-among-the-living natural baits.

**Offset hook point** A hook point bent out of line with the hook's shaft. If a hook's point is offset, it won't lie flat on a flat surface.

**Outrigger** A long pole projecting from the side of a boat. Almost always used in pairs, outriggers enable a fisherman to widen a trolling spread and reduce the chance of tangled lines. Of course, they also enable the fisherman to run additional lines, thus making possible far worse tangles.

**Party boats** Fishing boats that take out large parties, anywhere from two dozen fishermen on up. They anchor or drift, with the fishermen lining the rail. These boats usually supply everything needed, including bait and instructions.

**Port side** When you're facing forward in a boat, port is the direction to your left. No matter which direction you face, the port side of the boat does not change.

**Practice plug** A hard-rubber or soft-plastic weight, usually shaped something like a bank sinker. As a murder weapon, it admittedly leaves a lot to be desired, even in the hands of an expert. Still, it can do very serious damage to people's eyes or other delicate parts, including yours. Be careful with it.

**Quills** Small hooks dressed with nylon, bucktail, Mylar, or plastic. They are rigged multiple hooks to a line, a few inches apart. You jig them, continuously raising and lowering your rod tip a foot or so.

**Rip current** The meeting of two currents. They can both be surface currents, or one can be an upwelling or vertical current caused by a huge bottom formation.

**Setting a hook** Forcing a hook's point into the fish's flesh where it can find hold. The fish can do this to itself by biting down on the hook barb or applying pressure to the line. The fisherman can set the hook by applying pressure to the line with a backward jerk of his or her rod.

**Shock leader** A wind-on leader, attached to your line with a knot instead of a swivel so it will pass through your rod's line guides. Additionally, it is long enough to go a half dozen times around your reel's spool when you are in casting position. This allows the shock leader, not the relatively weaker line, to take all the force of your cast.

**Sloppy** When applied to water, this term means rough and covered with white caps or foam.

**Sloughs** Pronounced "slews," these are long, narrow depressions or channels between sandbars.

**Snag hook** A treble hook, sometimes weighted, used to snag (impale) fish. You cast it over a school of fish (usually bait fish), then violently jerk back your fishing rod in an attempt to snag (hook) one.

**Snap swivels** Swivels with connecting devices attached. They do the work of swivels, trying to keep your line from twisting, plus they enable quick connections of terminal tackle.

**Snell** A barrel-wrap type of knot used to attach line to the top of a hook's shaft instead of to its eye. The line runs through the hook eye if this eye is turned up or down. This enables a straighter pull, which defeats the supposed advantage of a turned-down eye – a superior penetration angle for setting the hook.

**Spincasting** An attempt to combine the advantages of conventional baitcasting tackle and spinning tackle. The close-faced spincasting reel, like the conventional reel, sits atop the rod. This enables the fisherman to release line simply by pressing a button. Line comes off the end of a fixed, nonrevolving spool, as with the spinning reel, facilitating easier casting with less danger of tangles.

**Spread** The arrangement, or pattern, of your trolling lures. It encompasses not only their position laterally behind the boat, but also vertically in the water column.

**Standing line** Any part of the line that is not the end of the line you're using to tie the knot (the tag end).

**Starboard side** When you're facing forward in a boat, starboard is the direction to your right. No matter which direction you turn to face, the starboard side of the boat does not change.

**Stringer** A heavy cord with a short stick attached to one end and a ring to the other. Fish are strung onto it by pushing the stick through a gill opening and out of the mouth. When all the fish are on the rope, the stick is passed through the loop to make sure they stay on it.

**Tag end** The end of the line you're using to tie the knot. The standing end is the other end.

**Temperature probe** A thermometer, lowered into the water on a cable, that transfers its readings to the surface where they can be read by the fisherman.

**Terminal tackle** All the equipment tied to the end of a fishing line.

**Test** The strength of a fishing line; refers to the amount of steady force the line can endure, measured in pounds or kilos. An 8-pound test line can lift about 8 pounds in air, and more in water.

**Thermocline** The meeting of broad layers of water of substantially differing temperatures.

**Trolling** A method of fishing that involves the dragging of baits behind a moving boat.

**Undertow** A flash current running from or near a beach, out toward the open sea.

**Weedless** When referring to a hook, one in which the barb is protected to keep it from picking up weeds or refuse.

**Windward side** The side closest to the wind.

**Wrap** A layer of thread used to attach the feet of a line guide to the rod shaft. The use of tape in place of thread is a sure sign of poor quality.

# Index

# Acknowledgments

AUTHOR'S ACKNOWLEDGMENTS
Despite the scars they left behind, honesty forces me to thank my opinionated
proofreaders (Dave Sneath, Jack Reece, and Steve Grogan) for making this a better book. I
would also like to thank Alan Moss, photographer extraordinaire and decent human being
to boot. Finally, I would like to thank my Super Agent, Jerold Roth, who breaks up my fish
diet by putting some meat on my table every once in a while.

PACKAGER'S ACKNOWLEDGMENTS
Sands Publishing Solutions would like to thank the following people for their help in this
project: Hilary Bird for compiling the index; Steve Gorton for photography; Andy Lush of
The Friendly Fisherman in Tunbridge Wells for the loan of lures; Barry Robson for the
dog illustrations; David Saldanha and Hayley Smith at Dorling Kindersley's picture library;
Phil Smith and Rob Earl of The Maidstone Angling Centre for advice and the loan of
equipment; Mariana Sonnenberg at ilumi for picture research.

PUBLISHER'S ACKNOWLEDGMENTS
Dorling Kindersley would like to thank Rebecca Studd for design assistance, Katy Wall for
the jacket design, and Beth Apple for jacket text.